P9-CFA-040

THE
·
HOUSE
·
OF
·
EMERSON

"Every spirit builds itself a house;
and beyond its house, a world;
and beyond its world, a heaven.
Know then, that the world
exists for you."
"Nature"

THE
·
HOUSE
·
OF
·
EMERSON

LEONARD NEUFELDT

University of Nebraska Press

Lincoln and London

ШM

Portions of this book have previously been published, in different
form, as "The Vital Mind: Emerson's Epistemology,"
Philological Quarterly 50 (April 1971): 253–70; "The Law of Permutation: Emerson's Mode," *American Transcendental
Quarterly* no. 21 (Summer 1974): 20–30; "The Science of Power:
Emerson's Views on Technology and Science in Ameri-
ca," *Journal of the History of Ideas* 38 (April 1977): 329–44; "Emerson,
Thoreau, and Daniel Webster," *ESQ: Journal of the American
Renaissance* 26 (First Quarter 1980): 26–37; and "The Severity of
the Ideal: Emerson's 'Thoreau,' " *Emerson Society Quarterly*
o.s. 58 (Summer 1970): 77–84.

Copyright 1982 by
the University of Nebraska Press
All rights reserved
Manufactured in the United States
of America

Library of Congress Cataloging in Publication Data

Neufeldt, Leonard.
The house of Emerson.

Includes index.
1. Emerson, Ralph Waldo, 1803–1882—
Criticism and interpretation. I. Title.
PS1638.N48 814'.3 81-16208
ISBN 0-8032-3304-3 AACR2

B14.36
E 53zn K_z
916144

for
Sherman Paul
and
Richard Thompson
with
affection

Contents

Preface   page 11

Acknowledgments   page 19

Note on Texts & Abbreviations   page 21

I. The House of Emerson

1. Man Thinking: Emerson's Epistemology   page 25

2. The Artist: Metamorphosis & Metaphor   page 47

II. Building the Commonwealth

3. Technology & Science: The Science of Power   page 75

4. Daniel Webster as Representative Man   page 101

5. Thoreau & the Failure of the Ideal   page 123

III. Rebuilding House & World: Emerson's Maturation

6. Metamorphoses of the Image: Emerson & Poetry   page 143

7. Tendencies, Forms, & Personae in *Nature*   page 169

8. Personae & Vision in Later Essays   page 201

Notes   page 243

Index   page 263

THE
·
HOUSE
·
OF
·
EMERSON

Preface

Thanks to Emerson's regimen as a writer, his prodigious literary production, his influence on subsequent American writers, and the appearance in recent decades of a number of major biographical and critical studies of him, his stature as one of the central figures in American literature is generally acknowledged. As for who Emerson really is, which is to ask what the Emerson text is or should be, there is much less agreement. The fact that various Emersons have been proposed reminds us that the text is in part Emerson's work, in part the critics'. The proportion has varied depending on whether the approach has been comprehensive or partial, biographical-historical or thematic, orginating in and passed through Emerson's forms or self-created, theoretical or non-theoretical and anti-theoretical, systematically analytical or evangelical and appreciative. To review the scholarship is to be reconvinced that with Emerson, as with most other literary artists, various critics work with various texts. As I see it, the dilemma is inescapable. I am neither distressed to admit the variety nor reluctant to acknowledge that *The House of Emerson* would not have been written except for the variety of studies in the last four decades.

And yet, to conduct still another critical study of Emerson requires one to choose between relativisms, to beware of myth proposed as biography or history, of a strict and narrow selection presented as representative, of commonplaces repeated in the face of evidence challenging their validity, of poignant romantic exuberance or agony trained on Emerson as soundingboard, and of post-formalist critical ecstasies holding up Emerson passages as a mirror to reflect the signs

11

and equations of their calculus. In recommending that Emerson be explored as a literary artist and preeminently as a corpus of literary achievements, Jonathan Bishop in the 1960s and Lawrence Buell in the 1970s chose between relativisms. They proposed an Emerson accessible primarily in his imaginative use of conventions and in his unconventional forms of voice, trope, syntax, and logic. Despite strictly limiting the text, they managed to expand it considerably by examining Emerson's forms of feeling and imagination as well as his thought and logic, whether these forms were uniquely his or a cultural inheritance. Their advances have been significant. In writing the present book I have assumed that the text needs additional identification, verification, and expansion.

One should not underestimate the difficulty of changing and expanding the Emerson text. The critic is like the textual editor in being forced to cope with the staying-power of widely accepted texts. The comparison by Henry James, Senior, of Emerson's *Essays: First Series* with *Essays: Second Series* and *Society and Solitude* produced a remarkably sensible observation, the cautionary element of which has been overlooked or ignored by most Emerson scholars: "The difference, of course, between the two series is only that between youth and age, or promise and fulfillment. . . . The sunset is just as admirable in its way as the sunrise; but every one knows that the latter excites . . . a very much more tender enthusiasm."[1] In recent years the prevailing view has held that the Emerson of the late 1840s and the 1850s was a one-time visionary defeated by the lords of life and stoically resigned to his fate, and, moreover, that a few essays between 1836 and 1844 constitute his literary achievements—in all the rest we may find, here and there, only a patch of eloquence or a reminder of a collapsed vision. An efficient assumption by now, one is tempted to infer, that conveniently throws Emerson into familiar relief and abbreviates both the reading and the critical analysis of his works. Whatever the reasons, the example is typical. Well-timed and energetically-stated critical interpretations have, in the absence of forceful counterstatements, become lords of the critical life.

As I have noted, to propose a somewhat different Emerson text is both risky and necessary. The ways of scholarship, like providence, are often a little rude. The persona of Emerson's "Experience" comes to mind: it is not easy for him to know even the surfaces of his world, yet he needs to master the surfaces before he is allowed a new reality. His "Reality" is by itself a presumptuous term that is saved from skeptical or derisive dismissal only by its context, a context that implies and enacts a dynamic, permutational process in which insight gives way to deeper insight, but usually not the one expected. This insight is received with joy and humility.

"Invisible or visible or both / . . . An abstraction blooded, as a man by thought" is one of those passages in Stevens's "Notes toward a Supreme Fiction" that wonderfully concentrate the complex intention and relentless urgency of the poem. Schools and critical fashions notwithstanding, literary criticism holds that the combination of "abstraction" and "abstraction blooded" is the real text. These two entities are mutually defined; in practical criticism each creates yet depends on the other. In the case of Emerson the abstraction encompasses a number of aspects of scholarly interest and concern. To name a few: the nature and particular quality of mind, sensibility, loyalties, prejudices, and ambition, and his sense of himself, friends, and associates and of his town of Concord (where he lived out his vocation), his America, and the human race. Trying to attend to these matters has not made my task easier than I had expected: Emerson is more complex and unlimited than any treatise on him has suggested. Both in his thinking and his literary compositions he refused to work inside the limits of those of us who have analyzed and interpreted him. According to him, reading with concentration and understanding requires a well-educated moral courage ("Will" in contrast to "willfulness") as well as native intellect. In the words of an instructive journal entry, "A man finds out that there is somewhat in him that knows more than he does. Then he comes pres-

13

ently to the curious question, who's who? which of these two is really me? the one that knows more or the one that knows less? the little fellow, or the big fellow?" (*JMN,* XIV, 259). If we ignore the ironies of this little fable we might be inclined to identify the author with one of the little fellows. To do that, Emerson implies, is to identify ourselves with the little fellow.

The most illuminating criticism on Emerson has on the one hand concerned itself with the "abstraction blooded" (bodied forth in the forms of the literary art) and has on the other hand conceded that the abstraction, like the mystery of Emerson's poem on the sphinx, was never fully bodied forth by Emerson and cannot be fully bodied forth by the critic. And yet the mutual dependence must be recognized. Emerson's mind, his sense of himself, his community, and America, shaped his experiences and loyalties, his literary compositions, and his literary choices in the process of composing. Likewise, all of these shaped his mind and his sense of self and world.

In my efforts to identify and expand the Emerson text I owe a special debt to my fellow editors of *The Writings of Henry D. Thoreau* and to the Textual Center at Princeton University. I have been taught the importance of studying autograph manuscripts (whether or not these have been published) and working accurately with them. Through my work on Thoreau's *Journal* I have been introduced to the major collections of Emerson manuscripts as well as the manuscripts of associates like Thoreau and Alcott. Moreover, I have been fortunate to cross paths with and receive useful information from editors of manuscripts of various New England transcendentalists: Thomas Blanding, John Broderick, Francis Dedmond, Walter Harding, George Hendrick, Joel Myerson, Margaret Neussendorfer, and Ralph Orth. The almost-completed Emerson *Journals and Miscellaneous Notebooks* have been enormously helpful, as has some of the unpublished Emerson correspondence. Etymology, lexical meanings of Emerson's words in his time and place, his reading, and his invention and manipulation of language are other interests fostered by the often mind-numbing work of establishing and glossing a reliable text for publication.

I wish also to note that an editorial interest in the genetic history of a work has carried over into my critical study of Emerson, whose changing and clarifying intentions can in a number of cases be traced through the process of composition and the several states of a particular work. Alterations Emerson introduced into later editions and changes over the years in trope, idiom, and syntax are also not without significance. In a paper delivered at the English Institute in 1973 Daniel Shea issued a plea that warrants repeating here. He called for "a thorough genetic study of Emerson,"[2] which suggests to me not only an examination of the genetic history of each work, insofar as that is possible, but also the genetic history reported by the sequence of Emerson's complete writings. With the help of such a study, I suspect, we may be able to reconcile the biographical-cultural and history-of-ideas approaches to Emerson with the recently fashionable and frequently instructive structuralist analyses. Understood in this context, genetic criticism brings into a proximity of reciprocal clarification several worlds: the incipient structures of Emerson the artist, the completed and formally disclosed structures of individual works, structures inhering in the writings as a whole, and the world of a life lived in a town, region, culture, and schedule of pressing activities that really existed. The note of victory so characteristic of Emerson's conclusions always involves something more than simply the literary tour de force. But an authoritative genetic study as called for by Professor Shea remains to be written.

Beyond this editorial interest in genetic study, my years of reading Emerson and an enduring fondness and admiration for a number of his essays, lectures, and poems not customarily identified with the essential corpus and therefore rarely if ever discussed, have been factors in expanding the text and redefining in my mind some of the salient features in the most familiar and most discussed works.

However limited a new book on Emerson is (the present book is both limited and incomplete), it will have served a salutary purpose if, among other things, it assists in demystifying and demythologizing Emerson, redefining his romanticism and transcendentalism, reassessing the nature and extent of shifts in views and art over the span of his literary career, recognizing *Nature* as the earnest rather than the centerpiece of his vision and career, and weighting the scales more on the side of the rigorously descriptive, systematic, analytical, and philosophical approach and somewhat less on the side of the moral, appreciative, and privately aesthetic.

Nonetheless, there is always an element in criticism that Emerson, in "Worship," characterized as the "state of the votary," a condition of awakening to a coherent and expanded sense of the particular world one is studying as well as of one's own being. This state, he informs us, is something he experienced many times over in his reading and writing. When the mind awakens, he noted in *Representative Men* in a passage personally revealing but also pointing to his readers as to the heroes of this volume, "a man seems to multiply ten times or a thousand times his force. It opens the delicious sense of indeterminate size and inspires an audacious mental habit. We are . . . entitled to these enlargements, and once having passed the bounds shall never again be quite the miserable pedants we were" (*W*, IV, 17).

At the risk of concluding these prefatory remarks on a pedantic note, I wish to remind the reader before the fact that the method in the first five chapters combines progressive development and argument with multiple approaches growing out of deliberate shifts in vantage point and interest. To employ the metaphor that informs both title and book, describing and interpreting Emerson's building of house and world requires a number of blueprints or building plans, each of which implicates, complements, and overlaps the others, yet has its own integrity and independence. The method falls somewhere between the process enacted by Stevens in "Someone Puts a Pineapple Together"

16

and Niels Bohr's principle of complementarianism, both of which are more characteristic of the fine arts, mathematics, and philosophy than of contemporary literary criticism. It is hoped that the resulting construction will do justice to Emerson's. What begins as the "casual exfoliations" of the Stevens poem finally resists the adjective "casual" although the mode of the critical construction is a kind of progressive exfoliation, an imitation, perhaps, of Emerson's man thinking and his law of metamorphosis.

Quite aware that Emerson is his own dictionary, I suggest that the figure best capturing and holding for clarification Emerson's view of man and world is "metamorphosis" and that the term that takes us to the center of his view of any creative activity, literary or other, is "metaphor." These two terms are causally and reciprocally related. In the state of constant metamorphosis the successful builder is man thinking, who in the context of his culture and history is representative man. Representative man takes many forms and appears in many versions, the most distinguished of these the poet as Emerson understood the role of "poet." Seen in terms of the house and world he was building, Emerson-as-representative-man is a poet who accepted the given in order to transform it, so as to counter and remake the present and create the conditions for a future centered by man thinking. It is in the nature of Emerson's literary work, in its modes and assumptions, that the more intrinsic our approach, the more extrinsic the implications. The better we understand his formal literary achievements, the more we are aware of how ideological his house and world building were and are.

To a large extent, Emerson's achievements in constructing a house and world are repetitive, which is to say they are repeatedly informed by the same impulses and convictions and take essentially the same form. The first two of the three parts of this book identify patterns of sensibility, inclination, belief, and practice that persist in most of Emerson's writings and career; these two parts, then, identify a text we can call Emersonian. Implicit in the discussion of prevailing patterns, however, is the recognition that Emerson's modes and emphases are the same and yet not the same. The third and longest part of the book, with its readings of a number of individual Emerson works, is, among other things, chronologically based in order to mark more sharply those lines of development in Emerson that I regard as central to his record of persistence and change.

Emerson's "house" was both a created and a containing structure, but above all it was a mediating structure between his experiencing, feeling, thinking, and inventing and the larger world in which he lived out his vocation. It both created and validated his life. On the other hand, the lifelong building and rebuilding strongly suggest that it always contained him too much. *The House of Emerson*, too, is a mediating structure—between the world of a critic's perceptions and organizations and the world Emerson built and inhabited.

Acknowledgments

Grateful acknowledgment is made to the following for permission to quote from copyrighted texts: Columbia University Press for material from *The Letters of Ralph Waldo Emerson* and *The Correspondence of Emerson and Carlyle;* Princeton University Press for material from *The Writings of Henry D. Thoreau (Reform Papers,* ed. Wendell Glick, copyright © 1973, and *Walden,* ed. J. Lyndon Shanley, copyright © 1971 by Princeton University Press); and New York University Press for material from *The Correspondence of Henry David Thoreau,* ed. Walter Harding and Carl Bode, copyright © 1958 by New York University. I also wish to thank the Houghton Library, the Huntington Library, and the Pierpont Morgan Library for permission to quote from manuscripts in their collections. The American Philosophical Society financially assisted the research for chapter four, the American Council of Learned Societies provided the means to spend several summers of work at the Textual Center of *The Writings of Henry D. Thoreau* and manuscript collections in New York and New England, and the Textual Center furnished useful information on several occasions.

Personal debts also need to be acknowledged. I owe much to scholarly encouragement from John Broderick, Kenneth Cameron, Hans-Joachim Lang, and Merton Sealts. Charles Mignon, George Hendrick, and Richard Thompson gave the typescript of this book a reading, from which it benefited.

As always, I owe much to my wife, Mera, and to the colleagues to whom this volume is dedicated, Sherman Paul and Richard Thompson.

Note on Texts
& Abbreviations

Quotations from Emerson's works are numerous in this book. For convenience and economy, titles of the following standard editions have been abbreviated throughout in parenthetical references by letter, appropriate volume, and page number:

CW   *The Collected Works of Ralph Waldo Emerson,* ed. Robert Spiller, Alfred Ferguson, Joseph Slater, et al. 2 vols. to date. Cambridge: Harvard University Press, 1971–

W   *The Complete Works of Ralph Waldo Emerson,* ed. Edward Waldo Emerson, Centenary Edition. 12 vols. Boston: Houghton Mifflin Co., 1903–1904.

JMN   *The Journals and Miscellaneous Notebooks of Ralph Waldo Emerson,* ed. William Gilman et al. 14 vols. to date. Cambridge: Harvard University Press, 1960–.

J   *The Journals of Ralph Waldo Emerson,* ed. Edward Waldo Emerson and Waldo Emerson Forbes. 10 vols. Boston: Houghton Mifflin Co., 1909–1914.

EL   *The Early Lectures of Ralph Waldo Emerson,* ed. Stephen Whicher, Robert Spiller, et al. 3 vols. Cambridge: Harvard University Press, 1959–1972.

RL   *The Letters of Ralph Waldo Emerson,* ed. Ralph Rusk. 6 vols. New York: Columbia University Press, 1939.

21

Acknowledgments

CEC   *The Correspondence of Emerson and Carlyle,* ed. Joseph
       Slater. New York: Columbia University Press, 1964.

It should be noted that in extended and continuous commentaries on individual Emerson essays and lectures,
documentation in each such discussion is limited to a reference at the outset to edition, volume, and pages.

Quotations directly from Emerson holographs are
documented in full in the notes.

Quotations from Emerson's texts in printed or holograph
form reproduce his text without emendation or normaliza-
tion and with a minimal use of *sic*.

I
THE
HOUSE
OF
EMERSON

"Written composition can surpass
any unwritten effusions
of however profound a genius;
for, what is already writ
is a foundation
of the new superstructure,
a guide to the eye
for new foundation,
and a provocation to proceed;
so that the work rises,
tower upon tower,
with ever new and total strength
of the builder."
"Literature" [1837]

•1•
Man Thinking: Emerson's Epistemology

In Emerson's essay, "Intellect," his most explicit epistemological treatise, he describes the mental action of man as follows: "In every man's mind, some images, words, and facts remain, without effort on his part to imprint them, which others forget, and afterwards these illustrate to him important laws. All our progress is an unfolding, like the vegetable bud. You have first an instinct, then an opinion, then a knowledge, as the plant has root, bud, and fruit. Trust the instinct to the end, though you can render no reason. . . . By trusting it to the end, it shall ripen into truth, and you shall know why you believe" (*CW*, II, 195–96). The language here leads us into the heart of what I regard as one of Emerson's central themes, the genesis, exfoliation, and limits of knowing, both in general and in each mental action. Germane to this theme is virtually everything Emerson wrote about men of the arts, technology, and science (he refused to distinguish between them except for reasons of expediency). Indeed, the discussion in "Intellect" touches and to a degree subsumes what Emerson wrote about the capacities and limitations of man in ordering and explicating his world, from *Nature,* published in 1836, to *Fortune of the Republic,* published in 1879. This persistent interest is reflected in the many remarkable discussions and statements in his lectures, essays, and journals, remarkable because they remind us how modern and intellectually attractive Emerson is—Jonathan Bishop describes him as "the

25

least limited, the most permanently suggestive" of American men of letters.[1]

The main thesis in "Intellect" is that the action of thinking begins in a pre-intellectual, hence pre-discursive mode, focuses as an initial conceptualization, and finally matures as thought. This process is a natural ascension from a sensuous reciprocity with one's world to the level of the symbolic and abstract. ("Progressive development" is perhaps a more appropriate description than "evolution." Emerson's favorite metaphors to describe the epistemological ascent are the plant, the expanding circle, and the ladder or staircase.) The same thesis is stated somewhat more abstractly in the journals: "Perception / Memory / Imagination / Metamorphosis / The Flowing & the Melioration or Ascent. / Then, as Dionysius described the orders of celestial angels, so the degrees of Intellect are an organic fact" (*JMN*, XIII, 455). "Perception" here refers to what we might call a pre-reflexive engagement of that world that is within the horizons of one's perceptions and relatedness. "Memory," following immediately upon "Perception" in the journal statement, suggests that individual perceptions are not suspended in isolation. The action of perceiving is susceptible to apperception; there is a tendency to assimilate one's perception with antecedent knowledge and experience. "Imagination" is another term for what in the essay "Intellect" is called "intellect constructive." "Metamorphosis" suggests transformation, in this case into higher "degrees of Intellect," that is, "knowledge." Metamorphosis is the key to Emerson's discussions in his essays of any vital intellectual action, and transformation is the quintessential trait of most of his poetry.

It should be clear that an epistemology that insists on mental life and sees it as "an unfolding, like the vegetable bud," is not on easy speaking terms with modern mechanistic approaches to the subject of the mind and the question of knowing. Knowledge is always more than a learned response, and ideas are more than habit formation, the result of inexorable conditioning. Although for Emerson there is no mental life unless there is a world present to consciousness, and making its imprint on that consciousness, knowing is always a concomitant of a reciprocity with one's world in which the individual acts creatively. Moreover, Emerson sees his thesis reflected in every human action that manifests some kind of mental life: development from infancy to adulthood, the genesis and growth of language, the action of the soul from primal organicism to intellectual and aesthetic initiative,[2] artistic creation, and scientific investigation and discovery, to name some of the notable examples. In each case he sees a purposive movement from inchoate beginnings to eventual dynamic forms.

The source of knowing for Emerson is, in a sense, the world of one's horizons, but, more precisely, it is the transaction between the individual and his world, "in a harmony of both" (*CW,* I, 10). The focus is neither on nature, nor on the self, but on the self in nature, that is, the engaging of one's world. This engagement is never a neutral or passive affair: "In every man's mind, some images, words, and facts remain, *without effort on his part* to imprint them, which others forget . . ." (italics mine). Man, then, always carries a tendency to his world, which adjusts his attention. We might call that tendency a pre-intellectual posture, a commitment or natural rapport that makes it possible for the world to be in a meaningful way. In each act of perception, and in experiencing the world in general, the individual, "without effort on his part," instinctively adopts a position. And this intrinsic involvement in his world is a commitment that is interiorly bound to one's whole being. The view here does not espouse the philosophical idealism of Emerson's day. In *Nature* he seems to invoke idealism, only to admit that it is unsatisfactory. In "Intellect" he warns that we "do not determine what we will think." Rather, we "suffer the intellect to see" (*CW,* II, 195). Yet, although we do not determine what we will see, we will see what we are instinctively ready to see (*CW,* II, 195–96). One does not automatically and passively receive the world's stimuli, but experiences them intentionally, that is, accepts and disposes "of all impressions from the surrounding creation after [one's] own way. Whatever any mind doth or saith is after a law." It has no random act or word. And "this native law remains over it after it has come to reflection or conscious thought" (*CW*, II, 194). "Native law" suggests an intentionality inherent in one's being. If the speaker in *Nature* was surprised by a moment of delight while crossing the muddy and bare Concord common, that moment was indeed a surprise, even though Emerson immediately proceeds to "explain" it within a teleological context.

Although not limited to personal experience, knowing is, for Emerson, always rooted in experience. The "unfolding" of this knowledge, according to "Intellect," is an exfoliation through two stages of knowing, the pre-personal or pre-reflexive and the personal or conscious. When he writes of "instinct" he has in mind a rudimentary consciousness that is the seedbed of knowledge. A number of suggestive images help us to venture into this world of "instinct." He speaks, for example, of the "darkness" of pre-reflexive reality (*CW*, II, 194) and of the "dark chamber" as the primordial antecedent to knowledge. Apparently "chamber" signifies both a repository (especially of significant points of interest that Wordsworth calls "spots of time" in Book XII of *The Prelude*) and a preparatory state, that is, a kind of vague notion or sense (*CW*, II, 198). This primal state is related to infancy (*CW*, II, 194), since instinctive action is the child's primary mode of experiencing his world. Infancy and the infancy of a thought are related. Emerson also speaks of "floating," "rapture," and "ecstasy," a natural, pre-conscious, yet intense experiencing of the world, an experiencing that is not yet knowledge but is a nascent possibility (*CW*, II, 194–95). It is apparent from most of these passages that Emerson rarely focuses on a distinctive faculty within man, some deep aboriginal region, as the progenitor of knowledge. Instead, he emphasizes an aboriginal engagement of the world as the basis for any knowing.

Jonathan Bishop describes this action as follows: "As he responds to actions that take place beyond his conscious control, he will become all the more deeply aware of the mode of being within himself that is equally given, equally an aspect of the natural order. And if these natural actions are the motions of living beings, animal or vegetable, they will reflect to their observer a renewed consciousness of himself, not merely as a natural event but as a living one, a being alive within an organic scene."[3] Such a condition, Bishop argues persuasively from Emerson's writings, was the basis for consciousness in Emerson's experiences and the initiating point in his epistemology. At this level, Emerson indicates, the perceiver is at one with his world; only when the incipient knowledge ascends to "intellection" does he begin to be aware of a separation from his world and think in terms of subject and object (*CW*, II, 193–94).

Emerson encourages his audience to "trust the instinct to the end." After all, it is no accident. Moreover, it is the all-important epistemological genesis. Such an organicism, which at best dimly forebodes the truth, does not pass with childhood. "This instinctive action never ceases in a healthy mind, but becomes richer and more frequent in its informations through all states of culture" (*CW*, II, 196). We could say that the wider the range and the more intense the energy of vital experiencing, the more likely the resources of the mind will be employed, and employed well.

"I knew, in an academical club," Emerson notes, "a person who always deferred to me, who, seeing my whim for writing, fancied that my experiences had somewhat superior; whilst I saw that his experiences were as good as mine. Give them to me, and I would make the same use of them. He held the old; he holds the new; I had the habit of tacking together the old and the new, which he did not use to exercise" (*CW*, II, 197). Several things in this illustration are important to us. First, instinctive action is incipient knowledge, but the transformation from one to the other is not guaranteed by any kind of necessity. Emerson's declaration that "you have first an instinct, then an opinion, then a knowledge, as the plant has root, bud, and fruit," does not imply an inevitable development but emphasizes the natural progression whenever knowledge has in fact been the "fruit." It was clear to him that instinctive action becomes for many a perdurable state. In *Nature* he noted with a touch of condescending irony the "sort of instinctive belief in the absolute existence of nature. In their view, man and nature are indissolubly joined." Later in the paragraph he notes that the "first effort of thought tends to relax this despotism of the senses, which binds us to nature as if we were a part of it" (*CW*, I, 30). The word "effort" should not be overlooked. In "Intellect" Emerson asks, "What is the hardest task in the world?" His answer: "To think" (*CW*, II, 196). Forestalling mental action is the common denominator of the conservative and the sensualist. It is in this respect that Emerson describes both as men of instinct alone, even though they might appear to be at opposite epistemological poles. To think is the hardest task in the world because the life of the senses all too readily becomes a way of life. Goethe's Mephistopheles, in contrast to the ever-striving Faust, is one of Emerson's examples of such an animal man. Alek Therien was Thoreau's example of a mind stifled by a "despotism of the senses." In such a life, and Emerson speaks of it as though it is omnipresent, the seeds of knowledge remain dormant.

The conservative, hidebound in institutions, is, of course, deprived of the strong sensuous contact with the world. But he is not deprived of instinctive responses. His mental life has fossilized because of his mindless (instinctive) acceptance of ideas and institutions at second hand. This fossil state is Emerson's definition of conservatism in the opening paragraph of *Nature*. In the sixth chapter he links the sensualist and conservative: "To the senses [sensualist] and the unrenewed understanding [conservative], belongs a sort of instinctive belief in the absolute existence of nature" (*CW*, I, 30). In "Intellect" the discussion of the man in the "academical club" reiterates a belief Emerson repeatedly expresses, that every opinion or knowledge is essentially a new creation, a new understanding or interpretation of the world. Knowledge, for Emerson, is always a miracle. Of conservatives he writes, "this class, however large, relying not on the intellect but on the instinct, blends itself with the brute forces of nature, is respectable only as nature is, but the individuals have no attraction for us" (*CW,* I, 172). The conservative, then, like the animal man, is unnatural; both have become victims of instinctive action. Higher modes of consciousness, arriving at new and unpredicted knowledge, are characteristic of the artist,[4] the dissenter, the theorist, the aspirant—in short, "man thinking." Emerson's acquaintance in the "academical club" apparently was able to progress ever so slightly beyond instinctive action—at least he came upon the new, although he was incapable of doing anything with it. His pre-personal relationship with his world had begun to give new meaning to his world and himself in the world, but he held the new in suspension while he lived by the old.

The progression from rudimentary consciousness to intellectual activity, especially as it crosses the threshold of knowledge, obviously is crucial in Emerson's epistemology. And because the misleading impression that for Emerson some have a special capacity or faculty and others do not is all too easily created, we need to investigate further his statements on how instinctive action generates conscious awareness, reflection, conceptualization, and, above all, discursiveness. The metamorphosis from experiencing to thoughts is contingent on several factors. One of these is that the mind takes its direction from its own life. It is not a tool that simply serves our business; it must be released from restrictions and prior allegiances (*CW,* II, 195; see also, for example, *W,* III, 27). If we keep in mind Emerson's definition of thinking we can appreciate his insistence that before knowledge is possible the mind must be free to generate its own forms. We do not determine that we will think or precisely what we will think. In Emerson's words, "We only open our senses, clear away, as we can, all obstruction from the fact, and suffer the intellect to see" (*CW,* II, 195).

The freedom of which Emerson speaks here is a notable concomitant of healthy organic vitality; hence we are reminded once again of the value he places on "instinctive action." This action, he has cautioned, can produce mental deadness. However, intensifying this action not as an end in itself but as an initiator of intellectual possibilities is something that man can and should do. In the words of "The Poet": "if in any manner we can stimulate this instinct, new passages are opened for us into nature; the mind flows into and through things hardest and highest, and the metamorphosis is possible" (*W,* III, 27). The "we" removes any doubt about Emerson's appeal for greater sensuous aliveness. Although the first person plural is probably the editorial "we" of the speaker, and although Emerson trusted himself with sensuous aliveness more than most of the recent critics have allowed,[5] the "we" also suggests a coterie of those who understand Emerson well and with whom he can take some rhetorical shortcuts. Those who embrace instinctive action at the expense of mental life are always referred to in the third person.

If the metamorphosis into thought is made possible, what makes it probable? On this point Emerson is understandably vague. A ripeness for thinking is not enough; the actual birth of "opinion" and "thought" is "spontaneous" (*CW,* II, 195–99). Emerson's language on this question is full of references to surprising insights, flashes of inspiration, sudden awareness. In "Intellect" he underscores this, employing the metaphor of the surveyor or architect: "With a geometry of sunbeams, the soul lays the foundations of nature" (*CW,* II, 204). ("Soul" here is a synonym for man thinking.) Spontaneity is easily reconcilable with Emerson's metaphor of gradual exfoliation, but suddenness presents some difficulties. Yet he wants us to see both the spontaneous coming into being of knowledge and the frequently sudden intuitive grasping that it entails as an indispensable part of the exfoliation. That is, the miracle of insight blesses the healthy, free, and exfoliating mental life.

The engendering of "opinion" and "knowledge" out of the incipient primordial consciousness as a spontaneous action is what Emerson refers to as "the intuitive principle" (*CW*, II, 195). Already in 1836 in *Nature* he described true learning (that which crosses the perimeters of our present knowledge and to that degree reorders what we know) as new insight, indeed, an organizing or reorganizing act. To know, man needs an environment. But conditioning, the "despotism of the senses," becomes a barrier to new knowledge, the blinkers that keep the horse's orientation as narrow and governable as possible. The intuitive principle implies a breaking out of this constriction. Emerson's favorite metaphors in this regard report liberation, expansion, and entering into the unfathomed. But chiefly they report man as a creative being—"himself the creator in the finite" (*CW*, I, 38)—and authentic knowing as creative activity. The intuitive principle is a natural expression of man's whole being. The light not so much breaks in upon man as suddenly shines within him. We are back to intentionality: just as man is naturally disposed to the world in a particular way on the pre-reflexive level, so man's intrinsic tendency is to be man thinking, constantly to fashion new knowledge. As Emerson says, "this native law remains over it [the mind] after it has come to reflection or conscious thought" (*CW*, II, 194). When this tendency in man is thwarted and rendered helpless, man becomes "a god in ruins."

The "intuitive principle," a teleological behavior central to the exfoliation of thought, is part of a more inclusive tendency in man: "It seems as if the law of the intellect resembled that law of nature by which we now inspire, now expire the breath; by which the heart now draws in, then hurls out the blood,—the law of undulation. So now you must labor with your brains, and now you must forbear your activity, and see what the great Soul showeth" (*CW*, II, 197; see also 198, 201, 203). Emerson introduces a new metaphor, "undulation," and with it a new problem. Is mental life undulation or exfoliation? Or do we have two basic epistemological experiences here? Several observations need to be made. First, Emerson's method is always to sidle up to his many-sided subjects with numerous metaphors. He is never satisfied with single metaphors or the "direct solving word" (see especially *JMN,* VIII, 23; IX, 259–60). Furthermore, the idea expressed by the reference to undulation is akin to Wordsworth's distinction between powerful experiencing and emotion recollected in tranquility. By insisting on the first, one will "sink into . . . sensation"; by rejecting it in favor of the detached and pensive mode one "may climb into the thin and cold realm" of abstraction. "Between these extremes is the equator of life, of thought, of spirit, of poetry" (*W,* III, 62). When Emerson described Alcott as a pail without a bottom (*JMN,* IX, 208) he was undoubtedly referring to more than domestic mismanagement and impracticality. Alcott is also described as "the fool of ideas" (*JMN,* VIII, 6).

Undulation, or respiration, then, is a more inclusive concept than exfoliation. Basic to exfoliation is the inspiring and the expiring, assimilation and relaxation. Exfoliation of thought is a continuous organic process. But vital mental life is not a lifelong nursing of a single thought; it is the sprouting and transformation of many thoughts and the growth of large thoughts in many successive stages. What makes each new thought or further growth possible is that consciousness relaxes and tends to revert for the time being to a more instinctive mode, only to anticipate another exfoliation. In "Intellect" Emerson describes the life of thought as a perpetual "undulation" in which instinctive action dilates into conscious thought, which then recedes as instinctive action becomes dominant again. Emerson is, of course, primarily interested in the exfoliation from instinct to thought, but simultaneously he affirms the endless undulation.

The ascendancy of "thought," its budding and ripening (to return to the analogy early in "Intellect"), includes two aspects of mental action that Emerson describes as "intellect receptive" and "intellect constructive" (*CW*, II, 198). These are in no way mutually exclusive. The first refers to the individual's capacity to appropriate and retain impressions of the world, to separate them from the world, and to disentangle them from rudimentary consciousness so that they are there for our contemplation. The second is a synonym for the recurrent term "genius," the creative power to fashion the impressions into an "advent of truth." Together they denote the simultaneously receptive and projective character of intellectual action. The metaphoric mode of the mind at once reporting the world and the mind that perceives it shows the two aspects as ultimately one unified action. In considering them, however, Emerson conveniently discusses them separately.

When man begins to contemplate his world intellectually, to grasp it not only as an aggregate number of impressions but as a world that is taking on meaning for him, the world moves into separation as the mind interprets it. In the words of Emerson, "intellect separates the fact considered from *you*, from all local and personal reference, and discerns it as if it existed for its own sake . . . cool and disengaged." He who is immersed in the world and cannot contemplate it does not experience this gulf, but neither can he "see the problem of existence" (*CW*, II, 193, 194). As Bishop observes, "This epistemological split between the subject of perception and the object perceived is very much a part of what Emerson has to say about the way the mind works; it is felt by him, organically, as a loss, an alienation from nature, but intellectually as a gain."[6] The alienating effect is noted in *Nature:* "The first effort of thought tends to relax this despotism of the senses, which binds us to nature as if we were a part of it, and shows us nature aloof" (*CW*, I, 30). The loss produced by "intellect receptive" (in *Nature* "the gymnastics of the understanding") is immediately also a gain. As the world moves into separation from man, a distance is also created between man and himself so that the mind is not simply caught up in rapture and, perhaps more frequently, overwhelmed by pain. On the latter, Emerson states that what we contemplate "is eviscerated of care." "We behold it as a god upraised above care and fear" (*CW*, II, 194). Or, as he writes in a late essay: "The intellect is a consoler, which delights in detaching or putting an interval between a man and his fortune, and so converts the sufferer into a spectator and his pain into poetry" (*W*, XII, 416). In short, despite the apparent gulf, "What is addressed to us for contemplation does not threaten us, but makes us intellectual beings" (*CW*, II, 194).

In Emerson's comment that the "intellect separates the fact considered . . . and discerns it as if it existed for its own sake," the almost too casual qualifier is "as if." On the instinctive level man is naturally at harmony with his world. "Intellect receptive" leads to a differentiation from his world, but "intellect constructive" establishes a new relatedness. If mental action replaces unity with diversity, it also discovers a new unity in diversity. According to Emerson, the artist (particularly the literary artist) and the scientist manifest a special degree of genius to unify, for constructive intellect "is the generation of the mind, the marriage of thought with nature." After all, "The world refuses to be analyzed by addition and subtraction" (*CW*, II, 198, 201). "We are too passive in the reception of these material or semi-material aids," he complains in "Uses of Great Men," reiterating the indictment of his age in the last chapter of *Nature*. "We must not be sacks and stomachs. To ascend one step,—we are better served through our sympathy." And thus he proceeds to call for the "man of vigorous mind" (*W*, IV, 13). "The sensual man conforms thoughts to things." We might add that the mind, simply by being mind, alienates man from things, but "the poet [more specifically his genius] conforms things to his thoughts" (*CW*, I, 31). This achievement marks not only the poet but also any mind whenever it is free to do its work. In the vigorous mind, perception "is not like the vision of the eye, but is union with the things known" (*CW*, II, 193). This "very high sort of seeing, which does not come by study," is "a secret which every intellectual man quickly learns, that beyond the energy of his possessed and conscious intellect [receptive and contemplative aspect] he is capable of a new energy (as of an intellect doubled on itself)" (*W,* III, 26). In *Nature* Emerson names this intellectual action "Reason." There he refers to two manifestations of "Reason," the adding of "grace and expression" to what we contemplate and, even more notable, the discovery of "causes and spirits" in what we behold. By "causes" he implies connections and relatedness. In the journals he observes that "Talent makes counterfeit ties. Genius finds the real ones" (*JMN,* IX, 220). "Spirits" in the context of Emerson's writings usually refers to spiritual energy or presence. One might submit point of view in literary art or perspective in painting as illustrations—we recognize and refer to something that is part of a perceiving mind, an expression growing out of the artist as he engages his world and at the same time vitalizes and orders that world. There are times when Emerson's comments on the constructive aspect of intellect suggest a private and subjective creation of a new order, very much like that of the singer in Wallace Stevens's "The Idea of Order at Key West." At other times this action of the mind is an uncovering of something that has always been there, but not available to the mind because of the constrictions of habit or fear of the new. Most often it is selecting, reshuffling, and reinterpreting already existing and familiar objects, facts, and ideas, and synthesizing them into a new order.

The genesis of new knowledge, in short, is both disjunctive and constructive. To begin with, a childlike devotion to instinctive action must be relaxed. Moreover, rigid patterns of mental organization must be broken so that the world can become meaningful again. Hence the constructive is allied to the disjunctive. Although old relations are broken and the world moves away from us, threatening to leave us in isolation, the mind moves into that world, discovers new relations, and closes the dichotomy of self and world. Emerson's best metaphor to express the two tendencies is the expanding circle. When the world moves outward the image is not pleasant—the circles leave us behind like a universe expanding more rapidly than our ability to contact it. When it is the mind that moves, the metaphor argues the infinite possibilities of man. We both receive the world and make the world. Emerson's heroes are individuals who distinguish themselves in these two respects.

To discuss the nature of thinking is to address the question of language. Emerson reminds us, "to genius must always go two gifts, the thought and the publication" (*CW*, II, 198). In *Nature* he observes, "A man conversing in earnest, if he watch his intellectual processes, will find that always a material image, more or less luminous, arises in his mind, cotemporaneous with every thought, which furnishes the vestment of the thought" (*CW*, I, 20). Most salient in this statement is that, according to Emerson, language comes into being just as thought does, and simultaneously with thought. The noun "vestment," which out of context might suggest a ready-tailored coat for the client (perhaps the authority-laden garb of the clergy), should not mislead us, for Emerson insists that verbal images exfoliate like our thoughts. The reference to "more or less luminous" images has a double meaning: the images are reasonably clear, that is, adequate to the thought, and the images may range from vagueness to surprising lucidity. The range from the very vague to the perspicuous covers the spectrum of instinct, opinion, and thought. Most important, language is not primarily a means, a handy vehicle, but a manifestation. The word is not there, ready to signify a concept that exists apart from it, but is the expression of the thinking itself. It too "must become." Our thoughts are not real and have no power in our lives unless and until they are expressed. "The rich, inventive genius of the painter must be smothered and lost for want of the power of drawing." On the other hand, the painter's vision is there when it descends "into the hand" (*CW,* II, 199).

Thought is incarnated in verbal expression. Through the word the thought seeks and finds its completion. Only when "the spiritual energy is directed on something outward," in this case the verbal image, is it a thought (*CW*, II, 199). In "Intellect," as in most of his other discussions of language, Emerson assumes that whenever language is an authentic incarnation of thought, it will communicate publicly; he rarely goes on to explain definitively how or why.

Since language is for Emerson the incarnation of thinking from its most inchoate to its most structured state, one must infer that some images in a special way attune us to the pulse of organic vitality and that primordial consciousness is a residual quality in all language. In other words, since language is incipient in rudimentary consciousness, one would expect some of the affective force of the primal state to be conveyed in the images of formal language. The power of "imaginative vocabulary," Emerson points out, flows in part "from experience," that is, organic experiencing (*CW*, II, 199). (If "instinctive action" is low, language will not have the desirable power, and to that degree the intellect is help-less.) In *Nature* Emerson states, "This immediate dependence of language upon nature, this conversion of an outward phenomenon into a type of somewhat in human life, never loses its power to affect us" (*CW*, I, 20). Here is the most basic kind of language, a sensory and affective order-ing, a kind of pre-reflexive gesturing, which Emerson finds most noticeable in the language of a child and primitive man.[7] Words in a primitive state tend to be word sentences that do not so much communicate a thought as tune us in to a kind of sense by gesturing. This primal expression in language is the gesture by which the world becomes a world according to man. Contrary to many modern archetypal critics, Emerson does not regard this sense as transcending time and place and the apparent meaning of the language in question. For him such gesturing is a function of style, which, by tuning us in to language, facilitates subsequent understanding of the language and, therefore, of the thinking.

"And yet," writes Emerson, "the imaginative vocabu-lary . . . does not flow from experience only or mainly, but from a richer source." That source is "the fountain-head of all forms in his mind" (*CW*, II, 199). Genius, the constructive capacity in mental action, expresses itself in metaphoric ability. "Imaginative vocabulary" is the result of the mind working analogically, bringing about "the marriage of thought with nature" by metaphors that thoroughly do the job. On the level of "opinion" this marriage is at best only a trial engagement, at worst a shotgun affair. "Opinion" suggests an initial pictorializing and conceptualizing that verifies the metaphoric capacity of the mind but has not reached that point in the mental activity at which the metaphor is authentic because as a mental and literary fact it works. Object and action concepts rise to the reflective level, an important progression in the genesis of metaphors as "imaginative vocabulary." But, if the metaphor has occurred, it is not as yet recognized as adequately relational to the larger background of environmental contingencies and the context of the thought being generated.

Verbally, "thought" is apparent as the culmination of the mind's action in inventing metaphors. It implies metaphors that successfully mediate between mind and world or ME and NOT ME. Knowing is impossible except through metaphoric action. For this reason all language turns on metaphor. Metaphor and metamorphosis share more than common syllables. As Bishop has noted, by the time Emerson returned from Europe to America in 1833 he recognized that a metaphor shares an identity both "with the facts it reports" and "the mind that invented it."[8] Through the metaphor one clarifies an aspect of the environment, an aspect of the self, and an aspect of the self in its environment. Thus metaphors are at once fully a product of the world and fully a product of man thinking. "Moments of intellectual discovery, scientific or otherwise, occur when someone invents a metaphor for the world that turns out to be the true name of the world."[9] The context of this quoted passage explains "true" for us—the metaphor is "true" because it succeeds. Or as Emerson puts it, "That which was unconscious truth, becomes, when interpreted and defined in an object, a part of the domain of knowledge,—a new weapon in the magazine of power" (*CW,* I, 23).

Understood in Emerson's terms, all language is metaphoric whenever the mind *knows.* And every authentic act of thinking implies the creation of metaphors. Subsisting on institutionalized ideas and culturally fixed words is not thinking, but a regression to instincts. But "imaginative vocabulary," which corroborates the ripening into knowledge, is always a new language. To some extent the mind acts as though there is no given language. Even those words that appear to be stock terminology the reader discovers to be fresh and natural in their new context (*W,* III, 22, 24). Emerson was familiar with the distinction in Hellenistic and Biblical Greek between *logos* and *rāma.* The latter means the precise, established, lexical word. "Logos," however, means both word and creative reason. It is "logos" that puts sense into the world and made sense of man. Indeed, "logos" is mind in its highest expression. And "logos" is Emerson's term for the verbal expression of the creative mind (*W,* III, 40; discussed more fully in chapter six).

If the preceding remarks give the impression that for Emerson language is never accidental or haphazard but that all men manifest in their discourse their intrinsic creativity, we need to take note of several qualifications in "Intellect." True, language, like primal and reflexive consciousness, is characterized as intentional. And Emerson firmly believes man's destiny is to be creative. Some individuals are able to exploit their genius, however, whereas others fail to do so. Many individuals have the capacity to engage their world poetically; only a few are poets. "There is an inequality," he concedes, "whose laws we do not yet know, between two men and between two moments of the same man, in respect to this faculty." Although Emerson pleads ignorance on this matter, he makes an observation that is not in keeping with popular romantic notions of genius and creativity: "the power of picture or expression, in the most enriched and flowing nature, implies a mixture of will, a certain control over the spontaneous states, without which no production is possible. It is a conversion of all nature into the rhetoric of thought, under the eye of judgment, with a strenuous exercise of choice" (*CW*, II, 199). Just what Emerson had in mind by the strenuous exercise of the will in thinking, speaking, and writing well is not entirely clear. We are reminded, of course, of the connection between the power of the word and the lived situation. But more seems to be implied here, a conscious commitment and volitional energy. Such a discipline protects against entrapment in the rapture of the moment, or bedazzlement by individual revelations on many sides. To create effective metaphors and thus clarify one's world requires that one be at the top of one's condition.

The passage once again underscores the high priority Emerson places on expression. "The most wonderful inspirations die with their subject, if he has no hand to paint them to the senses" (*CW*, II, 198–99). As we are reminded in "The Poet," "man is only half himself, the other half is his expression" (*W*, III, 5). And so "the true romance which the world exists to realize will be the transformation of genius into practical power" (*W*, III, 86).

Stephen Whicher noted that what mattered for Emerson "was not so much truth as truth-making, not thoughts but thinking." For man living his life and the student reading Emerson's essays, "the essential thing is not any given insight but the vital capacity to move from one to the next according to the natural rhythm of thought. The life of the mind is a perpetual voyage of discovery."[10] One recalls Emerson's image of mental activity as endless undulation between "instinctive action" and intellectual abstraction. On the other hand, there is Emerson's persistent emphasis on expression (verbal or otherwise) as the truest act and fulfillment of thinking. Without it, thoughts vanish like the Cheshire cat. Yet expression, particularly in language, implies a degree of fixation, for although the mind does not stop, the word, in a sense, is a stopping. As thinker and literary artist Emerson

42

was keenly aware of the paradox; he took up this matter in early essays like *Nature*, "The American Scholar," "Circles," "Intellect," "Art," and "The Poet." By his middle years, both in his essays and journals, the issue had become a brooding concern. Several journal entries register typical warnings: "The wise is not to be preached & not to be flattered out of his position of perpetual inquiry. The young & admiring tend to make him quit his apprenticeship & sit down & build homestead, church & state like other householders that have renounced their right to traverse the star lit desarts [sic] of truth, for the comforts of an acre, house, & barn. The Goodies on the other hand taunt him with inefficiency, with homelessness, with 'having no shelter', with pride in refusing to accept the revealed word of truth. . . . Nothing is so shallow as dogmatism. Your soaring thought is only a point more a station more whence you draw triangles for the survey of the illimitable field" (*JMN*, VII, 32). The surveying here is an action by which we make the uncharted our own, then continue on into the unknown. The self-evolving circle expresses the same—the appearance of another circle around the last, without end. "How many centres we have fondly found, which proved soon to be circumferential points!" (*JMN*, XI, 235). Momentary stopping is at once also the point of departure. "A wise man is not deceived by the pause: he knows that it is momentary: he already foresees the new departure, and departure after departure, in long series. Dull people think they have traced the matter far enough if they have reached the history of one of these temporary forms, which they describe as fixed & final" (*JMN*, IX, 301).

This last passage, in particular, explains the nature and strategy of language. It is a temporary form, and it acts as a motivation to discover new knowledge. Language as point of departure is Emerson's point in the last pages of "Intellect." When truths are fixed, and they, rather than truth-seeking, become our preoccupation, they turn into falsehoods. "How wearisome the grammarian, the phrenologist, the political or religious fanatic, or indeed any possessed mortal, whose balance is lost by the exaggeration of a single topic. It is incipient insanity. Every thought is a prison also" (*CW,* II, 200–201). The mind should always carry its theories and certainties lightly. Metaphoric action characterized by tentativeness, fluidity, and restlessness and onwardness exemplifies the vital mind. One can understand, then, why the man who dares to practice an honest skepticism becomes Emerson's hero of truth. As Emerson puts it, "Value of the Skeptic is the resistance to premature conclusions. If he prematurely conclude, his conclusion will be shattered, & he will become malignant. But he must limit himself with the anticipation of law in the mutations,— flowing law" (*JMN,* IX, 295). If the writer has learned this lesson well, then "each symbol is figured merely as a stimulus to send the reader on to new institutions."[11] His language is a blessing that, if it fossilizes, becomes a curse for writer and reader. The quality of true mind and language "is to flow, and not to freeze" (*W,* III, 34). But here precisely is the choice, to accept the fluxional, with its aspects of doubting and searching for better terms, or to turn to the easy security of the fixed—a "choice between truth and repose." "He in whom the love of repose predominates, will accept the first creed, the first philosophy, the first political party he meets. . . . He gets rest, commodity, and reputation; but he shuts the door of truth. He in whom the love of truth predominates, will keep himself aloof from all moorings and afloat." In so doing, man "respects the highest law of his being" (*CW,* II, 202).

Emerson's epistemology ends as an argument for man thinking. His faith in the possibilities of an energetic, explorative, and rigorously disciplined mind sustained his liberalism in an age that for many reasons horrified him. It was impossible for him, of course, to track down in a brief discourse like "Intellect" all the implications of such a mind for his age. Even all his writings together do not offer anything resembling an exhaustive analysis of the subject. This too is characteristically Emersonian. Nonetheless, in

"Intellect" Emerson draws his own surveyor's triangles, which serve as guidelines for more specific charting. These practical indicators (and "practical" is the best word if one remembers Emerson's interest in that which really works imaginatively, morally, intellectually, and communally) crop up recurrently, each time in a somewhat altered form.

For Emerson the vital mind is always the authorization of self-reliance. Self-reliance is the final exhortation of "Intellect" (*CW,* II, 203) as well as the title of an essay he is most commonly known by, and it is his noblest if rarely understood lesson. Divorced from his view of the mind and his rigorous demands on it, self-reliance is little more than sounding brass. Growing out of his views of the mind and man thinking, self-reliance is an intelligible and persuasive appeal. Commenting in "The Method of Nature" on man's record of productivity, Emerson advises his readers, "I do not wish to look with sour aspect at the industrious manufacturing village, or the mart of commerce. I love the music of the water-wheel; I value the railway; I feel the pride which the sight of a ship inspires. I look on trade and every mechanical craft as education also. But let me discriminate what is precious herein. There is in each of these works one act of invention, one intellectual step, or short series of steps taken; that act or step is the spiritual act: all the rest is mere repetition of the same a thousand times." These spiritual acts, Emerson goes on to say, are the works of a minority of individuals, yet embody man's "spiritual prerogatives" (*CW,* I, 120–21).

Each of these acts reports man thinking. A series of such acts in the span of an individual life is Emerson's definition of biography and fvorite metaphor for biography; the record of such acts over the span of more than one life is what he understood by the term history. To the extent that a single achievement by a Shakespeare or a Newton epitomized a constellation of achievements across the span of time, the metamorphosis in the achievement became itself a type of history. In this respect biography is history and history biography. Each is the record of the right kind of "departure, in long series." As such, biography and history are the record of a dynamic and progressive unfolding. Retrospective and retrogressive vision are quite out of keeping with them, whereas metaphors of exfoliation, expanding circles, the helix, undulation, and the series of advance are means of unfolding the subject. In asserting that "Man is endogenous, and education is his unfolding" (*W*, IV, 8), Emerson is also suggesting that "unfolding" is the principal form of education for man thinking and the unfolding of man thinking is the reader's truest education.

•2•
The Artist:
Metamorphosis
and Metaphor

If we focus on the act of invention described in "The Method of Nature" as a "spiritual act" and on Emerson's view of biography and history, we can begin to discern the essential Emersonian mode, which illustrates and enacts his view of metaphor and the nature of literary art. Inherent in his mode and presiding over most of his comments on man's perception and expression, especially in conjunction with language, art, and the artist, is the law of permutation, which implies a dual principle of concentration on a point and departure from the point, both of these actions serving metamorphosis. At the time when Emerson was beginning to use his journals to draft a number of discontinuous passages soon to become vital impulses and clarifications in the text of his new composition, *Nature*, he noted: "The truest state of mind, rested in, becomes false. Thought is the manna which cannot be stored. It will be sour if kept, & tomorrow must be gathered anew. Perpetually must we East ourselves, or we get into irrecoverable error." This passage was important enough to be incorporated by him into two of his lectures, "Religion" and "The Present Age." As though to sum up the implications of the journal passage, the next paragraph of the entry concludes, "Not in his goals but in his transition man is great" (*JMN*, V, 38).

The metaphors here express the same concern registered more forcefully in the opening paragraph of *Nature*. "Our age" has gotten into irrecoverable error by being "retrospective." The heart of Emerson's concern is reported by metaphors that excoriate experience, language, philosophy, religion, and poetry at second hand, an error pictured as groping "among the dry bones of the past." The scene is perhaps a musty closet of skeletons and badly faded and outmoded clothes, perhaps a mausoleum, perhaps a valley of bones and clothing remnants. Whatever the scene, these bones cannot live. In the past some vital minds enjoyed their works and days. Today perception is as eyeless as a skull, language is a fossil, and man is "a god in ruins." A startling and promising, if somewhat pompous, beginning. What can *Nature* say after such an introduction? The better question is, "Where does it go?" Like the manna of the journal passage, the statements of *Nature* cannot be stored. Paragraphs and chapters continue to gather new statements, which redefine the old. As soon as we stop reading *Nature* we have lost it, because the essay is still going; the next sentence is always Emerson's, and there is always a next step.

Reading Emerson, we should always be aware of the need for fresh considerations of what the art gives us if we read more, or if we read more fully and attentively. That should be the main expectation. Despite the fact that *Nature* was written a century and a half ago, it is new to us, and disturbing in its freedom of presentation. It is free in several ways, two of which are noted here: free from the backwash of traditional metaphoric material and from the traditional process of developing that material. The latter achievement, the Emersonian mode, is the principal subject of this chapter, as it is of chapter six, where it is discussed in greater detail and in the contexts of Emerson's poetry and his development as a writer. Emerson calls his mode by many names, including metamorphosis, mutation, transmutation, protean play, flowing law, Heraclitus's law, the active soul, and poetry.

For the reader demanding of the essays and lectures a traditional narrative or expository organization, it is no easier to get a handle on Emerson than it was for Henry James, Sr. A sentence or paragraph will not do, nor his favorite terms, nor those epigrammatic declarations by which many generations have come to know and represent Emerson, nor summations or concluding evocations in his essays, nor comments in his journals and letters about his essays. We have some Emerson thoughts in hand, but the thinking with its flowing law, the real art, is elsewhere. Emerson himself never furnished a systematically organized presentation of his philosophy or a grammar of his thinking. In and of itself "Intellect" does not explain Emerson's epistemology, much less diagram it. "We forget in taking up a cotemporary book," Emerson noted, "that we see the house that is building & not the house that is built" (*JMN*, VIII, 132). The essay on Montaigne quotes the journals in calling for a philosophical house that is not fastened to pilings and anchored in bedrock but resembles a sailing vessel that can cope well with a world "of fluxions & mobility" (*JMN*, IX, 222). In *Freedom and Fate* Stephen Whicher legitimately complained of Emerson's *Nature* without pressing hard his complaint: "One cannot always easily penetrate its rapid criss-cross of ideas and see its underlying intention."[1] What appears to have been a revised opinion a few years thereafter was simply a closer attention on Emerson as artist and the prevailing characteristic of the art: "What mattered, then, was not so much truth as truthmaking, not thoughts but thinking." And he added, "A failure to appreciate his method is responsible for a number of traditional errors about Emerson."[2]

In "Uses of Great Men" Emerson suggests that "the transmutings of the imagination" are "intellectual feats" a reader witnesses with pleasure and benefit (*W, IV*, 16). In the context of *Representative Men* this statement is more richly suggestive than when isolated as a representative declaration. In Emerson's art the intellectual feat we admire usually begins as an important philosophic problem and crucial questions directly connected with it. With few exceptions, however, his art proceeds from this initiating point into a mode he sometimes referred to as "poetic"—a process of metamorphosis in tropes, context, and reference. Such a process, in which metaphor is principal and agent, arrives not at a philosophic explanation but an artistic solution. Thus the philosophic problem is transmuted into artistic process and the literary enactments into a truth-making.

The more important signal in this sentence from "Uses of Great Men" is in the word "transmutings," a double-entendre in its context. On the one hand, it implies change, a continual shifting and departure—characteristics allied to the premise underlying Emerson's view of any vital mental life. This premise, alluded to in the preceding chapter, can be restated in the words of the journals: "The method of advance in nature is perpetual transformation. Be ready to emerge from the chrysalis of today, its thoughts & institutions, as thou hast come out of the chrysalis of yesterday" (*JMN*, VII, 524). Thus all life, including the individual mental life and the life of the kind of art Emerson proposed, "is an interim & a transition; this, O Indur, is my one & twenty thousandth form, and already I feel the old Life sprouting underneath in the twenty thousand & first" (*JMN*, VIII, 432–33).

The other meaning of "transmutings" is to concentrate and hold in relationship all the interim and partial elements, a holding action by metaphors in the art and representative men in the culture who establish, or reestablish, the center that Emerson's law assumes to be in motion. Occasionally, the metaphoric constructions are so concentrated, dynamic, comprehensive, and widely resonating that they approximate the definition of God that Emerson, in "Circles," attributes to Augustine: a logos "whose centre is everywhere, and its circumference nowhere." Such figures, although never static, immortal, or immutable, are fixed "to a millennium" (*JMN*, VII, 426) in that they exhibit extraordinary cultural and historical resonance and are allied to our best possibilities. To outwait the resistance of the moment and his narrow antagonists and to witness the elevation of his tropes to the level of such a logos is the hope of the patient and doggedly subversive Uriel. His ambition accounts for the fear and hostility of his heavenly peers, who understand themselves and the kind of concentration in Emerson's law of permutation as little as they understand Uriel.

To the extent that the metaphoric act approaches the definition of God in "Circles" it concentrates the entire literary work and thus is the work. As such it corresponds most closely to what Emerson regards as the ideal role of the scholar in his world. When the individual feat of man thinking measures up to the greatness celebrated in "Uses of Great Men," the scholar's private wealth encompasses the commonwealth and so is identified with it. In the work of such a genius, Emerson wrote, the "soul of all men circulates."[3] Emerson also contended that only when the particular wealth can be equated with commonwealth is man truly an individual (see *JMN*, VII, 441). Emerson's self-reliance is reserved exclusively for such an individual, and his essay "Self-Reliance" looks forward directly to *Representative Men.* In the work of this individual, no matter what his vocation, the great metaphor is self-regulating and self-justifying in a literary, biographical, and cultural sense. Seen in this context, *Representative Men* is as much a study of failures as successes. But in essay after essay, ferreting out failures of great individuals is part of the process of arriving at a literary definition of completeness and an artistic success.

Concentration and permutation, then, are the suggestive terms for discussing both man thinking and the internal structural principle of Emerson's art. "The metamorphosis of nature shows itself in nothing more than this," notes an Emerson journal entry, "that there is no word in our language that cannot become typical to us of nature by giving it emphasis. The world is a Dancer; it is a Rosary; it is a Torrent; it is a Boat; a Mist; a Spider's Snare; it is what you will; and the metaphor will hold, & it will give the imagination keen pleasure. Swifter than light the World converts itself into that thing you name & all things find their right place under this new & capricious classification" (*JMN*,

VIII, 23). The metaphor will hold, and will give the imagination keen pleasure, Emerson proposes. Yet how can such an arbitrary metaphorizing—he admits that as "classification" it is "capricious"—work reliably, or, to use his term, how will it hold? In this journal passage about the dance of figures necessary to express a world in constant metamorphosis, the holding action is, appropriately, the metaphor initiating the processive play of metaphor: "The world is a Dancer." Even while unfixing the semantic sureness in the language of the generalization that immediately precedes it, and while initiating a dance that is and is not defined by any of its metaphoric steps, the metaphor of the dance governs the sequence of metaphors and the dance of language. It is the holding action in a passage of extraordinary metaphoric permutation in which the permutation is inherent and implicitly announced in the very metaphor that holds.

The assumptions here are those of an Emerson who had already established a reputation as lecturer and literary artist and had thought and written much concerning the role of language in the engagement of mind and world. At the outset of his literary career, shortly after he had returned from Europe, Emerson expressed a rather simple, perhaps simplistic, view on the subject: "in all the permutations & combinations supposable, might not a Cabinet of shells or a Flora be thrown into one which should flash on us the very thought?" (*JMN*, IV, 288). Informing this passage was his visit to the famous botanical gardens of Paris and his subsequent reading and writing on the subject of natural history. Implicit in the passage is the assumption that "permutations & combinations" are largely a function of the artist, inventor, and scientist rather than the world they seek to define. Writing is seen as a game of combination and re-combination until the artist gets it right, that is, until his figures capture his thought perfectly. The various permutations, then, finally serve up a subjective correlative of one's keen perceptions of his world.

The view of *Nature* (*CW*, I, 1–45), although at times reflecting this earlier view, is the first major announcement and enactment of an argument we can call Emersonian because of its centrality to Emerson's thinking about language and his practice as artist during the rest of his career. In this work, which declares that "Nature is not fixed but fluid," the "Commodity" chapter opens with the assertion: "Whoever considers the final cause of the world will discern a multitude of uses that enter as parts into the result. They all admit of being thrown into one of the following classes: Commodity; Beauty; Language; and Discipline." These classes, one discovers, are not to be regarded as logical or biological categories, nor do they represent an exhaustive inventory. Rather than formal and fixed definition, true classification is, in the words of the journals, "merely full of tendency," which the journal entry explains as a classification that "will not present itself to us in a catalogue of a hundred classes, but as an idea of which the flying wasp & the grazing ox are developments" (*JMN*, IV, 290). As though to be more faithful in practice to the principle announced here, Emerson altered two key words of the trope in his original version to much more specific yet suggestive forms: "wasp" originally read "insect" and "ox" was altered from "cattle."

For Emerson to suggest that one role of metaphor-making in a fluid world is to catalogue or classify was, of course, to invoke a tradition from classical times down to Hugh Blair, several of whose books mentored Harvard students when Emerson was a student there, and who in his *Lectures on Rhetoric and Belles Lettres* defined metaphor as the "dress" in which the thought clothes itself, the proper appearance that enhances the thought.[4] Metaphor, Blair proposed, rendered a thought more concrete, more clearly diagrammed, and more identifiable generically, thus making it memorable, memorizable, and relational (harnessed to similar species of thought and expression). One does not need to read far into *Nature,* however, to realize that something other than Blair's view is being developed. The "classes" of nature into which the multiple uses and illustrations are thrown are large metaphors concentrating for the convenience of thought, expression, and the marriage of mind and nature the "multitude of uses that enter as parts" into the "final cause of the world." Each of the four chapters, "Commodity," "Beauty," "Language," and "Discipline," constitutes a sweeping metaphoric, which is to say "poetic," act. These acts suffice in their own way, not by means of arguable propositions and indisputable logical development, but as inventive, thoroughly functional, regulatory, forward-tending and open-ended achievements. The relation of the parts to each other within the chapter or of chapters to one another cannot be accounted for by Aristotelean logic, the dialectics of Plato's *Symposium* (although this model is more useful than Aristotle), the Neo-Platonists, Cambridge Platonists, Scottish Common Sense logicians, or Hugh Blair. Nor will modern dialectical theories do entirely, although their applications to Emerson have been instructive.

Emerson admits that as "classification" or "concentration" the metaphorizing in his essays is "capricious"; yet he also claims that it works reliably—to quote the journals, "the metaphor will hold." It holds, in Emerson's view, because at the moment the metaphor is invented under the pressure of the multiplicity of parts and the mind's rage for order it is a true enough naming of the world. It is true because it succeeds in concentrating the multifariousness of the scene in a large image or image web, thereby organizing and interpreting the many parts it reports according to nature, to each other, and to the mind. In short, it holds because it works, and it works because within a particular context the mind has invented and admitted into an important moment in the text of experience and literary expression a metaphor that will suffice. Each new metaphor of this order is "a new weapon in the magazine of power."

According to Emerson, such a strategy should be characteristic of all art. He explains his view in "Beauty," in one of the notable statements concerning his own method: "The poet, the painter, the sculptor, the musician, the architect, seek each to concentrate this radiance of the world on one point." This point is repeatedly found in response to changes in context, then established as a centering, only to be relocated, that is, superseded by another point that in its new way will "concentrate this radiance" or, to borrow another of his tropes, will be "the sunbright Mecca of the desert" (*W,* III, 72).

"Understanding" and "Reason" and the distinction Emerson makes between them need to be understood in this context. To explain them exclusively or primarily in terms of the Coleridgean source or the Kantian and post-Kantian distinctions between consciousness and the object of consciousness blurs Emerson's unique and metaphoric vision. Understanding admits, works in the midst of, and recognizes the "radiance of the world": "Our dealing with sensible objects is a constant exercise in the necessary lessons of difference, of likeness, of order, of being and seeming, of progressive arrangement; of ascent from particular to general; of combination to one end of manifold forces." Through her many stimuli and in conjunction with our attention nature tutors us. But when man's dealing with objects involves both the "sensible" and aspects beyond or outside of the sensory, and when "the combination to one end" includes a dimension Emerson calls "moral," then the action is a more comprehensive structuring and representing of objects, a centering according to man and not simply in terms of each other. This action, which is always seen as an action rather than faculty, Emerson calls "Reason." "The world's contracted thus," to borrow a line from John Donne's poetry. Such a combination, the "unity in variety," is not achieved through "addition or subtraction" but by "untaught sallies of the spirit." "The American Scholar" argues, however, that these sallies prefer to visit man thinking and that the scholar expects them even though they never cease entirely to surprise him. The degree and kind of metaphoric acts in a man's art, as in his inventions and scientific theorizing and application of theories, constitute his real natural history, and the "best read naturalist who lends an entire devout attention to truth" will be at once the best scholar and the best poet. "He will perceive that there are far more excellent qualities in the student than precise-ness and infallibility . . . and that a dream may let us deeper into the secret of nature than a hundred concerted experi-ments." As though to remind us of his qualifications, Emer-son's persona in *Nature* notes that his method of structuring is "by other principles than those of carpentry and chemis-try."

And so the "multitude of uses" of nature, brought into the sweep of attention and combination referred to as "under-standing" and "Reason," is organized and unified by each new chapter. The capacity to concentrate the radiance on one point or somehow capture it (without ever fully captur-ing it) in a figure makes idealists of us all, declares *Nature,* and helps us to explain the true poet and the new poetry, suggests "The Sphinx." (Emerson's poet and poetry are examined in chapter six.) For Emerson the only tenable kind of idealism is exemplified in the metaphoric concen-tration in *Nature* and the metamorphosis produced by metaphor-making throughout a work or career of literary composition. Not a Plato, Plotinus, or Berkeley; simply a scholar-poet who unceasingly makes his world even as he is finding it. "Every book is a quotation," observes the speaker of the essay on Plato, "and every house is a quotation out of all forests and mines and stone quarries" (*W,* IV, 42). And one continues to build the parts of the house and house after house. The ambition of the series of chapters in *Nature* should not be underestimated: "Each soul is a soul or an individual in . . . being a power to translate the universe into some particular language of its own; if not into a picture, a statue, or a dance, why then, into a trade, or an art, or a mode of living, or a conversation, or a character, or an influence—into something great, human, & adequate which, if it does not contain in itself all the dancing, painting, & poetry that ever was, it is because the man is faint hearted & untrue" (*JMN,* VII, 441). One should note in this catalogue the terms "conversation," "character," and "influ-ence," all of which refer in their particular ways to the persona, Emerson's most important metaphoric concentration and the subject of the last two chapters of this study.

In lauding "spermatic words of men-making poets" (*W*, VIII, 294) Emerson invokes both concentration and permutation: on the one hand, the image as figure so full of the complex life of what it reports and of its own literary energy that it becomes a new life; on the other hand, the image that does not raise itself to totalitarian pitch or final generation but immediately looks forward to and itself becomes the occasion for the new image, without end.

"Perpetually must we East ourselves" is the insistent advice of the journals, which also provided Emerson with most of his language concerning the metaphor as a concentration of a multiple and multifarious field. Although both ideas are based on a premise of movement rather than stasis, the one envisions endless dynamic permutation whereas the other sees a movement toward completion or closure. Perpetually to East oneself is the heart of Whicher's argument when he distinguishes between the critic's truths and Emerson's truth-making. To concentrate the radiance, on the other hand, appears to be more akin to the making of truths. Despite some of the several and somewhat unsatisfactorily reconciled inclinations of *Nature* and other early works by Emerson, the distinction just made is finally an artificial and misleading one. Throughout his writings, the flowing law of permutation and the act of metaphoric concentration depend on each other and imply each other.

If we take the chapters "Commodity" to "Discipline" as our examples once again, we might say that each chapter concentrates the radiance of the world in a new way and with a new center. The center of the holding action is repeatedly being found, used as a centering, then relocated, which is to say superseded by another centering. Each chapter, then, is at once another permutational impulse and advance and a major poetic concentration of numerous radii and circumferences that momentarily, at least, creates the illusion that the metamorphic process of the permutations has been stalled. The world is held at a particular kind of attention by the metaphor. Each chapter, however, makes and unmakes its version and is as susceptible to the next version as nature and wind are. "A wise man is not deceived by the pause: he knows that it is momentary," reads a cautionary reminder in the journals (*JMN*, IX, 301). This observation is but a small segment of a journal entry that in its rhythmic and strongly advancing procession of carefully shaped phrases and clauses and its commas and colons separating particular units of syntax and cadence creates an interesting doubleness: the restless, ongoing sentence, yet the periodic pauses poised against the movement, a miniature and compressed version of end becoming beginning and stopping serving as departure.

Or, we might say, the chapter of *Nature* poised against the movement of the essay even while inviting a new departure. Both dynamics are clearly implied and represented in terms of mutual dependence in another journal entry, which allows that the "poetic eye sees in Man the Brother of the River, & in Woman the sister of the River. Their life is always transition. . . . Heroes do not fix but flow, bend forward ever & invent a resource for every moment" (*JMN*, VII, 539–40). In Emerson's definition, the true poet, as the true scientist and the technological inventor, is an individual capable of inventing the appropriate and successful resource for every moment yet all the while committed to flowing law. Consequently in his redefinition of class in America he placed in the highest class the one always able to invent (*EL*, I, 228).

The end of the advances and concentrations in *Nature*, to summarize, is each new sally of the spirit, each metaphoric reorganization and its concomitant "self-recovery." Like the events of chapters and major tropes, the self-recovery is not a recurrence. Each time the world is re-formed the persona is remade and the vision recovered in a new version. They, too, participate in the metamorphosis, as the concluding paragraphs of "Prospects" make clear. In those paragraphs the diction and tone modulate into the language of devotion

58

and piety and an appeal for "humility": the arrogant are consistent, the dogmatist is proud. Prospectiveness is contingent on humility, on the ability to abandon moorages in order to chart new bearings and moorages. Those whose anchorage is "indisputable affirmation" have no further "Prospects."

What has been argued thus far in this chapter might suggest considerable discontinuity, both rhetorical and dialectical, in Emerson's writing. Occasionally Emerson himself was troubled by his discontinuity and expressed doubts about his method. "I am too quickeyed & unstable," he notes in a candid and revelatory admission. "My thoughts are too short, as they say my sentences are. I step along from stone to stone over the Lethe which gurgles around my path, but the odds are that my companion encounters me just as I leave one stone & before my foot has well reached the other" (*JMN*, VII, 327). The noble doubt expressed here implicates poet, nature, language, and audience, the first three of which figure in an earlier journal passage expressing doubts about his method: "The aim of the author is not to tell truth—that he cannot do, but to suggest it. He has only approximated it himself, & hence his cumbrous, embarrassed speech" (*JMN*, V, 51). As for the audience, Emerson sensed on his lecture tours that his intentions and the audience's expectation and interpretation were, at least on occasions, repellent forces. "People came, it seems, to my lectures with expectation that I was to realize the Republic I described, & ceased to come when they found this reality no nearer. They mistook me. I am & always was a painter. . . . Many have I seen come & go with false hopes and fears, and dubiously affected by my pictures." This entry, however, offers a private consolation: "I count this distinct vocation which never leaves me in doubt what to do but in all times, places, & fortunes, gives me an open future, to be the great felicity of my lot" (*JMN*, IX, 49).

At times such private consolation is either in question or absent. In one of several pessimistic statements in his journals concerning his poetry Emerson conceded, "A glance at

my own MSS. might teach me that all my poems are
unfinished, heaps of sketches but no masterpiece, yet when I
open a printed volume of poems, I look imperatively for art"
(*JMN*, VIII, 132). "How much is supposed in every discourse!" is another dark complaint in the journals. "O poet!
thou wert ten times a poet, if thou couldst articulate that
unsaid part" (*JMN*, VII, 34). And in still another passage,
"Ah! that I could reach with my words the force of that
rhetoric of things in which the Divine Mind is conveyed to
me day by day in what I call my life. A loaf of bread, an
errand to the town, a temperate man, an industrious man"
(*JMN*, VII, 488). Actually these expressions of doubt focus,
respectively, on the act of concentrating fully and definitively through the metaphor and the action of inventing a
succession of efficient tropes to articulate the "rhetoric of
things."

There is, of course, such a "noble doubt" in *Nature* as well.
"Discipline" registers doubt on the subject of the preceding
chapter, "Language," as though both language and the
treatise on language "cannot cover the dimensions of what is
in truth. They break, chop, and impoverish it." To clarify
and emphasize his pessimism about language, however,
Emerson turns to metaphors of correspondence and sexu-
ality. The effect is to emphasize yet overcome the remote-
ness and hostility of words in relation to truth-saying. In
"Spirit" the doubt exfloriates to the extent that "the heart
resists it." Here permutation is the main problem, the fear of
being imprisoned "in the splendid labyrinth" of the images
furnished by nature and metaphors developed in the essay,
a labyrinth, we are told, in which one can be condemned "to
wander without end."

The double-entendre on "end" alerts us to the complexity
of the problem, which in our century has been the problem
of poets like Stevens. Stevens's answer would not have gone
far enough for Emerson. Ultimately Stevens renounces everything except the poetic act, which justifies itself and its
primacy in the structure of the poem itself, an ambiguous
pattern that intensifies reality through its metaphoric asso-

ciations and heightens awareness, thus altering a dull sense of reality into an exceptionally keen one, but one inseparable from the world of the poem.[5] Each poem becomes its own end; in each new poem the imagination moves toward a conclusive structure of words, syntax, and associations. The discontinuity is accepted. Moreover, Stevens asks for a humility that will insist on the primacy of the metaphor and not the ego, the supreme fiction and not the self. Emerson, like Whitman and Browning, sanctified the splendid labyrinth with a belief in immanence, the view "that he was God when his vital consciousness acted,"[6] and that this vital consciousness cannot be thought of in narcissistic terms but must concentrate the genius of the commonwealth. Unfortunately, some of Emerson's favorite terms about poetry and metaphor-making have been read for generations as conventional romantic or platonic code words. Recently they have been read by some as buzz words or signifiers of particular modern (also vagrantly referred to as "postmodern") theories. An inevitable result has been to ignore the fact that at his most personal Emerson is also impersonal. To put this another way, individual and private metaphoric virtuosity, when successful by Emerson's standards, is a thoroughly depersonalized and culturally useful achievement.

To state it psychologically, what Emerson seeks through metaphor-making is always to reach a point of no return, which itself is also a point of "departure," an event that is true in its way, is unquestioned, and cannot recur any more than Heraclitus's river can repeat itself.

For Emerson, then, the creation of metaphors charts a direction rather than following a directive. This charting is functional when vision is richly tutored by nature and the angle of vision is comprehensive enough to center on a particular time, place, and event while going beyond them both in the moment of centering and the departure. Critics as early as W. T. Harris in the late nineteenth century have recognized an organization in Emerson's works that might be called evolutionary. What needs to be underscored, however, is that *Nature* does not feature an evolution of a single species of proposition and argument or rhetorical advance. "The meaning of nature," to quote Sherman Paul, "was its use."[7] All of the uses of nature are what Emerson regarded as metaphoric acts. The direction charted by these uses is from the rudimentary to the progressively more complex and from the relatively local, concrete, and psychological to the progressively universal, abstract, and philosophical.

Yet with its double character and tendency each chapter of *Nature* both suggests and qualifies such an evolution. Even nature as "Commodity" accommodates what Emerson describes as spiritual needs. Given Emerson's view of the spiritual, there are no rules to guide the persona of *Nature*—or the reader, for that matter—in the application of the spiritual scale. Progressive metamorphosis in metaphoric action, in the structural divisions such as chapters, and in the personae is the only norm of development. The chapters and their primary metaphors are not isolated presences searching unsuccessfully, like the fragments of *The Waste Land* or the soliloquies of a Beckett play, for their unity. But they are not really sequential stages of an inevitably developed argument, especially if we have in mind a development according to traditional rhetorical or logical principles. Each chapter and the persona of each chapter organize themselves according to their own life (some of which they share with previous chapters) and proceed to their own self-definition. The use they elaborate and enact creates the space for the next chapter and persona. That next version surpasses the former in the sense that it goes beyond it in terms of the evidence admitted, the metaphoric concentration achieved, and the persona at the dramatic center. A recognition of this achievement, it appears, lies behind a remarkably suggestive characterization of *Nature:* "something of a prose rhapsody."[8]

I suggested earlier that the nature of the chapter as metaphor has its correspondences in individual and lesser metaphoric sallies, including the image in a phrase or clause on which both sentence and metaphor turn. In short, Emerson uses "metaphor" to describe any image used beyond itself, a word that in itself is a poem, a memorable sentence, a chapter, an essay. One can infer, then, that the chapter as metaphor is the concentration and permutation of many smaller metaphors, raising them to the level of figurative and dialectical clarification. Such an art is entirely open-ended, and its suggestiveness is interminable. The method is best described by Emerson's paradoxical language about nature: "Its permanence is a perpetual inchoation. Every natural fact is an emanation, and that from which it emanates is an emanation also, and from every emanation is a new emanation. If anything could stand still, it would be crushed and dissipated by the torrent it resisted, and if it were a mind, would be crazed; as insane persons are those who hold fast to one thought, and do not flow with the course of nature" (*CW*, I, 124). Antitheses of Emerson's mode, the crazed persons alluded to here, are featured both in Emerson's works (in an essay such as "Demonology") and in American literary history. Melville's Ahab and Faulkner's Quentin Compson are two memorable examples (despite the long custom of the literature classroom to transplant Emerson's soul into the psychopathic Captain Ahab). Quentin Compson ironically chooses the river as his final refuge from the world of ceaseless flux and metamorphosis, and Captain Ahab's "iron-railed" pursuit leaves a shoreless ocean in its wake.

To chart Emerson's method throughout *Nature* and later essays requires more than this chapter or, for that matter, this book. And so I shall merely note it through brief and representative characterizations as a way of underscoring the persistence and centrality of this method in Emerson's work. The interest throughout the first chapter of *Nature* is in the "kindred impression" made by "natural objects." Primarily this interest is both in the fact that the "kindred impression" occurs and in how it happens—how consciousness hinges on images and how the imaging "is the suggestion of an occult relation between man and the vegetable."

In the bare common passage, for instance, the speaker can say "I am" and thereafter will say "I am not alone and unacknowledged." The incipience of being and understanding is always the elementary yet profound contact between mind and things. The images of chapter one do not report those things as autonomous events but as being experienced and perceived as connate facts. This process of becoming aware of things, self, and connateness is itself the argument of the chapter.

"Commodity" demonstrates how the contact of mind and nature and the kindred impression are manifested in the most ordinary use of nature (Emerson describes it as "low" yet "perfect in its kind"). The dance of metaphor is also a repeated metamorphosis of the central metaphor: "The field is at once his floor, his work-yard, his play-ground, his garden, and his bed." Viewed grammatically by the reader and passively by the man in the field, the "field" is the subject here. But the same field is also an opportunity for man to locate and define his connateness. Above all, it is the material of the metaphorizing that another subject (the mind) engages. The shift in the latter part of "Commodity," anticipating and corresponding to similar shifts in the next three chapters, centers the motion not in the field but in the process of metamorphosis, in which the metamorphic capacity of mind and language are crucial. "He no longer waits for favoring gales" is a perfectly timed announcement that turns on a carefully chosen verb. The rest of the chapter describes man who refuses to wait and be waited upon but chooses instead to harness multifarious images and energies and concentrate them in a humanly useful way. His response to "the two and thirty winds" blowing from as many directions at various times is to bag the winds, turning all moments, impulses, and directions into one action. Each time he does this—the winds and the bagging of winds cannot be held to a single version—he changes "the face of the world." This action, described in chapter three as art, in chapter four as metaphor, and in chapter five as Reason, is what *Nature* itself achieves chapter by chapter. The conclu-

sion of "Commodity" applies as much to the chapters that
follow as to "Commodity" and to the artist and scientist as
much as to the farmer and technological inventor: "A man is
fed, not that he may be fed, but that he may work." The
nature of that work has just been demonstrated by the
language and persona of "Commodity."

"Beauty" and "Language" describe, each in its way, the
multitudinous yield of nature and an answerable metaphoric working of the mind. Art, great actions, and literary
creation begin as a conspiring "with the morning wind" and
the "heavens" that "change every moment" and the "winds
and the waves." " 'The winds and waves,' said Gibbon, 'are
always on the side of the ablest navigators.' So are the sun
and moon and all the stars of heaven." Each plotting of
position organizes and concentrates the world being navi-
gated. Each is the central act in a series of "rapid transformations" that depends on "the plastic power of the human
eye," a centering, and a moving center. Hence the "beauty of
nature" continually "reforms itself in the mind, and not for
barren contemplation but for new creation."

Plato was right, then: " 'poetry comes nearer to vital truth
than history.' " This reminder in "Prospects" does not invoke an ancient philosophy but summarizes the mode and
argument of *Nature*. At this point both Plato and the various
personae of *Nature* step aside to admit the Orphic "poet,"
who in each of four independent yet related paragraphs of
rhetorical flourish seeks to concentrate a multiplicity of
concerns, prospects, and exhortation in one major figure.
Each, in short, behaves like the chapters of *Nature*. And
within each figure there is metaphoric permutation akin to
the permutation of tropes in the chapter and from chapter
to chapter in *Nature*.

Emerson's journals from the time *Nature* appeared until
his lecture in the early 1870s on the intellect are unmistakable reminders of his mode and of the view that Heraclitus's
flowing law pertains as much to man as the river. Language
and the literary artist are consistently given special responsibilities to bear in this respect: they are, for Emerson, the

linguistic embodiment of the truth about man and the river. Metaphor-making unnames even as it names, and proceeds on its way even as it holds.

In the mid 1840s appeared "The Poet," the full-grown descendant of *Nature*. And one cannot read the essays after 1848 (beginning with *English Traits*) without being returned repeatedly to the argument of "The Poet" and being reminded of its mode. We observe in these essays a mode and argument that, having been established as normative, continue to furnish the weight of emphasis. This Emersonian view of nature, mind, and art and its enactment in his compositions throw into intelligible relief his half-praise of Bacon and his discounting of Locke, Arthur Hallam, Dickens, and Thackeray in "Literature" *(English Traits)*. Moreover, it helps to explain the many-stringed instrument in "Fate" that can play more than one melody *(Conduct of Life)*. Through "pounding on each string . . . comes some reasonable hope of harmonizing them" *(W, VI, 4)*. It is also behind the pleas for "the old eye" and abandonment with respect to the American inventor and scientist in the hope that they will work with poetry and humanity ("Works and Days" in *Society and Solitude)*. It allows us to comprehend Emerson's criticisms of Thoreau in his strange eulogy ("Thoreau," *Lectures and Biographical Sketches);* to understand the less than optimistic plea—reminiscent of *Nature* —in "Fortune of the Republic" *(Miscellanies)* that "We want men of original perception and original action . . . who can live in the moment and take a step forward" *(W, XI, 536–37)*; and to appreciate the keynote in "Poetry and Imagination" *(Letters and Social Aims)* that "the creation is on wheels, in transit, always passing into something else" and that "the interest is gradually transferred from the forms to the lurking method" *(W, VIII, 4, 5)*.[9]

Rather than elaborate on any of these examples, I merely note them and proceed to another late work for brief analysis—*Natural History of Intellect*, particularly its first part, "Powers and Laws of Thought" *(W, XII, 3–64)*. Although the published version was prepared after Emerson's death by the editors, James Cabot and Emerson's son Edward,[10] Emerson began composing this "natural history" while under the influence of scientific lectures he had attended in Paris and London during his European visit in 1847–48. His design was to treat powers of thought as "facts," "objects of science" that "may be numbered and recorded, like stamens and vertebrae." Hence he divided "Powers and Laws of Thought" into three numbered sections and analyzed the mind and its matrix in two separate and succeeding essays. The scientific techniques he adopted would have been rejected by well-trained scientists, of which there were very few in Emerson's America. Even the largely self-trained first generation of scientists of his day would have been troubled by the assertion that "The analytic process is cold and bereaving and, shall I say it? somewhat mean, as spying." The three essays, completed for a series of lectures at Harvard in 1870, confirm Emerson's rejection of "the analytic process." A poetic and metaphoric mode comes closer to it, for the life of the mind is a miracle and "the use of a course on philosophy is that the student shall learn to appreciate this miracle." The essays will be an "ode," not a "surgical" performance. "Powers and Laws of Thought" proceeds to furnish a succession of images as its truest facts and creates metaphors instead of metaphysics. In this way the structure of the lectures imitates their subject: just as the mind continually turns a legion of perceptions into a figure according to man, thereby holding multiplicity by its centering action while creating the condition for transmutational movement, so the mind's truest words synthesize and reconcile, binding in order to unbind. The purpose of the essay is to delineate the law of permutation, the words of man thinking when they are free and capable of holding and giving keen pleasure. Emerson called these lectures "anecdotes of the intellect; a sort of Farmer's Almanac of mental moods" and "some sketches or studies" that were at best synecdoches of a more complete "picture" of human intellect.

The first section of "Powers and Laws of Thought" begins with the imaging of intellectual life as the ebbing and flowing sea, then shifts to the image of the river: "In my thought I seem to stand on the bank of a river and watch the endless flow of the stream, floating objects of all shapes, colors and natures; nor can I much detain them as they pass, except by running beside them a little way along the bank. But whence they come or whither they go is not told me. Only I have a suspicion that, as geologists say every river makes its own valley, so does this mystic stream. It makes its valley, makes its banks and makes perhaps the observer too. Who has found the boundaries of human intelligence?" The relation of perception to expression is described as follows: perceptions "hasten to incarnate themselves in action, to take body. . . . They take to themselves wood and stone and iron; ships and cities and nations and armies of men and ages of duration; . . . agriculture, trade, commerce;—these are the ponderous instrumentalities into which the nimble thoughts pass, and which they animate and alter, and presently, antagonized by other thoughts which they first aroused, or by thoughts which are sons and daughters of these, the thought buries itself in the new thought of larger scope, whilst the old instrumentalities and incarnations are decomposed and recomposed into new."

Nature invites and confirms this decomposing and composing, the second and third sections argue, because the mind's mode (from chaos to concentrated organization to permutation) is analogous to nature's. Here, of course, some of Emerson's descendants part company with him. Emerson easily finds evidence to support his belief in a correspondence between the modes of nature and mind (and, by extension, between nature and art). In our century Frost to some extent, and Stevens and the later Williams to a greater extent, bear witness to the assertion in Stevens's "Sunday Morning" that "We live in an old chaos of the sun," a chaos that in "The Idea of Order at Key West" is imaged in "the meaningless plungings of water and the wind." This chaos resists order and the ordering mind and, in the absence of the poet's most arduous and best work, leaves nature alien from man's rage for order, an order that in the case of each poet bears certain affinities to Emerson's flowing law.

The law of permutation, whose life is a "giant," indeed a giant "excited" (a metaphor Stevens may well have borrowed for his poem "A Primitive Like an Orb"), is more than the kind of transference observed in trade and commerce, Emerson notes. This reminder is the vis of the second essay of *Natural History* (*W*, XII, 65–89). The better man, whether painter, writer, inventor, scientist, or philosopher, does not transfer objects but transforms them by changing their arrangement. The best mind, man thinking, continually creates new forms, themselves as various as the shapes of leaves. One creates commodities, another machines, still another poems; one forms new social relationships, another a new theory. This continuing creation "never rests or repeats itself, but casts its old garb, and reappears, . . . the old energy in a new form." To apply this to the poet, in Emerson's view the prince of scholars, "No practical rules for the poem, no working-plan was ever drawn up. It is miraculous at all points."

To attempt an adequate account of Emerson's law of permutation is to be reminded that virtually every book-length critical study purporting to analyze Emerson's language and mode has gravitated into an investigation of his ideas, where, for the most part, it has stayed, a long-standing practice expertly documented in William Scheick's *The Slender Human Word*.[11] The few critics who have kept the focus on the language have, in the main, developed variations on Rusk's view that "Perhaps most passages could have been transferred from one paragraph to another or from one essay to another without harm. Only the sentences were indisputably units, but they were admirable."[12] Jonathan Bishop expanded the unit from sentence to the tonally, metaphorically, and rhythmically successful passage.[13] Several years later Morse Peckham seemed to refurbish Rusk's opinion when he declared that in Emerson's essays there is no argument, no sustained discourse, only sentences, "almost any one of which could appear in almost any essay." By extending the problem of style to philosophy, however, Peckham argued a necessary abyss between any two of Emerson's sentences, a trait Peckham regards as a distinctive feature of lyric poetry and poetic drama. For instance, poetic drama is presumed to confront the central character with "unassimilated aspects of his personality"; Emerson's essays, likewise, "emerge from . . . the condition of man—which, truly apprehended . . . shatters any man's self-image." The form of the essays mirrors a fragmented and incoherent human personality whose parts "come from he knows not where."[14] As exciting as it may seem to see Emerson as a composite of Poe and Samuel Beckett, one suspects that such a portrait will make the reader no wiser or better-equipped to handle his language. One fares better with *The Slender Human Word,* a welcome departure in its thesis that Emerson frequently developed "an essay around a central hieroglyph or picture created by numerous related motifs, resulting not only in a unique internal structural principle but in a visionary experience for the sensitive reader."[15] Scheick's thesis, this discussion of metaphor and metamorphosis has implicitly argued, needs additional unfolding and transmutings.

It is principally the Emersonian mode of a field of energies drawn together in a dynamically holding figure, and the energy of that figure reappearing "in a new form" with its new energy, that furnishes continuity and stability to Emerson's art from his work of the mid-1830s to the essays and lectures of the early 1870s, when he returned to lecturing and writing on the vital intellect even as his mind began to fail him. The world, to him, was both a "spectacle" awaiting form and an endlessly changing field. Like the world, the self too, according to Emerson, always lives on the border prospect of being defined, and redefined, never resting but always participating in the changing field. The stabilizing point for Emerson is not an inner faculty, or ego, or mystical eye, or over-soul. His stable center is a moving one, an ongoing activity in which the individual, true to the method of nature and the lesson of his own nature, knows himself through his world and knows his world in humanized terms. Much of the time, Emerson's discussion of the self is interchangeable with his poetics and the behavior of the persona in his prose. The language seeks out the "I" as the center to which all is to be related. Immediately, however, in such a concentration, the "I" shades into its basic denominator, a process of mutually dependent and reciprocally defined actions. The concentration is a point of departure toward a new and undefined circumference, and this movement is centered by still another figure, a figure that holds but to confirm "transition" and "mobility."

In this process there is no dimension except that created by the center on the move. Seen by themselves, apart from the flow of permutation, the individual acts or definitions often appear discontinuous. Followed through, Emerson would say, they are the life that makes us as we are and the life that makes and is the art. This mode accounts for the tension rarely absent in Emerson's art between the presence of the "I" as regulator of the world of its horizons and the recognition that the "I" is nothing even though it sees all. It is but a momentary clarification, a moment of conscious being or of definition of that being among related yet "self"-justifying clarifications that prove to be as transient as they are essential to flowing law. The true epiphany in Emerson is the trope that relates and centers the dynamic field and the splendor of permutation in experience, understanding, and language, none of which can be held—the serious play of metaphor and metamorphosis.

II
BUILDING
THE
COMMONWEALTH

*"He that speaks the truth executes no private
function of an individual will, but the world utters a sound by his
lips. He who doth a just action seeth therein nothing
of his own. . . . Compare all that we call ourselves, all our private
and personal venture in the world, with this deep of
moral nature in which we lie, and our private good becomes an
impertinence."*
Second essay on "Character"

*"Hence in each town there is some man who is, in his
brain and performance, an explanation of the tillage, production,
factories, banks, churches, ways of living and society
of that town. . . . We know in Massachusetts who built New
Bedford, who built Lynn, Lowell, Lawrence,
Clinton, Fitchburg, Holyoke, Portland, and many another noisy
mart. Each of these men, if they were transparent,
would seem to you not so much men as walking cities, and wherever
you put them they would build one."*
"Fate"

•3•

Technology & Science:
The Science of Power

The epigraphs of the preceding page represent two versions or permutations of a central and, in a number of Emerson's works, centering metaphor of the hero as "man thinking" or, to use another Emersonian term, representative man. In chapter two we noted the equivalence of the metaphor as linguistic-poetic event in the art and representative man in the culture, and examined the former. In the next three chapters the shift is one of focus rather than argument: from the role of language-as-metaphor in a paragraph, essay, or lecture to man thinking in his culture. To discuss metaphor-making is to discuss truth-making, which is to discuss man thinking, which is to deal with a number of permutations of the true scholar in Emerson's writings. In the commonwealth the chief versions are the artist (already examined in chapter two and reexamined in chapter five in the analysis of Emerson's "Thoreau"), the inventor and the scientist (the subjects of this chapter), the politician (chapter four), and the true citizen (chapters three, four, and five).

As the epigraphs from "Character" and "Fate" reveal, man thinking represents the commonwealth, that is, he thinks and acts in a context and out of a world much greater than the "private and personal." Merely private and personal venturings are incompatible with self-reliance and the role of representative man. Also clearly implied by the epigraphs, especially by the passage from "Fate," is that the scholar as concentrating force is fundamentally involved in building the world he represents. His responsibility is to be informed by, encompass, concentrate, and thus both represent and create the commonwealth in his individual achievements. When Emerson writes about the habitable environment of man thinking, he sometimes refers to an American culture (or part of it) as community. At other times he is creating or reporting a world that spans the culture like a vision, and that organizes, centers, and identifies new and important meanings in, and implants a new dynamic into, the culture in the interest of growth and metamorphosis. This latter sense of habitation and inhabiting strongly informs essays such as "Progress of Culture."

The nineteenth century in Western Europe and America, particularly the middle years, confirms Alfred North Whitehead's observation that the most important nineteenth-century invention was the method of invention, by which he meant the acquisition of the necessary technical and scientific knowledge and the ability to work systematically, empirically, and experimentally in order to translate insight and hypothesis into practical reality. It was an era in which inventions, machines, and the coming of age of the sciences increasingly dominated the thoughts of artists, captains of industry, social theorists and reformers, and the public at large, not only in England and the Continent but also in the United States. The rapid sweep of the Industrial Revolution in Great Britain would appear to indicate that this characteristic of the age was exploited primarily by industry or manifested itself principally in the proliferating industries and industrial cities. In retrospect, however, we can trace back to Emerson's age something more central to modern Western history and culture. The results of research in pure science were increasingly applied to industry and technology, while technology made invaluable tools and mechanisms available to scientists. It was, in short, the beginning of a lasting nexus between science, technology, and industry. The century is crowded with examples of technically-oriented scientific investigations leading unpredictably yet surely to what can be referred to as pure scientific knowledge. Conversely, pure knowledge led to a legion of applications in the practical affairs of men. Although industrialization was a brooding and often brutalizing omnipresence, especially in the Old World, both in Europe and America conditions placed a premium on invention, machines, and progress in the sciences. In fact, an exhaustive inventory of invention in nineteenth-century Britain and America alone would require more pages than a history of technology for these years. And most of our modern sciences—botany, zoology, chemistry, astronomy and astrophysics, cartography, and nuclear studies, to cite the notable examples—outgrew their infancy.

The prevailing tendency was, as Lewis Mumford has pointed out, to identify the new characteristics of the age with progress.[1] Even the low-hanging smoke of the industrial valleys, slum cities and worker unrest, and the increased savagery of war as a result of the invention of modern firepower did little to check an unexamined and smug optimism. Literary artists, however, were exceptions. William Blake's angry indictment of the "dark Satanic mills," machine mania, and scientism of his age was not a lonely cry in the wilderness. Most literary artists in England and America and a number of philosophers and scholars in the humanistic tradition shared his alienation from both science and the Industrial Revolution. Looking into the future with fear and moral indignation, they envisioned something similar to the "Unreal City" of Eliot's *The Waste Land*.[2] This alienation produced some of the most acute and useful criticism of the age as well as some of the most uninformed and deploringly mindless resistance to it.

Emerson devoted much of his energy as artist and lecturer to exploring a habitable future for man thinking in an America characterized by phenomenal technological advances, industrialization, and popular fascination with science and machines. Rarely did he address himself to the industrial machine and the inventions that transformed eastern Massachusetts into one of America's first industrial regions. His most negative appraisal of modern factory technology and impoverished workers resulted from visits to Manchester during his 1847–48 stay in England, not from tours of the mills in Lowell, Worcester, Waltham, and other nearby New England industrial centers. He spent virtually no time observing New England factories. One needs to remember, moreover, that shipyards and iron foundries were at an infant stage until mid-century, and that when Henry Thoreau and his brother took their eloquently memorialized two-week excursion up the Merrimack in the summer of 1839 there was little industry along the banks to disturb the idyllic world reported by Thoreau. After the Civil War his account would not have been the same. In 1834 Harriet Martineau, on her visit to America, confessed surprise at the prejudice throughout much of the country against factories and at the relatively small number of factories. As late as 1850 almost no steel was produced, and iron rails were brought from England. But as traveling lecturer Emerson came into physical contact with several of the most impressive technological advances of his day, including railway passenger service. The fact that technology could so conveniently serve the scholar was not lost on him.

In Europe very few literary artists shared Emerson's cultural vision and efforts. The reaction to science was considerably less ambiguous and ambivalent than that of Mary Shelley's *Frankenstein*. As for technology and inventions, one does not equivocate about dark, satanic factories that deface the countryside and machines that dehumanize man. Even Emerson's friend Carlyle, although he tried in several early essays to defend a technology based on humanitarian and humanistic principles,[3] inevitably resorted to images from technology in castigating the blindness and mediocrity of his age. The imagery reaches its strongest expression when Teufelsdröckh sees the universe as "one huge, dead, immeasurable Steam-engine, rolling on, in its dead indifference, to grind me limb from limb." The teller may seem to bluster, but the tale makes its case.

Among American literary figures of his time, too, Emerson was virtually alone in his endorsement of the possibilities of technology and science for the individual and the culture.[4] In Leo Marx's *The Machine in the Garden* the list of antagonists is striking in part because Emerson is the only exception,[5] in part because Marx restricts his pulse-taking to literary people. Were the investigation extended to a larger, more representative company, the rule and exception would probably have to be reversed.

This reminder is as pertinent to an investigation into the relationship between Emerson's view of the scholar and literary artist and his attitude toward technology and science as it is to an assessment of that attitude. His views on technology and science are neither simple nor easily accounted for. As his ambivalence toward America increased in the 1850s and '60s, he turned even more to technological and scientific progress for signs of intellectual, moral, and imaginative growth in his generation and the next. That he never ceased looking indicates both a stubborn hope and the lack of evidence to support it.

The reason for Emerson's hope is summarized in a passage from "Progress of Culture":

one of the distinctions of our century has been the devotion of cultivated men to natural science. The benefits thence derived to the arts and to civilization are signal and immense. . . . The chief value is not the useful powers he obtained, but the test it has been of the scholar. . . . It taught him anew the reach of the human mind, and that it was citizen of the universe. (*W*, VIII, 220–21)

The reference to citizenship recalls the concern already in Emerson's earliest writings over the potential and actual estrangement of man as an intellectual being from his environment. An important qualifier of the passage just quoted is the additional observation, "But over all their utilities, I must hold their chief value to be metaphysical." Implicit in the judgment is the converse—their lowest value is the physical (this point is made nonpejoratively in the "Commodity" chapter of *Nature*). "Metaphysical" is a favorite Emerson term, which he usually understood, as he does here, in an etymologically literal sense: beyond the physical, in short, the moral, imaginative, intellectual. To say that the chief value of the railroad is metaphysical is in keeping with his view of man thinking and is an endorsement quite different from the one Leland Stanford or Henry E. Huntington might have made.

A similar view and conscience informed the hope of William Ellery Channing, the renowned Unitarian minister, who observed in a speech in Philadelphia in 1841:

Science has now left her retreats . . . and with familiar tone begun the work of instructing the race. . . . Its professors, heard not long ago in the university or some narrow school, now speak in the mechanic institute. . . . There are parts of our country in which Lyceums spring up in almost every village for the purpose of mutual aid in the study of natural science. The characteristic of our age, then, is not the improvement of science, rapid as this is, so much as its extension to all men.[6]

Throughout his writings Emerson expresses annoyance over those who are inclined to understand and refer to power in terms of the steam engine and railroad. Like the child and the purely instinctive person, they are victims of their surroundings. Emerson's endorsement of technology and science, like self-reliance, is not a starting point in his thinking but the end of an argument. The antecedents include distinctions that make the conclusion tenable. For instance, Emerson trusts the work of those who are reminded at the end of *Nature,* "Know then that the world exists for you"—the few who work with the world as lovingly and patiently as the Emersonian artist with his materials, who do not deny and mistrust themselves, who are not gods in ruins, and who do not approach nature with the "penny-wisdom" of moral and imaginative bankruptcy.

The relationship Emerson sees between technology and science, too, helps to illuminate his point of view. (He does not employ the word technology; in its present sense the word has gained popular currency in our century.[7] Emerson's terms are "machine" and "invention.") At times he lists the celebrated technological advancements of his age to leave no doubt about his reference. The new machine testifies to man's capacity for working intelligently with his environment. Like trade, invention should be "a very intellectual force." Furthermore, "the only rule & condition of merit & noteworthiness is . . . vitality," not only of the "Engineer" but also "the railroad builder, & the manufacturer" (*JMN*, VII, 436).

As a natural response (both instinctive and intellectual) to the environment, technology was, for Emerson, self-justifying. In most of his discussions touching the subject, however, inventing, building roads, canals, and steam-powered ships, and pushing railroads across the continent are related to one of his fundamental notions, discussed at length in "The American Scholar"—action. Through "doing" the inventor becomes the scholar and the mind awakens to its possibilities. Man's technological efforts should discipline the mind to become an interpreter of its world, to discover the world's laws and its own and the correspondence between the two. Technology is clearly the means, the "science-armed" man the end. In "Works and Days" the motivation behind the emphasis on technological progress is to urge man beyond a "respect" for his "works" to "wonder" at his world, from an "economy which reckons the amount of production *per* hour to a finer economy which respects the quality of what is done, and the right we have to the work, . . . then to the depth of thought it betrays, looking to its universality" (*W*, VII, 185). Through work man discovers laws; through machines he learns his first lessons in influencing the world so as to augment its natural ministry to him.

Such a view of technology is close to synonymous with what the classic Greek term "techne" denoted, a term that, as Mumford has noted, "characteristically makes no distinction between industrial production and 'fine' or symbolic art; and for the greater part of human history these aspects were inseparable, one side respecting the objective conditions and functions, the other responding to subjective needs."[8]

The term "science" occurs at least as frequently as "machine" and "invention" in Emerson's writings. When in conjunction with inventions, science always enjoys a special priority. A passage from "Uses of Great Men" helps to explain why. In praising the "zodiac of sciences, the contributions of men who have perished to add their point of light to our sky," Emerson cites the "engineer, broker, jurist, physician, moralist, theologian." This list of scientists, curious to one not familiar with the traditional sense of the word "science," clarifies Emerson's meaning. Each individual, "inasmuch as he has any science,—is a definer and mapmaker of the latitudes and longitudes of our condition" (*W*, IV, 12–13). Science, then, is any vital intellectual discipline—not a faculty, curriculum, area of investigation, or prescribed method, but a quality of mental action. Hence this pointed observation in the journals about scientific inquiry: "I do not wish to know that my shell is a strombus, or my moth a Vanessa, but I wish to unite the shell & the moth to my being" (*JMN*, VII, 111). Or in his essay "Success": "We are not strong by our power to penetrate, but by our relatedness" (*W*, VII, 302).

Through Emerson's classes with John Gorham at Harvard, his associations with people like C. T. Jackson, Francis Cabot Lowell, and Louis Agassiz, and his meetings with several European scientists during his transatlantic visits, including John Davy and Gay-Lussac, he came to understand that despite the overcrowding of popular lectures on science in New England's lyceums, American science was still in its infancy. Furthermore, it lacked original, speculative, and authoritative leaders. And by the late 1840s Emerson was beginning to voice the European criticism that America's interest was crass materialism, not culture, arts, and science. On the other hand, he recognized the same opportunity that spurred Agassiz's enthusiasm. Agassiz was determined to interest American scientists in the philosophical aspects of their fields of interest and research endeavors. What he and colleagues such as Spencer Fullerton Baird, Asa Gray, and Joseph Henry discovered, among other things, was the need to create a new generation of scientists, that is, a first generation. The American Association for the Advancement of Science was founded in 1848 by a fledgling scientific community to realize this objective. Two years earlier, Congress, enthusiastic with much of the country over new technology and scientific discoveries, had created the Smithsonian Institution. In the 1850s, under the superintendence of Henry and Baird, the Smithsonian began to develop a scientific museum of international reputation. In 1859 Louis Agassiz, with the help of undergraduate students, was able to move his books and specimens into his new Museum of Comparative Zoology at Harvard. Despite the sound of artillery and politics of the Civil War, the National Academy of Sciences was created by Congressional Charter in 1863. It is not coincidental that the first formal technological programs were instituted in the same generation.[9]

Emerson's visit to the Jardin des Plantes of Paris did not transform him into a scientist of the new school, and he lacked any intimate knowledge of how men like Agassiz or Gray carried on their research in and out of the laboratory, but, as a scholar who celebrated man perceiving, guessing, symbolizing, theorizing, he welcomed a new age of science in America even as he praised the Keplers, Lamarcks, Newtons, and Daltons. And so he can suggest in "Progress of Culture" that at the moment progress in technology and science implies "the appearance of gifted men, the rapid addition to our society of a class of true nobles" (*W,* VIII, 210).

Much of what Emerson wrote over a lifetime about technology is summarily brought together in his lecture "Works and Days" (*W,* VII, 155–85), delivered first in Cincinnati in 1857 and published in *Society and Solitude* in 1870. Jottings as early as the 1830s reveal Emerson's keen interest in the proliferation of the machine, and that interest accounts in part for his admiration for Carlyle during these years. In 1844 in the lecture entitled "The Young American" Emerson pulled together into a sustained visionary statement many of his optimistic responses in the 1830s and early '40s to the prospect of increasing invention and mechanization in America. This essay is regarded by Leo Marx and Michael Cowan as the basic document in understanding Emerson's position and by Sherman Paul as close to that.[10] One needs to take into account, however, the rhapsodic evocation in the essay, a view of history that is subsumed by a millennial dream in which the continent and culture look through the open spaces of the present to utopian possibilities. The vision needs and gets reinforcement from the spreading mechanization and industrialization. But the issues of technology and science are not given the separate and sober consideration they receive in "Works and Days." In his earlier years Emerson was witnessing the beginning of a thoroughgoing shift in America from tools to machines, a change that initially he welcomed as enthusiastically as anyone, since machines would free men hitherto bent tiredly over their tools for worthier pursuits. Technological change came swiftly and industrial production centers developed along the seaboard, rivers, canals, and newly-laid railroads. According to the census of 1860, one-third of America's population was sustained by manufacturing industries, this largely as a result of industrialization during the last fifteen years. During the next sixty years industrial production would multiply thirty-threefold and the number of workers and managers employed in the technological and industrial sector would rise from 1.3 million to 9.1 million.[11] Emerson checked his enthusiasm in the 1840s, especially after his British tour. As Alfred Ferguson's textual apparatus shows, the revisions Emerson made for the 1849 printing of "The Young American" deleted several long, ebullient passages and toned down the celebratory pitch in other instances (*CW*, I). With the subsequent intervention of the Civil War and old age, Emerson never again returned to the subject with the concentration and conviction of "Works and Days."

"Works and Days" confronts the rapidly multiplying inventions and the enthusiasms these have produced in

84

America. Because labor was both scarce and expensive, the ability to make devices that would do man's work was important; a "knowing why they worked was not. The folkhero of American technology was the ingenious gadgeteer with little or no formal training."[12] The international expostions of the next several decades bore witness to this apotheosis of mechanical genius: enormous crowds, lavish spending by the United States (almost entirely for displaying technological accomplishments), and unreflective, nationalistic pride and delight. "Works and Days" scores this tendency as "Greatness begotten of paltriness," a narrow, religious enthusiasm for "selfish, huckstering Trade" (*W*, VII, 166). Whereas "Commodity" is a rudimentary chapter in Emerson's *Nature,* America has made commodity its ultimate chapter.

Emerson's rhetorical strategy is reminiscent of the "Divinity School Address": at the outset, tone, mood, and ideas undoubtedly are shared by speaker and audience, but halfway through, to borrow an Emerson metaphor, "when we think our feet are planted now at last on the Adamant, the slide is drawn out from under us" (*JMN*, IX, 295). The first few paragraphs of "Works and Days" enumerate and praise recent inventions that cause us to "pity our fathers for dying before steam and galvanism, sulphuric ether and ocean telegraphs, photograph and spectroscope arrived, as cheated out of half their human estate. These arts open gates of a future, promising to make the world plastic and to lift human life out of its beggary to a godlike ease and power" (158). Emerson could have extended his enumeration to include the mass-produced clock, assembly-line firearms, the cotton gin, the McCormick reaper, textile mills, the lathe, axe factories, rail locomotives, and Singer sewing machines.

What we are to make of this encomium to modern inventions becomes clear later. But several observations are crucial here. First, Emerson rejects the popular distinction among artists of his time between the mechanical and the natural, for machines have as their ultimate origin "the same

85

Spirit that made the elements at first." In a late essay, where he discusses the utility of all things "in the hands of thinking man," Emerson sees the "gods" of nature and technology as a single community—Bacchus, Ceres, Arkwright, and Whitney (*W*, XI, 513, 512). But already in his first major work, *Nature,* Emerson argues that inventions enhance the environment in its ministry to man. A machine is the wit and will of man combined with the will of nature. Otherwise the machine has no use, physical or metaphysical. Nature is defined as "essences unchanged by man; space, the air, the river, the leaf." Inventions are "reproductions or new combinations . . . of the same *natural* benefactors" (*CW,* I, 8, 11; italics mine). A new element, then, has entered man's conditions; an element has gained new possibilities. Through his ingenuity and artistry man can apply technology to adapt external conditions to his needs instead of waiting, perhaps painfully, to adapt to external conditions.

Such a view sees technological invention to be as natural as language, art, and nature itself. A technological world need not be a horrible aberration. "We talk of deviations from natural life," Emerson complains, "as if artificial life were not also natural. . . . If we consider how much we are nature's, we need not be superstitious about towns, as if that terrific or benefic force did not find us there also, and fashion cities. Nature, who made the mason, made the house" (*W*, III, 182–83).[13] This marriage of man's inventions with the natural order lends a special emphasis to a number of Emerson similes, such as the comparison in *Nature* between the train and the eagle or swallow. Moreover, man's progress in the mechanical provides a provocative source of metaphors for Emerson's exploration of how the mind works. Rarely does he discuss the genesis, growth, and limits of mental action without resorting to analogies from man's interaction with nature in the technological sense. In fact, these analogies allow us to assess the prominence and the kind of importance of particular inventions in Emerson's consciousness and that of his age: metaphors borrowed from the railroad, canals, steamships, the steam engine, hot air balloons, factories, and the telegraph, among others. In its use of nature, technology explains the mind's natural and necessary use of the world.

It is this view of technology that informs every statement in the first ten paragraphs of "Works and Days." The tone becomes more and more commanding as the speaker builds up to a paean of praise reminiscent of the final chapter of *Nature:* "There does not seem any limit to these new informations of the same Spirit that made the elements at first, and now, through man, works them. Art and power will go on as they have done,—will make day out of night, time out of space, and space out of time."

"Art and power" will transform, will bring about changes on the order of reversals. But are technology and the prolific rate of inventions part of "Art and power"? Perhaps. Still, the entire paean of praise may be undercutting itself as a way of insisting on a less superficial vision and a more astute reading of this essay. The eleventh paragraph signals a considerable change of tone: "Yes, we have a pretty artillery of tools now in our social arrangements," a comment that clearly fails to match the earlier superlatives, such as "vast," "grand," "excellent," or "enormous." This paragraph continues, "Much will have more. Man flatters himself that his command over Nature must increase." With "flatters" there is a further shift in tone. But the main shift occurs with the extended metaphor in the following paragraph:

Tantalus, who in old times was seen vainly trying to quench his thirst with a flowing stream which ebbed whenever he approached it, has been seen again lately. He is in Paris, in New York, in Boston. He is now in great spirits; thinks he shall reach it yet; thinks he shall bottle the wave. It is however getting a little doubtful. Things have an ugly look still. No matter how many centuries of culture have preceded, the new man always finds himself standing on the brink of chaos, always in a crisis. . . . Can anybody remember when sensible men, and the right sort of men, and the right sort of women, were plentiful? Tantalus begins to think steam a delusion, and galvanism no better than it should be.

With the Tantalus metaphor the reader can no longer be excluded from Emerson's ironic design. After all the insistence on the basic harmony between the technological and natural, and the celebration of man's inventiveness and tools, Emerson chills expectations any reader may have of further celebration. The millennial language is checked with "Things have an ugly look still." As he notes later in the essay, "We are coaxed, flattered and duped from morn to eve, from birth to death; and where is the old eye that ever saw through the deception?" If the reader is familiar with Emerson's mode of progression in other essays, he will suspect a new center of concentration here that checks and transforms the old without repudiating it. It is the kind of reorientation that not only requires a new attention and recognition at this stage of the essay but also raises some doubt as to whether one has been listening adroitly enough to the language from the very beginning of the essay. A second reading of the opening paragraphs of "Works and Days" leads one to suspect considerable ironic hyperbole that anticipates the sudden and deft switch of perspective. There is, for instance, the vision of rubber putting "every man on a footing with the beaver and the crocodile." Perhaps the same kind of irony operates in the apparently enthusiastic statement, "We may yet find a rose-water that will wash the negro white."

To find the old eye that sees through tantalizing deceptions becomes, in the essay and elsewhere in Emerson, a cutting of anchors, a drifting away from an easy mooring in order to see the dangers. The shift is not in the subject but in the location of the reader: "Many facts concur to show that we must look deeper for our salvation than to steam, photographs, balloons, or astronomy." Such a quasi-theological statement throws light on the intellectual and moral dilemma. "Every victory over matter ought to recommend to man the worth of his nature," but the man with a "great, equal, symmetrical brain, fed from a great heart, you shall not find." What has gone wrong? "Works and days were offered us, and we took works." Hesiod, the Greek farmer-scholar-poet of the eighth century B.C.E. and author of a work from which Emerson culled his title, had written of "work" that it "is no disgrace; it is idleness which is a disgrace. . . . Whatever be your lot, work is best for you." Emerson has added much to the terminology, refusing to find a beatitude in either man's work or his works, both of which may reflect spiritual poverty and mental idleness.

"Works and Days" continues on this new note—both disgust over a bad faith and a desire to work out a new salvation. One of the manifestations of the "deception" that has come with technology is man's reliance on inventions instead of himself. Mechanical power is confused with and substituted for mental action. Tools and engines are permitted to become limbs and brain. By degrees technology-minded man relinquishes his inner life and abnegates his individual responsibility as a moral and creative being. "Machinery is aggressive," Emerson warns; the "weaver becomes a web, the machinist the machine. If you do not use the tools, they use you." To "use" tools points to more than utilitarian exploitation. For Emerson, using is synonymous with discovering the meaning and meaningfulness (for the self) of anything, a view both argued and invoked in *Nature*. If man surrenders to complacency, "man is no longer free," that is, the mind is not free to do its work, to reconcile and integrate mind and environment without rejecting either. Just as established forms can choke the power of the artist's work, man's inventions can constrict his life, his alternatives, and his ability to fashion the circumstances that will make his destiny, to where his technology determines his options. When that is the case, action, one of the three tutors of the "American Scholar," is no longer the stuff "out of which the intellect moulds her splendid products" (*CW*, I, 59). Rather, man is "a part of the machine he moves; the man is lost" (*CW*, II, 83).

Mechanical expertise, Leo Marx notes, "is morally neutral, thus potentially dangerous." He might just as well have written "potentially beneficial." Yet his explanation makes his terminology permissable if somewhat unsatisfactory:

"Men of Understanding . . . perfect the means by which society functions, but they fail to define the ends. A nation dominated by men of this type could become passive in the face of history."[14] Although Emerson would have welcomed the typewriter, Xerox machine, computer, X-ray, by-pass cardiac surgery, and pocket calculators, his concern in "Works and Days" is succinctly expressed by a passage in Charles Sanford's "The Will to Power": technology, when "incorporated into the fabric of human society, . . . willy-nilly inculcates certain values associated with its leading characteristics. These are: causal sequence, order, functional efficiency, impersonality, uniformity, number, utility, power and motion."[15] Although releasing man from mind-dulling, body-aging work and the curse of poverty, and freeing him for a healthier mental life, the machine is just as apt to invade his consciousness to a point where it constitutes the authoritative metaphor for how an individual, the mind, the community, or a nation should run. "The Iron Madonna," Howells was to call this phenomenon; the "Virgin" become the "Dynamo" was Henry Adams's characterization—the modern world's version of *deus ex machina*. It is in this sense that, according to "Works and Days," "The machine unmakes the man. . . . Every new step in improving the engine restricts one more act of the engineer." This mechanization of man, which tends to outstrip the humanization of the machine, forms the basis of Emerson's opposition to slavery. Slavery, he argues in "American Civilization," is a "destitution," not an "institution." It is when man believes that physical and mental labor are "vile" and his inventive work is under Adam's curse that he is given to technological excesses and human slavery. "We want men of original perception and original action," not those who steal their labor, lapsing into "a comatose tendency in the brain" (*W*, XI, 297, 302, 300).

An ancillary problem in "Works and Days" is the vulnerability of the believer in amelioration, which becomes a tawdry doctrine when applied only to the removal of any and all forms of friction from one's life. Emerson seems particularly drawn to the image of diminishing friction associated with the iron tracks of the railroad. In the first chapter of *Nature* this reduction of friction promises new and more extensive exploration, faster travel, and new ties between human communities. But when "remov[ing] friction from the wheels of life" is divorced from the cultivation of "Thought, virtue, beauty" and linked merely to freeing man from headaches, wet feet, and cold rooms, "the old aims have been lost sight of, and to remove friction has come to be the end" (*W*, III, 191). Society "must be catholic in aims" (*W*, VII, 26). "A strenuous soul hates cheap successes" (*W*, VIII, 231). At present, Emerson fears, expectations are too easily met. Man particularizes and atomizes success to the point where his horizons shrink to inventions that, if mechanically serviceable, promise a personally and collectively satisfying future. As he particularizes, "the advance of his character and genius pauses; he has run to the end of his line" (*W*, X, 280). Blinded by the particularization (as Milton's Eve is), man becomes an enemy of culture and the future. "No matter how many centuries of culture have preceded, the new man," by contrast, "always finds himself standing on the brink of chaos" (*W*, VII, 163–64). Chaos is a negative term neither here nor elsewhere in Emerson. The journals report that the creative man always lives near "chaos" or the "abyss," that is, this source of his power must never be far away (see especially *JMN*, IX, 325). The terms refer to recesses of consciousness, the instinctual and organic life, and the environment yet unexplored, which the mind is under mandate to explore and claim. Clearly it is an uncivilized energy. But its pull is to the very world in which man must work and help to shape the future. And work and learn he shall if not alienated from this source of power, Emerson contends. Here, as in "Intellect," the alternatives are simply truth and repose.

A further source of danger is the intoxicating power of technology. Here Emerson's fear is not complacency but recklessness, "an easy self-reliance that makes [man] self-willed and unscrupulous" (*W*, XI, 522). The "balance of man" is threatened by a "new Universal Monarchy more tyrannical than Babylon or Rome" (*JMN*, VII, 268). If with all his technological progress man "is a felon," Emerson notes sardonically in "Works and Days," "we cannot assume the mechanical skill or chemical resources as the measure of worth." Bonaparte and Czar Alexander are cited as recent examples. Their science has been the science of power. In "Success" Emerson complains that the public is no better—they zealously believe in the invention and the power it promises in a way that the inventor does not. "We are great by exclusion, grasping and egotism. . . . 'T is a haggard, malignant, careworn running for luck" (*W*, VII, 289). An invisible force of mind and habit is organizing the individual and society into worshippers of power, or what Mumford has called the "megamachine." The prime mover of the age is infatuation with power rather than respect for man, who he is and who he should be. Emerson, then, observes in his own age what Mumford observes in Western history: "In a series of empirical fumblings and improvisations, with little sense of the ultimate end toward which society was moving, that great mechanical Leviathan was fished up out of the depths of history."[16] Technological Fausts cannot understand or appreciate the proportioned balance of "power and form" advocated in the essay "Experience," a balance that must be maintained "if we would have it sweet and sound" (*W*, III, 65). To be sure, "Experience" is concerned with the larger question of how to live and does not specifically explore the question of man and his machines. "Demonology," however, does. The essay explores the demonisms at work in American culture, not the least of which is intoxication with inventions—a conspiracy "to win from Nature some advantage without paying for it." The "steam battery" recommends itself as a notorious example: so fatal as to put an end to war by the threat of universal murder." "It is curious to see," Emerson notes, "what grand powers we have a hint of and are mad to grasp, yet how slow Heaven is to trust us with such edge-tools" (*W*, X, 20). A prayer Emerson noted in the journals has an understandable urgency: "Don't trust man, great God, with more power than he has, until he has learned to use that little better. What a hell should we make of the world, if we could do what we would!" (*JMN*, III, 320).

Still, Emerson refuses to renounce the machine and the inventor even though they seem to promise at once more and less freedom of experience, growth, thought, and expression. A comment in *Conduct of Life* puts the dilemma clearly: "All the elements whose aid man calls in will sometimes become his masters, especially those of most subtle force. Shall he then renounce steam, fire and electricity, or shall he learn to deal with them? The rule for this whole class of agencies is,—all *plus* is good; only put it in the right place" (*W*, VI, 68). As Whitman put it in his 1855 "Preface," where he applied the doctrine to poetics: "Nothing out of its place is good and nothing in its place is bad." In the first number of the *Massachusetts Quarterly* Emerson argues the duty of patriots to question the "infinite glut of their production." Our progress should lead not to a landscape cluttered with excesses but to a "Columbia of thought and art" (*W*, XI, 386–87).

Nor is Emerson sympathetic with any "back to the primal state" longing. He writes mockingly: "It must be admitted, that civilization is onerous & expensive; hideous expense to keep it up; let it go, & be Indians again; but why Indians, that is costly too; the mud-turtle & trout life is easier & cheaper; & oyster, cheaper still" (*JMN*, XIV, 90). His attitude toward the machine is not adequately explained by what Marx calls the "pastoral impulse" and what Lovejoy (quoted with favor by Marx in a discussion of Emerson, among others) calls "semi-primitivism."[17] One should really not be surprised to read in "Nature" (1844): "We may easily hear too much of rural influences. The cool disengaged air of natural objects makes them enviable to us, chafed and irritable creatures with red faces, and we think we shall be as grand as they if we camp out and eat roots; but let us be men instead of woodchucks" (*W*, III, 183).

If our salvation is not to be found in renouncing the

ambiguous power of technology in favor of a simple order, where is it? Emerson's answer in "Works and Days" takes us beyond the subject of technology to the higher end served by invention—vigorous mental life. There is a problem in such an approach. If, in fact, America "is a vast Know-Nothing Party" (*JMN*, XIV, 133), what purpose can be served in calling for an active mind and the creative sensibility that characterizes it? The essay itself and before it the lecture in Cincinnati are Emerson's implicit answer: "Works and Days," like most of Emerson's essays, aims to become a way of seeing and understanding for the listener or reader. What Emerson has to say in this essay about the sensibility of the true man of science is simultaneously the one legitimate but also compelling rationale for technology.

"The Science of power," Emerson states just before the allusion to Tantalus in "Works and Days," "is forced to remember the power of science. Civilization mounts and climbs." The almost immediate reference to Tantalus suspends the statement in dubiousness. The concession that "Things have an ugly look still" directly challenges it. The urgency in the second half of the essay is to rescue "power" and "science" from the mindless aggressiveness and complacency of the age. Not talent but sensibility is lacking in America. And to quote "Success," "in the scale of powers it is not talent but sensibility which is best" (*W*, VII, 295). It is this imaginative, moral, and intellectual sensibility that Emerson saw in Copernicus, Kepler, Newton, and Dalton, all of whom he cited in the journals as models of the truly scientific man.[18] In Emerson's explorations of the power of science in "Works and Days," we meet with words such as "sweetness," "wonder," "magical," and "abandonment." Ostensibly not scientific terminology. Behind them, however, lies a concern with a quality of mind.

The point is clear enough—until American culture progresses from the quadruped and consumer-commodity interests to a wonder and respect for one's world and one's mind, technology can be entrusted only to the true man of science, for he has gone beyond "works" to "days." The striking terminology in the latter pages of "Works and Days" applies to the American Scholar. It is he who practices "perfect timing and consent," refusing to "turn [his] ability indifferently in any particular direction by the strong effort of will." "Timing" suggests a harmonious and functional action, "consent" a sober and loving regard for one's work—a regard that resists both alienation and gluttonous appropriation. In his first essay on "Art" Emerson borrows from the language of the lover in discussing science. Thoughtless faith in the machine has been estranging man from his world. The kind of scientism it generates, the "compact organization and drill of parts" (*W*, IV, 273) confirms the separation. To learn science in love is to learn through one's work to be at once a scientist and an ardent lover of one's world. In Newton, Archimedes, Linnaeus, and Franklin, Emerson is impressed by "the like sweetness and equality." "Sweetness" in this context is ancillary to "love." "Equality" reports a persistent quality of mind and respect for the world. Of Newton Emerson writes, "science was as easy as breathing; he used the same wit to weigh the moon that he used to buckle his shoes; and all his life was simple, wise, majestic."

The preeminent manifestation of the sensibility called for in "Works and Days," and basic to the other characteristics mentioned, is "abandonment": "There can be no greatness without abandonment." Of this principle the pedestrian savant is negative proof in his tendency to equate tools and dogmatic methods with truth and to ignore or reject flowing law. Abandonment implies freedom from obsessions, particularizing, cultural blinkers, artificial methods, direct and fixed formulas. It also suggests boldness of exploration and a refusal to overload hypotheses, theories, scientific methods, or inventions with faith.[19]

The appeal for abandonment gains a special poignancy in Emerson's late years. Recognizing that the nation and he had been exhausted by the Civil War and that events did not bear out his hopes for a political and cultural regeneration, he sought signs of a more hopeful age in industrial growth, technology, and science. His journal entries on the subject, however, are filled with doubt,[20] not because of a lack of expansion in these areas, but because a tired and uneasy population was much too willing to chop the insecure present into specific technological and scientific programs in the hope of making it manageable. The utilitarian was triumphing over the theoretical, things crowded out ideas, scientific endeavors were being translated into practical forms but invention was not bringing on a new generation of "science-armed" men. What was acted as life, to paraphrase one of the ringing declarations of *Nature*, but now in the negative, was not apprehended as truth. Man's work needed to be humanized; the moral needed to keep pace with technological and scientific advances rapidly outstripping it. This recognition was undoubtedly a factor in Emerson's decision after the war to return to the subject of the intellect.[21]

Prospectively Emerson could celebrate the "science-armed man," even after the war. But he tired more quickly over the course of an argument or essay in his later years. It is possible that he suggested more tiredly than not, now that his essays tended to be more labored, that the inventor will become the scientist, the scientist will work with "poetry and humanity." If "Works and Days" is not in the best of spirits, Tantalus is—and he is "in New York and Boston." Neither Tantalus nor the inventor and scientist as yet recognize a culture crowded with phalanxes of vulgar aggressiveness for what it is, a culture in which it might take "20,000 years for the dream of one hour to be fulfilled" (*JMN*, XIII, 27). Nor do they perceive that "We are too passive in the reception of these material or semi-material aids. We must not be sacks and stomachs. To ascend one step,—we are better served through our sympathy" (*W*, IV, 13). At best, then, the culture is explained by Tantalus. It is not at all certain that America will progress beyond a respect for "the works of man . . . to a delight in the faculties which rule them." Yet this progression, in the concluding words of "Works and

Days," is "the only definition we have of freedom and power."

"Freedom and power": it is the freedom and power of man thinking to create beyond his private house a world and to epitomize his world, that is, make his thinking and acting a continual transaction between house and world and himself the nexus of the two. For most of Emerson's contemporaries this was too much to ask. Over the years we have enshrined in our scriptures of favorite Emerson epigrams "Know then, that the world exists for you." We probably would not have done so had we really understood him.

Emerson's admission that he is often defeated yet to victory born has its other versions: that the metaphoric action in his art and therefore the art as such are often magnificent failures; that ventures *en passant* in a world *de passage* may appear to be games but are in fact ordeals; that as one builds one's world some innocence is necessarily and continuously being lost; that prospectiveness is as important an ally of the inventor, scientist, and political leader as it is of the artist and the language of his art; and that the quandary of "Uriel" is persistingly manifest and manifold in an American culture that loves machines and is fascinated with science.

The problem Emerson analyzes in "Works and Days" and his dilemma over it are still with us. His attempt to resolve the dilemma of technology with his view of man thinking, science, the building of a world, and true citizenship in the world is not only relevant but painfully so. His ambivalent answers also find a strong resonance among American scholars today. Perhaps what is most exasperating about his approach is that we have finally caught up to it after World War II only to discover that it no longer solves our problem (individual and collective) although it resolved Emerson's more respectably than anyone else in his time could resolve it for him.

What Emerson sought to overcome is clear enough. There is, first of all, the problem of mindlessness, which he sought to counter by calling for the vital mind, or, as "Works and Days" puts it, the "right sort of men, and the right sort of women." But the contention that the mind is "a factor in political economy" is followed by the discussion of Tantalus. To believe that the act of thinking, rightly done, will lead the culture to its best destiny is a belief he and we are able to share and yet not know what to do with. It can become as bewildering to us as Lot pleading that Sodom and Gomorrah be spared because of their righteous members. His prayer was based on the proper belief; it was only that he was much too alone in that belief, and the judgments of history were passing him by.

Emerson also sought to avoid the trap of cheerless skepticism, which so easily turns into fatalism. He understood the crisis of faith of his generation. Moreover, he anticipated the dilemma of scholars like Henry Adams because it was already part of his inner struggle. What he resisted most of all was the view succinctly formulated and endorsed by Adams a generation later: "Nobody knows anything. Nobody controls anything. Nobody sees ahead. We go because we must, and we are becoming necessitarians and fatalists with most astonishing rapidity."[22] Invention and the machine were not special providential signs to Emerson, but they were natural, that is, creatures of the mind and hence part of nature as of the culture. The issue was to create and maintain one's place in the world while always noticing how tentative the footing must be. Although more useful and perhaps even more honest than Adams's view, his attitude, too, has its escapist tendency, since the matter of establishing one's place in an unsettling world means also not to commit oneself to any one step. This refusal to commit himself one way or the other provides a structural solution of sorts for "Works and Days" even as it leaves the problem in a maybe-here, maybe-there position.

And yet, to suggest escapism without qualifications is too easy not to be misleading. In a journal entry quoted earlier in this chapter Emerson expresses his fear of that which threatens the "balance of man." The balanced man is a recurrent metaphor in Emerson's writings. To keep one's

98

equilibrium in an ever-shifting world of mind, nature, and history is an important ideal already underscored in his early writings, as Martha Banta has shown in "Gymnasts of Faith, Fate and Hazard."[23] The enemy here is not invention and the machine, nor a holy war against technology and science, but lopsidedness. To quote a particularly poignant journal notation: "Even the great & gifted do not escape but with great talents & partial inspiration have local cramps, withered arms, & mortification. Proportion is not. Every man is lobsided [*sic*] and even holding in his hands some authentic token & gift of God holds it awry" (*JMN*, VII, 149). 216144

"Works and Days" is a balancing act, a dialectic that shifts weight from both sides like the pole in the grip of the high-wire artist. It appears there is no net underneath in this or any other late essay touching on the subject, though the tendency of the scholars in the last two decades is to ignore the older Emerson or to chide him for nets too large and comfortable. It is simply a question of how well the essay, the mind, and the culture can keep the equilibrium even as they continue to move. What Emerson's metaphors of balancing imply is that we must heed the rules of a sport that is ours whether or not we want it and whose danger increases in proportion to our unwillingness to think about it. It is here that Emerson is most timely and most archaic—we recognize his problems as ours, but the sport has undergone several revisions, the rules have been altered, and the threat of lopsidedness, with its newest terms, is more ominous and far-reaching than even Emerson was willing to allow. If in his treatment of technology and science he was more comprehensive than Poe, more ambitious and philosophically rigorous than Thoreau or Hawthorne, and more practical than Whitman, still "Works and Days" is a modern prophetic statement only as we practice the discipline of abandonment called for in the essay, move away from Emerson's footholds, and find our own in a modern world of flowing law and dangerous fixations.

99

•4•

Daniel Webster as Representative Man

As already noted, the credentials Emerson required of the artist, philosopher, inventor, and scientist extended to political leaders. The role of representative man in the commonwealth was based on assumptions that fostered and reinforced his disdain for much of American politics. Like slavery, the American political process was as much a destitution as an institution. More often than not his characterizations of American politics, especially at the national level, note a process and class of people described in "Works and Days" as refusing "Days" but greedily accepting the offer of "Works." In his view, political representatives were, on the whole, intellectually and spiritually impoverished, vulgar, aggressive, and given to a grasping and careworn running for luck. They represented not the commonwealth but their own limited interests. In contrast, the true political leader was known for his "spiritual step," which helped to create and enlarge a young America even while representing it at its best. In such a person the "private and personal venture in the world" is a public good, and the method of nature as well as the "deep of moral nature" richly inform the personal act and word (*W*, X, 94). "The moral element invites man to great enlargements, to find his satisfaction, not in particulars or events, but in purpose and tendency" (*W*, X, 95).

Given Emerson's views of the individual and the commonwealth, his admiration for Daniel Webster is explained only superficially by family ties, personal acquaintance, or respect for eloquence, although these factors influenced

Emerson's attitude. A better explanation lies in the physiological metaphor in "Works and Days" of a "great, equal, symmetrical brain, fed from a great heart," and in Emerson's insistence in that essay on original perception and action. As spokesman and political power Webster belonged to the same American pantheon as the new American artist surmised in *Nature* and "The Poet" and the small new generation of scientists paid high respect in the journals.

The reasons for Emerson's regard for Webster were clearly and uniquely his own; nonetheless he was not alone among the intelligentsia of his region in his admiration for the senator. One recalls the early enthusiasm of Richard Dana, Jr., which he recovered to a large extent after Webster's death, the strong and deep loyalty of men like James T. Fields and George Ticknor, the unbridled adulation of a young Jones Very, the magnificent old-age reminiscences of James Russell Lowell, the personal and ideological respect of both elder and younger Oliver Wendell Holmes, and the reverence of Longfellow, who despite his anger at Webster's concessions to slavery, wrote a memorable tribute upon learning of his death: " 'Les dieux s'en vont.' In England, Wellington; here, Webster, a greater than he intellectually."[1]

Yet the very same character, actions, and eloquence that so impressed Emerson and other notables also evoked hate, revulsion, and indignation during Webster's political career and after his death. Henry Thoreau, for example, held a view of Webster almost diametrically opposite to Emerson's, a difference of attitude and principles that reveals much about these two Concord writers and helps to account for the suspicions, strains, and incompatibility in their relationship after the mid 1840s. Despite the support Webster enjoyed from a majority of educated and notable New Englanders and Concordians (in part, perhaps, because of it), Bronson Alcott suspected Webster, many transcendentalist ministers publicly challenged him (especially as the abolitionist movement gained momentum in the 1840s and '50s), and a few Harvard students and the Peabodys regarded him as beyond the pale of moral civilization.[2] Charles Sumner—with the help of William Cullen Bryant's New York journalism—worked against him politically, and Whittier wrote "Ichabod" as his version of the devil and Daniel Webster. As for Thoreau, Webster was one of the scoundrels he could not suffer gladly. His attitude, like Emerson's, grew out of his views of the individual and the commonwealth.

In this chapter my purpose is to examine the nature of Emerson's understanding of Webster. To discern his view of Webster is useful as a means both of plotting the progress of his view of the role of man thinking in the political life of the commonwealth and of identifying the chief reasons why Webster as United States Senator approached, as closely as any American, the representative man of Emerson's America. Emerson's view of Webster provides a striking contrast to Thoreau's, whose position, although not a factor in Emerson's attitude toward politics or Webster, helps to explain why Emerson's view of Webster was a factor in his attitude toward Thoreau. To Emerson, Webster symbolized the exfoliating mental life, a proper reciprocity between sturdy roots in the physical and instinctive and a perennial flowering of the mind in constructions and reconstructions of the world. Furthermore, Webster demonstrated an admirable balance between "l'abandon" inherent in permutation ("power") and the centripetally holding force of intellectual design ("form"). Above all, he manifested a capacity to translate that power and form into the life of the commonwealth. This view of Webster is thrown into sharper relief if one extends the examination to Thoreau—to Thoreau's dislike for Webster and Emerson's gathering disappointment with Thoreau.

Emerson never tired of citing Webster as one of the heroes of the age. An inventory of the indexes to *The Journals and Miscellaneous Notebooks* from the time Emerson moved to Concord in 1834 until Webster's death in 1852 and a close scrutiny of the volumes concerned will reveal

103

that Webster figures as prominently as Jesus, Plutarch, Dante, Michelangelo, Montaigne, Milton, Bonaparte, Wordsworth, Alcott, Thoreau, and Ellery Channing, and more prominently than Homer, Socrates, Mohammed, Coleridge, Scott, and Tennyson. Only a few receive greater attention: Plato, Shakespeare, Swedenborg, Goethe, Carlyle, and God. No American and no contemporary except Carlyle received higher praise. Until the Senate slavery debates of 1850–51, Webster was one of very few countrymen to survive inside the shrinking circle of Emerson's heroes.[3] He was, moreover, the only American to approach the stature of the individuals treated in *Representative Men*.

Emerson's earliest references to Webster reflect juvenile partisanship and hero worship (*JMN*, I, 9; and II, 39; *RL*, I, 123–24), but in the 1830s his view matured philosophically. He mentions Webster in an early attempt to define greatness:

I mean that elevation of reason that sees clearly great principles & trusts magnanimously to them in the face of present odium because it has some insight into their wholesome nature. . . . It takes advantage of that moral advancement which the world has made & is a tribute to that. This has been done by the Pitts & Burkes & Websters & is second only to the praise of Godliness. They do not act as unto *men as they are,* but to men *as they ought to be,* & *as some are.* (JMN, III, 224–25)

Throughout this decade, Emerson's prolific journal lists of great men include Webster with few exceptions. These lists are both consistent and normative in their attempt to profile greatness through galleries of names. In the "Encyclopedia" notebook he listed Burke, Bonaparte, Makintosh, Webster, Goethe, and Schiller, in each case providing statistics of birth and death. Webster is the only member still alive (*JMN*, VI, 192). A similar list groups Webster with Copernicus, Kepler, Newton, Shakespeare, Cervantes, Milton, Scott, Washington, Biot (*JMN*, IV, 235).[4] Milton, Burke, and Webster illustrate the "intimate connexion between goodness & knowledge," that is, wisdom aided and enforced by goodness (*JMN*, III, 238–39). Journal entries and letters are sometimes specific in their praise. Webster demonstrates that "only a virtuous will is omnipotent" (*JMN*, IV, 257); he and Socrates are "faithful registers of all their past hours" (*RL*, I, 426); his "superiority of intellect is as settled a fact . . . as the existence of Bunker Hill Monument" (*JMN*, VIII, 327); the Bunker Hill obelisk and Webster "seemed to understand each other well enough" (*RL*, III, 180–81). Webster's arguments compare in excellence to Shakespeare's dramas (*JMN*, IV, 315), and Webster should be recruited as professor to Emerson's ideal college (*JMN*, VII, 198).[5]

This striking use of Webster to embody aspects of Emerson's vision, both general and specific, extended to the writing of major essays. At the time he was drafting *Nature,* and as though he were anticipating the pronouncement that "If the Reason be stimulated to more earnest vision, outlines and surfaces become transparent," revealing "causes and spirits" (*CW*, I, 30), Emerson wrote in his journals that the public goes to hear Webster in order to "rend the thin rinds of the visible & finite & come out into the world of sentiment & truth" (*JMN*, XII, 49). Another journal passage, incorporated into the "Language" chapter of *Nature,* reads, "Good writing & brilliant conversation are perpetual allegories." The entry adds, "Webster is such a poet in every speech" (*JMN*, V, 63). On the contrast between a tradition-mediated and original relation to one's environment (which he would use to open *Nature*), he noted, "Burke's imagery is much of it got from books. . . . Webster's is all primary. Let a man make the woods & fields his books then at the hour of passion his thoughts will invest themselves spontaneously with natural imagery" (*JMN*, V, 106). Prototypical of the speaker in *Nature,* "Mr Webster never loses sight of his relation to Nature" (*JMN*, V, 199), "the sun & moon water & fire met his eye & heart as they do mine, precisely" (*JMN*, V, 244).

"The American Scholar," too, is informed by Webster. Late in 1834, a year before he began to draft lectures on the philosophy of history and two years before he began work on "The American Scholar" (both are attempts to define the complete, undivided man), Emerson wrote that the "greatness of Homer, of Shakespeare, of Webster & Channing" is "the truth with which they reflect the mind of all mankind" (*JMN*, IV, 353). The call in the Phi Beta Kappa address for "active soul" recalls a journal entry of the same year: "Where I see anything done, I behold the presence of the Creator. Peter Howe knows what to do in the garden . . . & Webster in the Senate, & I over my page" (*JMN*, V, 296).

"The Divinity School Address" unambiguously identified the complete, unified man with divinity. In this essay Jesus rather than Webster is the heroic man who in "sublime emotion" naturally accepted and asserted his role "to take possession of his world." In the journals, however, "The sublime envelopes" Webster, among others, and recommends his mission to him (*JMN*, V, 346). As though answering all the unsettling and condemnatory questions raised in the address concerning the contemporary preacher, Emerson wrote in the journals, "Tell them that a true preacher can always be known by this, that he deals them out his life, life metamorphosed, as Taylor, Webster, Scott, Carlyle do" (*JMN*, V, 464–65). Like Jesus, Webster, and Emerson, the preacher must be the man of the logos, the word as "Original Cause" or "proper creation," and leave to others the dialogos (between men, and between their words and his word).

The glow of enthusiasm for Webster and other Emerson heroes and close associates diminished noticeably in 1841–44, for him a period of mounting doubts, difficult reappraisals, increasingly radical and unorthodox shifts in his thinking, and some depression. "Friendship" signals the change, especially in its tone. The affirmation and celebration of transcendental friendship is sustained for less than half the essay; the remainder takes on the circumspect and even gloomy tone of Emerson's current statements on friends in the journals. The celebratory and hortatory fade, likewise, in "Heroism," which concludes by congratulating Washington for having died long ago, immune to the common and mean present generation and its leaders. The debility that Emerson ascribed to his age in "Experience" applied to Webster as well as to other luminaries, including Emerson himself (*JMN,* IX, 83). Along with Carlyle and Wordsworth, Webster is one of the "cheap contemporary models" (*JMN,* VII, 527); "too plainly, too plainly he was one of us" (*JMN,* VIII, 111).

Events in Emerson's life contributed greatly to this period of depression. In 1841 his step-grandfather, Ezra Ripley, died. Ripley had assumed the role of protector, supporting Emerson through his change of vocation, taking in Emerson and his mother at the Old Manse when they moved to Concord, making his study and library available for the drafting of the "Historical Discourse" (1835) and *Nature* (1836), and defending Emerson against some of the local criticisms of his lectures and essays in the later '30s. Shortly after Ripley's passing came the tragedy of Waldo's death, in the wake of which Emerson's wife, seeking emotional and theological consolation, turned from her husband's views to orthodox Christianity. A further blow followed quickly with the death of Dr. Channing, an Emersonian hero in the mold of Webster and even more of a spiritual father than Ezra Ripley had been.

Dispiritment came from other quarters. Bronson Alcott was proving a disappointment as a writer, an exasperation as a manager, and, with the collapse of Fruitlands, a financial burden to Emerson. Brook Farm, likewise, troubled Emerson, first the strong personal appeals of George Ripley, then the smug and self-congratulatory reports coming out of the unsteady venture, finally his own attempts at modified communal living.[6] Thoreau overstayed the year he was to spend in the Emerson household in lieu of the Alcotts, and Hawthorne's move to the Old Manse did not result in the mature friendship Emerson had hoped for. And, since Margaret Fuller, George Ripley, and Thoreau became engaged elsewhere, he was saddled with the major editorial responsibilities of *The Dial* during much of this time.

On the national scene, the first extensive debates over

territorial expansion were taking place. On this issue, Webster turned out to be as fallible as friends close to home: "Any form of government would content me in which the rulers were gentlemen, but it is in vain that I have tried to persuade myself that Mr Calhoun or Mr Clay or Mr Webster were such; they are underlings, & take the law from the dirtiest fellows. . . . they are not now to be admitted to the society of scholars" (*JMN*, IX, 17). Webster's refusal to condemn slavery confirmed the lesson recently refracted in much of Emerson's life and described in "Experience" as "the Fall of Man." As "long as they are themselves," great men are praiseworthy. Webster was not himself (*JMN*, IX, 36).

Nor was Emerson, according to the candid autobiographical revelations of "Experience." "I have set my heart on honesty," he reminds his reader (*W*, III, 69). Deliberately and relentlessly the essay steers toward its central paragraph on debility, which opens with the proposition that in life the proportion of "power and form" must be kept if we are not to be victimized by flaws in ourselves and our world (p. 65). Supposed embodiments of completeness had become a treachery: "You who see the artist, the orator, the poet, too near, and find their life no more excellent than that of mechanics or farmers, and themselves victims of partiality. . . and pronounce them failures, not heroes, but quacks,—conclude very reasonably that these arts are not for man, but are disease. . . . A man is a golden impossibility" (p. 66). This passage has a corresponding version in the journal for 1844: "What a company of brilliant young persons I have seen with so much expectation! the sort is very good, but none is good enough of his sort. Every one an imperfect specimen, respectable not valid. Irving thin, & Channing thin, & Bryant & Dana Prescott & Bancroft. There is Webster, but he cannot do what he would; he cannot do Webster . . . all promising failures. No writing is here no redundant strength, but declamation, straining, correctness, & all other symptoms of debility" (*JMN*, IX, 83). Webster, too, was a golden impossibility.

Despite the discouragements close to home and in the nation, Emerson arrived at a kind of balance during this period. His crisis should not be over-dramatized as a loss of faith or inconsolable grief. Several full-blown romantic treatments of the Emerson of these years, out of impatience or overcommitment, have ignored much of the evidence.[7] Despite his disappointment, he never viewed Webster cynically or with hostility as he did the "new troop . . . of lordlier youths" who judge the times: "It is a bad fact that our editors fancy they have a right to call on Daniel Webster to resign his office, or, much more, resign his opinion & accept theirs. . . . I account it a good sign indicative of public virtue in the Whigs that there are so many opinions among them, & that they are not organized & drilled" (*JMN,* VIII, 102).

In a reference to Webster's conduct, Emerson described himself as sufficiently liberal and generous to allow the "barbarous & semi-beast life to pass" (*JMN,* IX, 450). Serious flaws notwithstanding, Webster belonged in the "class of superior men" (*JMN,* IX, 235). To such a "right aristocracy," including Hercules, Walpole, Napoleon, and Webster, "of course every thing will be permitted & pardoned, gaming, drinking, adultery, fighting—these are the heads of party who can do no wrong,—every thing short of incest & beastliness will pass." On the other hand, if the trivial "handkerchief gentleman" who in no way serves or adorns the people "go about to set ill examples & corrupt them, who shall blame them if they shoot him in the back, or burn his barns, or insult his children?" (*JMN,* X, 75).

Emerson's powerful sense of the debility and defects of his generation, rather than heroism past and present, prepared him to compose the essays of *Representative Men,* none of the subjects a great man of the present or, for that matter, of America, but all epitomes of his pronouncement in the journals, "We are tired of asking for a great man, & now ask for a great deal of a man, somewhat satisfying; Buonaparte, Webster, even Captain Rhynders" (*JMN,* IX, 388). Not surprisingly, in the same journal entry Emerson could both praise Webster as "a man by himself of the great mould" and

109

blame him in that he "underlies the American blight" (*JMN,* IX, 444). Like the models of *Representative Men,* he was blessed with "great superfluity of strength" (*JMN,* IX, 89).

In short, Emerson's definitions of good and evil did not undergo significant revision in these years. His assessment of his generation, however, had changed. It was a more imbruted age than he had thought, given to base interests and naïveté. The name of the new Know-Nothing party described the public more accurately than Whig or Democrat did. One of the new and prominent terms in the journals is "stupid." "How hard to find a man," reads an entry made at the time Thoreau was building his house on Emerson's lakeside property. "Otis talked too much. Webster has no morale. Choate wants weight. . . . Alcott is a pail of which the bottom is taken out" (*JMN,* IX, 208). The search for Protean models who in such an age might through their performances recommend "a great deal of a man" became the motif of *Representative Men.* Despite his defects, Webster more nearly approximated the models than Thoreau or Alcott, both of whom Emerson had patronized in the hope that they would influence their age.[8]

Planning another excursion to London and Europe, Emerson described Webster's grandeur and vitality as wasted on Concord, where he had recently argued the Wyman case in the County Court: "he seems like a great actor who is not supported on the boards, & Webster like the actor ought to go to London" (*JMN,* IX, 251). In April 1850 a more telling response was provoked by Isaac Hill, former congressman and senator from New Hampshire and owner of the *New Hampshire Patriot,* who bitterly attacked Webster in print. Emerson reacted as he did to the beating of Sumner some years later, but here only in his journals: commendation of Webster and vicious characterization of Hill.

Shorn of completeness, Webster was not shorn of his glory except in 1851, when Emerson drafted and delivered the first of two addresses on the fugitive slave provisions of the 1850 Compromise. The "abomination of our Fugitive Slave-Bill drove me to some writing & speechmaking," he wrote Carlyle, "without hope of effect, but to clear my own skirts" (*CEC,* 470). Characteristically, it was several months after the enactment of the essential bills of the Compromise before he expressed his dismay at Webster in his journals: Webster is but a small man masquerading as a Roman (*JMN,* XI, 435), is "low, has no character, could not conceive a great design & put it through, lives with little people, & is easily led" (*JMN,* XI, 409). But soon he could write in a jocular but serious letter to Henry James, Sr., that Webster is one of the "prophets of the East" (*RL,* IV, 280), east undoubtedly referring to more than New England. Denunciations of Webster diminished markedly in number and tone after the spring of 1851; for the rest of the year the journals contain a few scattered reminders of a lingering disappointment.

Emerson's moving eulogy of Webster, occasioned by his recollection of walking the shore south of Marshfield (the seat of the Webster estate) through the salt spray on the day of Webster's death, betrays a touch of that disappointment. The predominant emotion, however, is sadness over the death of a monumental human being who had deserved and claimed his youthful and adult loyalty.

The sea, the rocks, the woods, gave no sign that America & the world had lost the completest man. Nature had not in our days, or, not since Napoleon, cut out such a masterpiece. He brought the strength of a savage into the height of culture. He was a man in equilibrio. A man within & without, the strong & perfect body of the first ages, with the civility & thought of the last. "*Os, oculosque Jovi par.*" And, what he brought, he kept. Cities had not hurt him, he held undiminished the power & terror of his strength, the majesty of his demeanour

He had a counsel in his breast. He was a statesman, & not the semblance of one. Most of our statesmen are in their places by luck & vulpine skill, not by any fitness. Webster was there for cause: the reality; the final person, who had to answer the questions of all the faineants, & who had an answer.

But alas! he was the victim of his ambition; to please the South betrayed the North, and was thrown out by both. (*JMN,* XIII, 111–12)

In an age of lopsidedness and its sinister threats, Webster

was, for Emerson, a balanced man, a composite of many strengths, a near-perfect mixture. Four years after Webster's death Emerson transcribed verbatim a passage on Carlyle he had transcribed previously, about the time of Webster's death: "He is respected here by all sorts of people,—understands his own value quite as well as Webster,—(of whom, his behavior sometimes reminds me, especially when he is with fine people,) & can see society on his own terms" (*JMN*, X, 541).

In contrast to Emerson, Thoreau wrote as little of Webster as he thought of him. His aversion, once rooted, persisted.

Thoreau's earliest references to Webster, in the journal of 1842, a letter to his mother in 1843, and the "Herald of Freedom" review essay in 1844, range from positive to neutral, the journal citing Webster as a modern analogue to Philip, the famous seventeenth-century Sachem (although Thoreau wonders if Webster's character contains enough of the American Indian), the letter expressing regret for having missed Webster's speech in Concord. "Herald of Freedom" is essentially neutral.[9] Thoreau's revision of "Wendell Phillips Before the Concord Lyceum," specifically the cancellation of a positive reference to Webster, strongly suggests that by the mid-1840s Webster was losing favor with Thoreau.[10]

The compositional history of "Resistance to Civil Government" (1848–49) features the opposite strategy, eventual inclusion of a passage on Webster, in this case negative.[11] By the turn of the decade Thoreau's opinion had become fixed, never to waver thereafter, especially in the period in which he mentioned Webster most frequently, the three years spanning his visit to the Marshfield area and the Webster estate in 1851, Webster's death the following year, and the completion and publication of *Walden* and "Slavery in Massachusetts" in 1854. In these references, Webster figures in relation to two of Thoreau's most compelling themes.

The more obvious theme, and the only one discussed

with respect to Webster in the scholarship to date, is the issue of slavery and the Fugitive Slave legislation, on which Thoreau found Webster's stand despicable. The basis for his disapproval is disclosed for the first time in "Resistance to Civil Government." The lecture version, delivered either in installments or in different versions in 1848, did not castigate Webster. When Thoreau revised it the next year for publication, however, he inserted a passage upbraiding Webster as one who "never goes behind government, and so cannot speak with authority about it." His mind is limited both in "range and hospitality," his frame of reference is purely political, he is a "follower," and he lacks foresight and farsightedness.[12] The few positive points Thoreau makes here about Webster occur only in comparing him to yet worse politicans.

In 1852 and 1853, unflattering references to Webster's pomp and his role in the Fugitive Slave debates appeared in the *Walden* text in the fourth and fifth versions and survived in slightly altered form in "Conclusion" and "Brute Neighbors" respectively. The latter is particularly interesting in that the journal entry on the war of the ants, made early in 1852, reveals Thoreau deliberately fictionalizing an aspect of the struggle: "The battle which I witnessed took place in the Presidency of Polk, five years before the passage of Webster's Fugitive-Slave Bill."[13] Whereas in the journal the ant war invites comparison to the North Bridge fight and to "Austerlitz or Dresden," it now suggests analogies to Polk's campaign against the Mexicans, to Thoreau a fitting precedent for Webster's Fugitive Slave campaign in the Senate.

Thoreau's angriest attack on Webster's politics appeared in "Slavery in Massachusetts," published by both Garrison and Greeley in 1854, eighteen months after Webster's death. In this broadside against the Fugitive Slave Law, which "rises not to the level of the head" but has its "natural habitat . . . in the dirt," Thoreau added that "he who walks with freedom, and does not with Hindoo mercy avoid treading on every venomous reptile, will inevitably tread on it, and so trample it under foot,—and Webster, its maker, with it, like the dirt-bug and its ball."[14]

The majority of Thoreau's references to Webster, however, concern not slavery but the preeminent theme of Thoreau's life and writings, proper economy in the sense of the original Greek word for true stewardship and correct management and order. One can see Thoreau placing Webster in the context of his developing concept of economy in the journal entries that recount a brief walking tour Thoreau made in July 1851 in the vicinity of Webster's Marshfield estate and that summarize his assessment of Webster as economist. Recalling that the land once belonged to the Winslows of the Mayflower passage and one of the most distinguished New England families, and learning that the Winslow house, too, had been purchased by Webster, Thoreau wrote a passage about Emerson's favorite brother, Charles, much of which was suppressed by the editors of the 1906 *Journal of Henry David Thoreau:*

Took refuge from the rain at a Mr. Stetson in Duxbury—told me an anecdote which he heard Charles Emerson tell of meeting Webster at a splendid house of ill fame in Washington where he (Emerson) had gone unwittingly to call on a lady whose acquaintance he had formed on the stage. Mr Webster coming into the room unexpectedly—& patting him on the shoulder remarks "This is no place for young men like you" I forgot to say that I passed the Winslow House now belonging to Webster—This land was granted to the family in 1637.[15]

Although it may be overly speculative to suggest that the splendid Winslow house is, by association with the new owner, a house of ill fame, Thoreau's proximity to this famed estate calls to his mind Charles Emerson's presence in the Washington brothel.

Whether Webster's comment to Charles is more than a humorous, compressed, and sharply critical conclusion to the anecdote is not clear. The next two sentences of the entry, however, report ambivalence about the residence: on the one hand a strong tug toward its history and direct link to the Plymouth Colony, on the other an estrangement from what it has recently come to represent. The latter sentiment is confirmed in the rest of the text on Webster—Marshfield's changes suggest loss and only loss. How Webster could afford to purchase the estate and enlarge it through annexation apparently did not mystify Thoreau, who here and elsewhere charged Webster with venality. He knew the senator to be the hero of shipbuilders, shipowners, and millowners of Massachusetts, who for years had contributed to him, although Thoreau could not have known how handsomely.

Unflattering throughout, this Marshfield journal entry is most damning in its comments on Webster's incompetent farming and management and his lack of higher laws, two aspects of the economy theme that preoccupied Thoreau at this time. He cites numerous intolerable faults: the discrepancy between Webster's omnivorous acquisition of real estate and his cultivation of only a small portion of it, his high eating and hard drinking, his dependence on the labor of fifteen Irish tenants who do the work of fifty and for subsistence wages, and his low view of work. On the return trip, Thoreau visited with one of Webster's neighbors, whose small acreage Webster "surrounds & endeavors in vain to buy." The neighbor is "proud of the quantity of carrots he had raised on a small patch. It was better husbandry than Websters."[16] In the same passage Thoreau expresses reservations about the farmer and his farming—both fitting candidates for the farming population in *Walden*. Yet the farmer is preferred over Webster, and his superiority extends to social courtesy and neighborliness. Webster's neighbor willingly visits with Thoreau and answers his queries. He also tells Thoreau of periodically paying Webster respect with a social call and perhaps a small present of food, only to find that Webster has nothing to say to him and is impatient to see him go.[17]

About the time of this trip, Thoreau was expanding the theme of economy in the opening section of the *Walden* manuscript and extending it to become the book's major motif.[18] Webster is mentioned by name only once in *Walden*

115

in relation to the theme of economy—in the fifth-to-last paragraph amid a welter of tragic-comic images of mismanagement, perverted interests, and triviality. But Thoreau's discussion of the Concord farmers peopling his manuscript, who, with the exception of John Farmer, clarify economy by negative definition, specifically recalls charges he had registered against Webster in the journal. These farmers, Thoreau writes in 1852–53, degrade husbandry, deform the land, and lead mean lives immune to higher laws because of "avarice and selfishness, and a grovelling habit."[19] The strictest definition of "grovel," etymologically speaking—"to be down on one's face," that is, "to take pleasure in base things"—appears to be operative here.

The standard Thoreau formulated at this stage of his career was high: "The true husbandman will cease from anxiety . . . and finish his labor with every day, relinquishing all claim to the produce of his fields, and sacrificing in his mind not only his first but his last fruits also."[20] Even the hoer of beans falls short of this model economy, which has progressed from proper cultivation of the field to the successful planting, cultivating, and harvesting of virtues such as "sincerity, truth, simplicity, faith, innocence."[21] The self-criticism by the tiller of beans, too, was introduced in 1852 or '53, when Thoreau added not only much material on farming but also most of the "Higher Laws" discussion.

In 1857, five and one-half years after his visit to Marshfield and four and one-half after Webster's death, Thoreau, in the midst of lengthy journal entries on the sudden destruction by fire of Concord's distinguished old Lee House on Nashawtuc Hill, abruptly interrupted his discussion of the ruins with an apparently unrelated comment on Webster's wasteful ways:

Webster prided himself on being the first *farmer* in the South parish of Marshfield, but if he was the first they must have been a sorry set, for his farming was a complete failure. It cost a great deal more than it came to. He used other people's capital, and was insolvent when he died, so that his friends and relatives found it difficult to retain the place. . . . How much cheaper it would have been for the town or country to have maintained him in the almshouse. . . . How many must have bled annually to manure his broad potato-fields, who without inconvenience could have contributed sufficient to maintain him in the almshouse! (Thoreau *Journal,* IX, 261–62)

The oldest surviving house in Concord, built and inhabited for two centuries by one of the most reputable families, invites associations similar to those of the Winslow house, as does the destruction of the house and its legacy, almost as though Webster had put the torch to it. A greatness has passed, according to Thoreau; the rubble recalls both Webster's management and the mess he left behind.

In the years that followed, Thoreau continued to assail Webster for bad economy and base laws. Several passages to this effect appear in the journal, the last, longest, and most interesting one omitted by the 1906 *Journal.* In this passage, which appears in revised state in "The Allegash and East Branch," Thoreau reported the account by Joe Polis, Indian guide and friend, of his two meetings with Webster. The significant variants between journal and published text are in the beginning and conclusion. Near the outset of the journal account, Thoreau noted that Polis remembered "calling on [Webster] once in Boston—I think it was the day after he delivered his Bunker Hill oration— He did not like him—declared that all he said 'was not worth talk talk [*sic*] about a musquash'—." Many words, but little force and value, was Polis's assessment, echoing the observation in *Walden* that "a man is rich in proportion to the number of things which he can afford to let alone."[22] Further, when Polis called on Webster at his Senate office, Webster first ignored him for much of the day, then raised his hand as if to strike him, behavior that Polis found unworthy of Webster's reputation and that Thoreau regarded characteristic of the man.[23] Webster's treatment of Polis was only a little worse than his abuse of land and hired hands at Marshfield.

Thoreau was aware of Emerson's allegiance to Webster and the adjustments in Emerson that made it possible to continue one's loyalty to men whose flaws were as convincing as their greatness. The moral superiority with which Thoreau referred to Emerson in his journal of the 1850s is that of the man of an uncompromising view of right economy toward the apostate. Two months after returning from his walking tour to the area of Webster's estate, Thoreau wrote of Emerson:

Ah, I yearn toward thee, my friend, but I have not confidence in thee. . . . I am afraid because thy relations are not my relations. . . . We do not know what hinders us from coming together. But when I consider what my friend's relations and acquaintances are . . . then the difference between us gets named. I see that all these friends and acquaintances . . . are indeed my friend's self. (Thoreau *Journal,* III, 61–62)

Emerson's journals for this period are equally enlightening. A month or so earlier he had observed with irritation: "H. T. will not stick. . . . He is a boy, & will be an old boy. . . . He speaks at Lyceum or other meeting but somebody else speaks & his speech falls dead & is forgotten. He rails at the town doings & ought to correct & inspire them" (*JMN,* XI, 404). Webster, in contrast, was an example of "right aristocracy," which Emerson defined as being "incomparably superior to the populace in ways agreeable to the populace" (*JMN,* X, 75). The goal of such ways acceptable to the times and the people is described in the concluding sentence of "Experience" as "the transformation of genius into practical power" (*W,* III, 86).

Thoreau's economy served quite another purpose, a personal integration of nature and human nature, a formal ecology of character, world, and word in a moral-aesthetic order. In his younger years he found his ideal characters in an earlier golden age.[24] By the 1850s he was convinced of the failure of his New England culture, town, and acquaintances to practice proper economy in their occupations, avocations, leisure, social relations, art, religion, ethics, and education. Generally speaking, the greater an individual's reputation, the more disappointing Thoreau found him. It is not surprising that his growing dislike for Webster coincided on the one hand with his falling out with Emerson, on the other with the cultivation of friendships with men like H. G. O. Blake, B. B. Wiley, Daniel Ricketson, Franklin Sanborn, and the Englishman Thomas Cholmondeley.

As for his literary use of Webster, his deletion of Webster from the revised text of "Wendell Phillips" gives the case away. Unimproved means to his aesthetic-moral ends were of little use. There are comparatively few passages on Webster in the journal, a literary work in its own right as well as a notebook of materials for subsequent literary compositions. Like the state and army, Webster was to be resisted, that is, consciously and deliberately transcended, much as the narrator effectively transcends the restricting power of the state in "Resistance to Civil Government."

The act of drafting for possible literary composition was itself an opportunity for transcendence. When drafting journal entries that seemed especially promising for later literary use, Thoreau often disguised the identity of the people referred to, a practice that probably helps explain the paucity of references to Webster and the many composite types that include features Thoreau identified with Webster. More revealing is the record of Thoreau's mining the journal for his essays. Very little material on Webster is admitted into his literary compositions, although several proximate passages are used. This rejection of the Webster material for literary use helps define his allegiance and vision. On the one hand, Webster could not give shape or vitality to the literary daemon; on the other, even in the days of John Brown's arrest and execution, Thoreau was reluctant to write essays on demonology.

In contrast, Emerson not only wrote prolifically of Webster in his journals but also used these passages strategically in lectures and essays, as a rule dropping the name without significantly altering the thought. Emerson's views on race help to explain his attitude toward and literary use of Webster. He saw him as an animal man or savage type, with his excess of simple brute energy; as the quintessential Saxon man, whose strong physical energies were combined with an ability to act in a concentrated, practical, and intellectually astute manner; and as the natural aristocrat, born to command, to be the world's soul.[25] In combining all three, Webster more closely approximated Emerson's ideal of the complete man, a vigorous hybrid who in and through himself reflected the nation's strength, a union of many races and energies. In 1859 and '60 Lincoln did not measure up to Emerson's standards; he would have preferred a cultivated and forceful Yankee as President, a philosophic and eloquent version of Judge Samuel Hoar of Concord, of whom Emerson wrote: "if one had met him in a cabin or a forest he must still seem a public man, answering as sovereign state to sovereign state" (*W*, X, 441).

Several names on Emerson's lists of the cultural elite were known primarily for their oratory, an art that Emerson (unlike Thoreau, the man of written words) admired and practiced. Admittedly Webster turned out to be less of a "primary" force in politics than Emerson saw himself to be in literature. Despite Emerson's criticisms, however, Webster's name persisted on the lists of orators. In his "superfluity of strength" he was at least "somewhat satisfying."

"Uses of Great Men," the opening essay of *Representative Men*, sums up Emerson's case for Webster and helps toward understanding Thoreau's case against both Emerson and Webster: "Once you saw phoenixes: they are gone; the world is not therefore disenchanted." In the Thoreau home was such a phoenix, a Samuel Rowse engraving of his portrait of Webster, which he had given to the Thoreaus as a gift and which was hung conspicuously in the diningroom to serve, for Aunt Louisa at least, as an enchanting and religious emblem.[26] For Thoreau the fact of the picture will not have been a problem; his treatment of character and his use of ideal heroes reveals an imagination and conscience inclined toward the fixing of character and the fixed type—a consistency and concentration raised to the level of emblem and thus in keeping with portraiture. Whereas nature and languages change, the character of the hero does not, and life and literary art are a formal integration of the fixing hero and the unfixing world. Both Webster's and Emerson's capacity for departure from what Thoreau identified as their center, or what their center should have been, was reason for disenchantment. The sense of the picture was as wrong for him as it was right for Emerson, who added to his observation on phoenixes: "The vessels on which you read sacred emblems turn out to be common pottery; but the sense of the pictures is sacred" (*W*, IV, 34).

•5•

Thoreau & the Failure
of the Ideal

How to live wisely and what to expect from life had become a preoccupation of Emerson as well as Thoreau. About the time that Thoreau moved into his one-room shanty on Emerson's land on the north shore of Walden Pond, Emerson noted in his journals: "There are many skepticisms. The Universe is like an infinite series of planes, each of which is a false bottom, and when we think our feet are planted now at last on the Adamant, the slide is drawn out from under us." This statement is followed by a paragraph that gets to the heart of Emerson's view: "Value of the Skeptic is the resistance to premature conclusions. If he prematurely conclude, his conclusion will be shattered, & he will become malignant. But he must limit himself with the anticipation of law in the mutations,—flowing law" (*JMN*, IX, 295).

One of Emerson's favorite and most affirmative metaphors in his lectures and essays of the late 1830s and early '40s, the circle, was rejected, in this journal entry at least, in favor of the infinite series of planes, the special effectiveness of which becomes apparent as soon as we arrive at his reference to false bottoms. The sense of endless search suggests continual exasperation as much as sublime infinitude of possibility. It is man's moral and emotional tendency to think that "our feet are planted now at last on the Adamant." In "Montaigne" Emerson had written, "We love whatever affirms, connects, preserves; and dislike what scatters or pulls down" (*W*, IV, 170). Lyceum listeners nodding in assent to this declaration, which poignantly invites assent, will have had the slide drawn out from under them.

123

This passage is thoroughly ironic; moments later the speaker drops his irony to encourage the thoughtful man "to avail himself of the checks and balances in nature, as a natural weapon against the exaggeration and formalism of bigots and blockheads" (*W*, IV, 171). Otherwise, as he warns in the entry about false bottoms, one's premises and beliefs will become identified with one's life and designs on life, and the periodic shattering of conclusions will threaten the life and embitter the individual. The disturbing aspect of the journal passage has nothing to do with Emerson's attitude but is directly related to the metaphor employed. The would-be absolutist, who has insisted on finding the adamant in order to place both feet firmly on it, is glimpsed disappearing into dark recesses.

Approximately one year after Emerson had made this journal entry, Thoreau began to draft his first version of *Walden,* a version that originally began with material that eventually formed the core of chapter two, "Where I Lived, And What I Lived For" and in which the narrator states that "The Intellect is a cleaver; it discerns & splits, and rifts its way into the secret of things," and that "I would mine & burrow my way through these hills."[1] It was several years later, however, in his next version of *Walden,* that he wrote of wedging downward through the mush and sludge of opinions and interpretations, ever downward until one would hit solid bottom, reality. And even though the speaker in *Walden* several times treats with ironic reservations the quest for absolutes and adamantine footing, the evidence of Emerson's journals reveals that this quest was a part of Thoreau that Emerson failed to discover or take seriously. Thoreau, he was convinced, was too adamant in both attitudes and ideas. "The absolutist is good & blessed," he noted, "though he dies without the sight of that paradise he journeys after" (*JMN,* IX, 317). And several years before Thoreau first wrote about his design to "drive life into a corner, and reduce it to its lowest terms,"[2] Emerson had lectured college students that "We can never surprise nature in a corner; never find the end of a thread; never tell where to set the first stone" (*CW*, I, 124). Or, as he put it in a miscellaneous worksheet and in a quite different metaphor, "My attention, my love, can only be commanded by the single aperçus [*sic*]. I think we must not presume wholeness."[3]

The growing rift between Emerson and Thoreau in the 1840s and '50s was, to a notable degree, the result of changes in the views of both men—Emerson in the direction that his flowing law took him and Thoreau in the direction of anticipating nature and driving it into a corner so as to discover the laws behind growth and change in nature and human nature. In *Walden* the theme of defining nature does not imply the rigorous, exact, and comprehensive endeavor that Thoreau's major unfinished project at his death indicates. The ambition behind the latter, which at his death had produced five essays and three extensive but unfinished studies of which more than a thousand holograph pages have survived,[4] appears to have been a large-ranging attempt to define nature's ways, both patterns of persistence and the order of change, in order to take as far as personally possible the exclamation in *Walden*: "To anticipate, not the sunrise and the dawn merely, but, if possible, Nature herself!"[5]

An equally significant factor in Emerson's and Thoreau's mutual disenchantment, as their radically different responses to Webster reveals, was their view of the individual's role in the commonwealth and the kind of individual who warranted "heroic" associations. At the time when Emerson was making final arrangements for Thoreau to leave the Emerson household for the home of his brother William Emerson of Staten Island, where Thoreau was to test his literary wings (this was one of many instances in which Emerson relied on William to help solve his domestic problems), Emerson wrote revealingly in his journals: "Young men like H[enry]. T[horeau]. owe us a new world & they have not acquitted the debt: for the most part, such die young, & so dodge the fulfillment" (*JMN*, VIII, 375). Not surprisingly, Emerson incorporated this passage into his discussion in "Experience" of defects and golden impossibilities. As usual, he dropped the personal reference without significantly altering the sense of the passage: "We see young men who owe us a new world, so readily and lavishly they promise, but they never acquit the debt: they die young and dodge the account; or if they live they lose themselves in the crowd" (*W,* III, 51). From Emerson's perspective, given his definitions of the scholar and his obligations to his age, Thoreau was dodging the account.

This had not always been Emerson's opinion of Thoreau. In the journals from 1838 to 1842 he usually expressed unqualified admiration for Thoreau. Thoreau's pertinacity and stoic toughness were especially impressive. He could even admit, "I like Henry Thoreau's statement on Diet. 'If a man does not believe that he can thrive on board nails, I will not talk with him' " (*JMN,* VII, 497). But by 1843 Emerson was cooling toward Thoreau and, when Thoreau decided to settle down at the pond, was cool toward the enterprise. There are indications at the end of the chapter "Former Inhabitants; And Winter Visitors" and in the compositional history of this chaper in *Walden* that while at the pond Thoreau was disappointed in Emerson's coolness, a disappointment that increased in later years.[6] Like Thoreau, Emerson revealed his attitude. Two months before Thoreau moved back to Concord, Emerson wrote that "T. sometimes appears only as a gen d'arme good to knock down a cockney with, but without that power to cheer & establish, which makes the value of a friend" (*JMN,* X, 106–7). He admits that Thoreau gives him "in flesh & blood and pertinacious Saxon belief, my own ethics. He is far more real, & daily practically obeying them, than I; and fortifies my memory at all times with an affirmative experience which refuses to be set aside" (*JMN,* XIII, 66). There are many entries, however, that criticize Thoreau's "Puritan" inflexibility, moral and conceptual implacableness, and habit of working in opposition. According to Emerson, one of their infrequent meetings in 1850 was held at Emerson's proposal, "with malice prepense, & take the bull by the horns" (*JMN,* XI, 283). This contrariness was rarely a desire to explore or express still another point of view. With irritation and impatience Emerson observed, "The Purist who refuses to vote, because the govt does not content him in all points, should refuse to feed a starving beggar, lest he should feed his vices" (*JMN,* XIII, 20).

From the time that Thoreau began to call Emerson by his first name, and especially when he recognized a considerably changed Emerson in the man who returned some months later from his European journey of 1847–48, and when thereafter he increasingly allowed himself to challenge Emerson openly and then withdraw from his imperious friend for months at a time, his journal began to be a record of a shift in Emerson. He was half-right in saying that it was Emerson who had changed, not he.

The major differences between the two men are most fully expressed in Emerson's eulogy of Thoreau, published serially three months after Thoreau's death and in the *Complete Works* (*W,* X, 449–85). The point of view is Emerson's; Thoreau's version would have been different. The interest here is not the accuracy of Emerson's backward glance over Thoreau's life—and, indirectly, over his own—but the congruence between this eulogistic essay and his essays and journals of the 1840s and '50s. To a large extent this eulogy, and its theme of the severity of Thoreau's ideal, is a restatement of opinions he had expressed in his journals. Almost two decades before Thoreau's death Emerson had forecast that Thoreau would not acquit his debt to his times, and that individuals like him tended to die young "& so dodge the fulfillment." Notwithstanding the possibility of a mean-spirited side to Emerson, his assessment of Thoreau acknowledged assumptions and attitudes that governed Emerson's view of Webster.

Although tone in Emerson's prose writings is a subject that has not sufficiently troubled scholars, an essay like "Works and Days" is an unmistakable reminder that Emerson's prose must be listened to with care and that it resists superficial reading and excludes superficial readers. In "Thoreau" tone is very much at issue. The ironies are less obvious than in "Works and Days" and do not depend on an easily recognizable and telling shift after which a number of points begin to double back on themselves. Rather, Emerson signals the reader in the second paragraph that there is more to say about the subject of Thoreau, more than we have imagined and different from what we might have expected. This message to the reader is postponed to the second paragraph to allow for the usual brief identification of the subject of the eulogy.

The first sentence of the second paragraph promises historical resumé: "He was born in Concord, Massachusetts, on the 12th of July, 1817." But if Emerson proceeds from there with historical data, these are extremely selective, remarkably similar, and quick to establish a point of view. "An iconoclast in literature, he seldom thanked colleges for their service to him, holding them in small esteem, whilst yet his debt to them was important. After leaving the University, he joined his brother in teaching a private school, which he soon renounced. His father was a manufacturer of lead-pencils, and Henry applied himself for a time to this craft, believing he could make a better pencil than was then in use. After completing his experiments, he exhibited his work to chemists and artists in Boston, and having obtained their certificates to its excellence . . . he returned home contented. His friends congratulated him that he had now opened his way to fortune. But he replied that he should never make another pencil. 'Why should I? I would not do again what I have done once.' "[7] Although the mood is reflective, as we might expect, it lacks the meditative aspect one associates with the beginning of a eulogy. And despite the fact that the traits are enumerated in an agreeable and entertaining manner, they are not in themselves entirely agreeable. The eulogy seems to be saying, "There is something here that points to itself and you would do well to understand it and me." At the outset there is the suggestion of slight whimsy; by the end of the paragraph, despite the speaker's modesty and politeness, the reader is a little surprised by the irony. Moreover, the critical detachment alerts the reader to observe the difference between the speaker and the one eulogized. The intellectual smile is less than innocent, especially when the speaker mimics Thoreau's supposed words. Yet the tone also includes a somewhat amused informality that suggests affection. Emerson creates the initial relation to his subject by citing several of the widely known, because idiosyncratic, facts of Thoreau's life, the kind of qualities that in life annoyed some of Thoreau's acquaintances but in death generated a legend. In short, the tone prepares us for a remark a few paragraphs later, " 'I love Henry,' said one of his friends, 'but I cannot like him.' " This statement Emerson culled from his 1843 journal, where it opens the paragraph already cited, in which Emerson declared that young men like Thoreau "owe us a new world" and that Thoreau will likely "dodge the fulfillment." Since Thoreau is dead and recently buried, one would expect the liking and disliking (a function of life and relationships of the living) to be subsumed by a prevailing love for a most unusual friend. Such will not be the case in this essay.[8] Emerson's indirection is strategic. In the initial essay draft of this paragraph he did not attribute the remark to a friend, or to Elizabeth Hoar as he did in the journal entry, but made it as a personal observation.[9] With the revision he politely mutes the criticism, maintains critical distance, and does not invite unnecessary resentment toward the speaker.

Yet as a eulogist the speaker seems in a hurry to point to tendencies in Thoreau that he will track down in the rest of the essay: reductionism, fixation, love of the absolute, and implacability—characteristics that hurt his productivity as a writer and often produced minor or major collisions with friends and society. Emerson implies that Thoreau had reduced Harvard's role in his life to two alternatives—much influence or none. Since Thoreau perennially sought to cultivate his independence he had to insist on the latter.

Emerson typically does not specify the degree of influence colleges had, but the speaker states flatly that Thoreau's "debt to them was important." The word "renounce" as it is used in the context of Thoreau's teaching experience does not suggest that he gave up an idea or belief, but that he gave up a desirable profession and professional development for the sake of an idea. This is amplified in the next paragraph: Thoreau refused "all the accustomed paths" and kept "his solitary freedom at the cost of disappointing the natural expectations of his family and friends." The adjective "natural" is carefully chosen for someone who had expressed love of nature and the life of the naturalist, and one of whose nicknames in Emerson's journals was "Sylvan." As for "natural expectations," Emerson includes both himself and his expectations here. As for "family," Sophia, at least, regarded Thoreau's literary achievements with admiration bordering on religious awe. "He was a born protestant," the speaker continues. Here the critical voice is recessive. "If he slighted and defied the opinions of others, it was only that he was more intent to reconcile his practice with his own belief." Perhaps here too a little pique is revealed. A gesture of approval, however—Thoreau's interest was "the art of living well"—is the dominant one. Yet we should detect the discriminating voice when we are told that Thoreau was "*exact* in securing his own independence" (italics mine). This capacity to mingle admiration and ironic detachment is particularly apparent in the remark on Thoreau's pencil-making. Striving to make the perfect pencil recalls Thoreau's efforts to find bottoms or perimeters, unshakable foundations, and the ungraspable. Or, as he exhorted his readers in *Walden,* to build castles in the air and put foundations under them. Emerson would probably refuse to move into such a castle; at least he would never cease to remodel. And he would hardly have "returned home contented" having achieved his goal.

The fifth paragraph is more openly critical. Here Emerson expands the subject of Thoreau's peculiar protestantism: "He interrogated every custom, and wished to settle all his practice on an ideal foundation. He was a protestant *à outrance,* and few lives contain so many renunciations. He was bred to no profession; he never married; he lived alone; he never went to church; he never voted; he refused to pay a tax to the State; he ate no flesh, he drank no wine, he never knew the use of tobacco; and, though a naturalist, he used neither trap nor gun. He chose, wisely no doubt for himself, to be the bachelor of thought and Nature." The first habit noted is a positive one. Endless interrogation is something Emerson would be quick to notice and praise in another person. In "Circles" he had allowed a somewhat too enthusiastic pronouncement: "I am only an experimenter. . . . I unsettle all things. No facts are to me sacred; none are profane; I simply experiment, an endless seeker, with no Past at my back" (*CW,* II, 188). Emerson's reservations about the speaker at this point in "Circles" notwithstanding, he allows the pronouncement to stand. The eulogy goes on to note that Thoreau "wished to settle all his practice on an ideal foundation." The word "wished" is a little cool: Thoreau's achievement did not measure up to his intention and probably could not have measured up. And with the adjective "all" Emerson returns to Thoreau's absolutism. "He was a protestant *à outrance.*" This is the second time Emerson has used "protestant." He may simply be saying that Thoreau was a Protestant to the extreme even if it might kill him as it did some of his Huguenot forebears. For years Emerson had warned of the potential destructiveness of a lopsided commitment. To Emerson, Thoreau's protestantism was particular, however, and consisted of a long regimental line of certainties, some of which are cited in rapid-fire fashion. A little later the speaker adds, "There was somewhat military in his nature, not to be subdued, always manly and able, but rarely tender." The original version of nine years earlier is less muted and gracious: "H is military/ H seemed stubborn & implacable" (*JMN,* XIII, 183). Humor dresses up the criticism just enough when Emerson recalls how Thoreau has been compared to an elm tree. Perhaps the most instructive comment in paragraph five to someone listening to the tone is the following: "He chose, wisely no doubt for himself, to be bachelor of thought and Nature." The qualification "wisely no doubt for himself" has a ring of superiority. Emerson begs to differ.

The most remarkable aspect of the passage is that it consists largely of a series of negatives. Thoreau's clear-cut response to life manifested itself in negations. Several paragraphs later we are informed, "It cost him nothing to say No; indeed he found it much easier than to say Yes." Emerson had admitted more than once than he preferred *No* people to *Yes* people. But he was speaking of something other than a penchant for renunciation. The essay "Fate" is illuminating in this respect. In the midst of chaos, which negates some of man's power and threatens to negate man himself, he dare not practice resignation or invoke cheap affirmations. The labored quality of the prose and the powerful denials establish a speaker who dares to say No as far as his perceptions and honesty require and then to fashion some kind of Yes. For the later Emerson survival, belief, and work depended on that Yes, a condition that will be discussed in a later chapter.

The other side of Thoreau's renunciation was his sense of opposition. It was "as if he did not feel himself except in opposition," Emerson pointedly notes. "He wanted a fallacy to expose, a blunder to pillory, I may say required a little sense of victory, . . . to call his powers into full exercise." Again the tone is cutting. Thoreau's journal, with which Emerson was acquainted, included many passages expressing the importance of acquiring greatness through opposition. Indeed, "He cannot be said to succeed to whom the world shows any favor. In fact it is the hero's point d'appui, which by offering resistance to his action enables him to act at all. At each step he spurns the world. He vaults the higher in proportion as he employs the greater resistance of the earth."[10] In the essay "Wild Apples," which he completed on his deathbed, Thoreau had defended such a style of life on moral and aesthetic grounds. Yet it was this living in opposition that repeatedly exasperated Emerson. On the occasion of Thoreau's refusal to pay his poll-tax and his subsequent jailing, Emerson wrote, "Don't run amuck against the world. Have a good case to try the question on. It is the part of a fanatic to fight out a revolution on the shape of a hat or surplice." Knowing that the Abolitionists' dogmas would never fully satisfy Thoreau, Emerson also noted, "The Abolitionists should resist, because they are literalists; they know exactly what they object to, & there is a government possible that will content them. . . . They are the new Puritans, & as easily satisfied. But you, nothing will content. No government short of a monarchy consisting of one king & one subject, will appease you. Your objection then to the State of Massachusetts is deceptive. Your true quarrel is with the state of Man. . . . This prison is one step to suicide" (*JMN,* IX, 446, 447).

To underscore his point in the eulogy Emerson cites another anecdote from his dealings with Thoreau: "Talking, one day, of a public discourse, Henry remarked that whatever succeeded with the audience was bad. I said, 'Who would not like to write something which all can read, like Robinson Crusoe. . . ?' Henry objected, of course, and vaunted the better lectures which reached only a few persons." In "The American Scholar" Emerson had described the influence of the vigorous mind as far-reaching in the culture and in history, and the scholar as one with the capacity to inspire his generation, "one who raises himself from private considerations, and breathes and lives on public and illustrious thoughts" (*CW,* I, 62).

The next paragraph of the eulogy begins with a discreetly subdued summation that readers have since tended to lift out of its context and transform into a beatific aphorism on Thoreau. "He was a speaker and actor of the truth," Emerson begins. The comment is a notable epitaph, but it continues, "and was ever running into dramatic situations from this cause. In any circumstance it interested all bystanders to know what part Henry would take." The speaker then lists a number of Thoreau's actions, some of which are censured in Emerson's journals. But the mildly ironic "running into dramatic situations" is hint enough.

One of Emerson's best known poems, "Uriel," reveals much on the subject of running into dramatic situations. The young deities are sitting about, discussing the heavenly orthodoxies of the moment. But Uriel breaks into their monotonous harmony with an opinion of his own, truly original and thoroughly unorthodox. In other words, he not only runs into a dramatic situation, he creates it. As usual in Emerson, orthodoxy is a function of miserably limited perspectives. Only Uriel sees through insignificant particulars to the central issue and true relations. And he shakes the realm with his vision and words. But something happens in the second half of the poem that is perhaps as important to our understanding of Emerson as the content of Uriel's speech. Uriel withdraws into silence, which tends to be regarded by the other gods as recantation, and fades into angelic anonymity. The reason has to do with a certain "sad self-knowledge." Exactly what this might be is not clear, but it seems to include a recognition that his words will not be given a fair hearing, and that by pressing them without any regard to anything or anyone will create for him a condition too demanding and debilitating. In any case, Uriel does not press his view. What purpose then can the utterance serve, if he permits even heaven to smooth it over? The poem explains that although Uriel withdraws his personal force from the statement, the statement itself still stands and occasionally triumphs by censuring the heavenly host into a collective blushing. "And the gods shook, they knew not why." Uriel, it seems, refuses to lead an open and frontal revolution because he will be crushed. More likely, if he persists in his unorthodox pronouncements and open opposition, he will be laughed at, or eventually ignored. Hence he does not stubbornly persist. He has the integrity and the powerful words to make his statement and to make it count, but he has enough knowledge of his local and larger community to sidestep or pull back, as saddening as this may be, when it is strategically imperative. Thoreau did not have the "sad self-knowledge" and the dark but wise rebelliousness of a Uriel. When Thoreau was arrested for refusing to pay what he regarded as an unjust tax, Emerson revealed much more annoyance with Thoreau than with the state of Massachusetts.

The eulogy also has words of unmixed praise. For several paragraphs the tone loses much of its doubleness. "He lived for the day," the speaker says of Thoreau, "not cumbered and mortified by his memory." This was important to Emerson; the past could easily have haunted Emerson and drained the springs of his energies. For the Emersonian scholar heroic action was possible only as he found the courage, energy, and discipline to bring all his resources to bear on the present moment, but to do so wisely. In 1836 Emerson had written that "The sun shines to-day also"; in a late essay first published in 1879 he scorned the "backward creeping crab" and called for individuals "who can live in the moment and take a step forward" (*W,* XI, 537).

Especially praiseworthy was Thoreau's ability to think and write metaphorically, to concentrate his rich and various thoughts in attractive tropes. With him the metaphor was not an "ornament" but "an unsleeping insight." He "liked to throw every thought into a symbol. The fact you tell is of no value, but only the impression. For this reason his presence was poetic, always piqued the curiosity to know more deeply the secrets of his mind." Emerson's tribute here is unabashed. One recalls his fondness for Thoreau's memorable metaphors both in his speech and writings, metaphors that from time to time Emerson recorded or transcribed in his journals and other notebooks, in a few cases trying to improve on them by making them serve his convictions. More than once Emerson expressed a special admiration for one of Thoreau's famous statements in *Walden:* "I long ago lost a hound, a bay horse, and a turtle-dove, and am still on their trail." In the notebook of the eulogy is a leaf originally loose but in more recent years tipped in by proprietors of the manuscript. This leaf, of an excellent quality of paper and much finer and more attractive than the notebook paper, has text on only one side. With a fine nib and in a very large and artistic hand Emerson had transcribed the passage from *Walden* concerning the hound, horse, and turtle dove. It is the only writing on the leaf. After Thoreau's death Emerson apparently inserted this leaf, without changes, into the notebook in which he was drafting the eulogy. Here was an example of sidling up to that reality ungraspable by the direct word. There is no reservation in the paragraph of the eulogy consisting solely of the complete version of this passage from *Walden* or in the paragraph that follows, which begins, "His riddles are worth the reading, and I confide that if at any time I do not understand the expression, it is yet just."

Emerson is attracted to the passage for another reason, however, which recalls much of the address up to this point. The quotation tells him of the pilgrim soul in Thoreau, the searcher who moves onward and outward pursuing what for Emerson has to a considerable degree become the ungraspable phantom of life. Such a pilgrim soul is commendable, indeed so attractive that speaker and subject appear to have merged. Yet at this moment the speaker recalls how Thoreau had one day heard the night-warbler, a bird he "had been in search of twelve years, which always, when he saw it, was in the act of diving down into a tree or bush, and which it was vain to seek." "I told him he must beware of finding and booking it," the speaker reports, "lest life should have nothing more to show him." Thoreau's answer merely confirmed Emerson's fear: "You seek it like a dream, and as soon as you find it you become its prey." The polite reprimand he reports to have given Thoreau betrays once again his desire for mobility and a fear that in his language, thinking, or experiencing a rigor mortis might set in. Likely for the same reason Emerson's discussion of Thoreau's keen interest in the Indian is both brief and off-handish. He did not share Thoreau's interest in finding an aboriginal saint, a man of primordial innocence, virtue, and strength. Perhaps Emerson was no longer able to understand Thoreau's aspirations in this regard. Moreover, it seems that he was not sufficiently familiar with the essays "Chesuncook" and "The Allegash and East Branch" to be aware of Thoreau's dissillusionment with the Indian, who, it turned out, shared the Yankee's fears and vices.

Soon the tone becomes ambivalent again. The dissenting voice makes its presence felt in an extraordinary fashion. Thoreau is honored as "a person of a rare, tender and absolute religion, a person incapable of any profanation, by act or thought." The adjective "absolute" does not quite fit with "rare" and "tender" unless it is read as "pure" or "perfect." Even then it causes the reader uneasiness in the light of what Emerson has said thus far. Our dubiousness lingers with the sentence that follows: "Of course, the same isolation which belonged to his original thinking and living detached him from the social religious forms." But he adds, surprisingly, "This is neither to be censured nor regretted." And Aristotle appears to furnish additional sanction and approbation: " 'One who surpasses his fellow citizens in virtue is no longer a part of the city. Their law is not for him, since he is a law to himself.' " Then, while this reference to Thoreau's surpassing virtue is still uppermost in our thoughts, Emerson continues, "His virtues, of course, sometimes ran into extremes." The "of course," which appeals to the common knowledge and bias of the audience, does not suggest approbation. The word "extremes" perhaps strikes the reader as mild, but behind it is a history in the journals and essays like "Montaigne" of insistence that the wise man recognizes and accepts "that human strength is not in extremes, but in avoiding extremes" (*W*, IV, 156). One must learn to live productively in that "narrow belt" of the "mid-world" discussed in "Experience." An effective way of avoiding destructive extremes—for Emerson, running to extremes is potentially suicidal—is to practice greater skepticism and mobility. For friends and acquaintances of Thoreau, Emerson continues, "It was easy to trace to the inexorable demand on all for exact truth that austerity which made this willing hermit more solitary even than he wished." Emerson has just stated that "This is neither to be censured nor regretted." Perhaps "censure" is too strong a word for what he proceeds to do, but he is censorious. Furthermore, there is noticeable regret that Thoreau's demand upon his fellows was so *inexorable,* that the truth he sought was the *exact* truth, and that his life was excessively *solitary.* "I think the severity of his ideal," Emerson adds, "interfered to deprive him of a healthy sufficiency of human society." At one point in the manuscript Emerson had noted the following, then changed his mind and cancelled the passage: "When a man for whom he once had a great regard, but who had become intemperate, came to see him on some business, Thoreau perceived that he had been drinking, and declined to deal with him, but advised him to go home and cut his throat, and that speedily."[11] That man likely was Alek Therien, one of Thoreau's closest friends while he lived at Walden Pond, and one of his loyal bedside visitors when Thoreau was dying of tuberculosis. "The severity of his ideal" might well serve as a subtitle for the eulogy.

The comment on "healthy sufficiency of human society" should not be sentimentalized. Emerson, like Thoreau, was at war with society—this is abundantly clear from his less popularized writings, especially his letters and journals. But since it was war, Emerson sought to know the ground rules. There are at least two ways out, given a society that Emerson and Thoreau agreed was there to reduce you to its mediocrity—retreat or wise co-habitation. In sketching plans for *The Conduct of Life* Emerson wrote the *dissidentia* for man thinking and hence for himself and individuals like Webster: "A topic of the 'Conduct of Life' under the head of *Prudence,* should be how to live with unfit companions: for, with such, life is, for the most part, spent" (*JMN,* XI, 370). Thoreau had little use for society and, as "Resistance to Civil Government" and its several manuscript antecedents make clear, for politics and influential public figures. Emerson did have use for society (*use* is probably the best word applicable). His writings had a public appeal, he was a public figure with a consciousness of his audience, and his ideal was to translate genius to the commonwealth. The severity of Thoreau's ideal, Emerson believed, forced him to misspend his resistance and to retreat too far.[12] Thus he adds, and one can hear the keenly disappointed patron, "with his energy and practical ability he seemed born for great enterprise and for command; and I so much regret the loss of his rare powers of action, that I cannot help counting it a fault in him that he had no ambition."

In the conclusion of the eulogy the tone shifts once again. The critical voice recedes and Emerson finally pays a moving tribute that manifests both admiration and affection. In a few sentences he refers to a summer alpine plant of the same genus as New England's "Life-Everlasting," the small, wooly, white flower the Swiss call *"Edelweisse,"* which he translates as *"Noble Purity."* In developing the metaphor he states that "Thoreau seemed to me living in the hope to gather this plant, which belonged to him of right." The sentiment is a noble one, yet even here one detects an important reservation-as-concession: that Thoreau lived *in the hope to gather.* That is as much as Emerson says, and perhaps can say, of a friend who lived in the commonwealth but was not of it to the degree that Emerson was and insisted on being. If Thoreau seemed to live in the hope of perfection, Emerson can pay his respects without claiming the hope for himself. The realization he had made about his life was radically different from the one Thoreau pursued: "It is indeed a perilous adventure this serious act of venturing into mortality swimming in a sea strewn with wrecks, where none indeed go undamaged, / It is as bad as going to Congress none comes back innocent" (*JMN,* XI, 417). "It seems an injury," the speaker exclaims, again betraying the large hopes Emerson had pinned on Thoreau and his disappointment, "that he should leave in the midst his broken task which none else can finish, a kind of indignity to so noble a soul that he should depart out of Nature before yet he has been really shown to his peers for what he is." Thoreau had departed from nature and life before he was able to realize and appreciate the prospects and exfoliations of his nature and to make those crucial new departures in his life that Emerson had expected.

The conclusion reminds us once again that in Emerson's view he and Thoreau had not built the same house and world. With that reminder the essay ends somewhat abruptly and with a final note of discontent. But Thoreau, "at least, is content. His soul was made for the noblest society; he had in a short life exhausted the capabilities of this world." The conclusion of the essay is indeed conclusive; the subject is closed, the essay has no further prospects, and initiatives of the kind the reader has learned to expect in the end of an Emerson essay are absent as the words focus exclusively on Thoreau. Emerson's "Thoreau" is one of only a few of his essays of the middle and late years that do not culminate in an end-as-beginning.

III

REBUILDING
HOUSE & WORLD:
EMERSON'S
MATURATION

"A man serves his work.
A man is a housekeeper,
—yea, verily, he builds a house,
& it is his task thenceforward
whilst he lives
to paint, shingle, repair, enlarge,
& beautify that house."
Journals

"We forget in taking up
a cotemporary book
that we see the house
that is building
& not the house that is built."
Journals

•6•
Metamorphoses of the Image:
Emerson & Poetry

However much we may wish to qualify Emerson's characterization of the real Webster as "in equilibrio" and the real Thoreau as incomplete yet severe, these characterizations should remind us of the metaphor of balancing in "Works and Days." This metaphor of balancing can be paraphrased in terms of style as follows: style is another way of speaking about man thinking and about the actions of man thinking; style is a large term that requires artist, inventor, scientist, and politician to heed the rules of a sport that is inescapable and serious. The survival of art, culture, and man are at stake. In the words of the journals, "You cannot build your house or pagoda as you will but as you must." That observation is followed by a typical Emerson criticism of a contemporary English writer whose reputation, Emerson suspected, was transitory: "Landor has too much willfulness; he will not let his genius speak but must make it all himself. A writer must . . . be content to stand aside & let truth & beauty speak for him, or he cannot expect to be heard far" (*JMN*, V, 164).

In the light of Emerson's conclusion in *Nature,* and the strategic reference there to "educated Will," the journal entry on Landor can be rephrased as follows: "Landor writes from the will; he has not developed beyond personal willfulness to the educated will. He does not write from an individual imagination attuned to nature, human nature, and the commonwealth." By Emerson's standard, then, Landor is much too small to be a representative man. One can also make the point negatively. Landor's kind of willful-

143

ness does not allow one to shift one's footing repeatedly, as required, so as to recover and maintain balance, poise, and strength in a precarious world.

To explore Emerson's style is to discover how thoroughly he served his work, and how a consistent emphasis produced notable development and change. "The great man," he wrote, "even whilst he relates a private fact personal to him, is really leading us away from him to a universal experience" (*W*, XII, 314–15). Translating this observation into practical criticism of Emerson, we can say that to examine Emerson's "facts" is to probe a quality of mind, sensibility, loyalties, ambition, affirmation, and vision, and, above all, to attend to metaphoric concentrations and permutations and the voices of personae. The result is not as much a definition of Emerson as it is an identification of the Emerson text that seriously warrants our attention. According to Emerson, the imaginative and intellectual steps of man thinking establish his true history, and it is that history that surmises and enlivens the commonwealth. In Emerson's case the text is the true history and vice versa. After a lifetime of composition and revision, Emerson's text became, and still is, its own compelling metaphor for the law of permutation. Such is the case in the poetry (the subject of this chapter) as in the essays and lectures (the subjects of the final two chapters).

If we remember that most of what Emerson had to say about style he said in the context of the poet and poetics and that his major essay on style is "The Poet," we can agree with David Porter that in the end Emerson's "defense of poetry stands as the defense of his prose."[1] Moreover, it stands as a defence of his own poems, and his best poems are his strongest defence of "The Poet."[2] Yet Hyatt Waggoner has suggested that the poetry has been ignored and, when not, read and explicated with surprisingly narrow sympathies; our most urgent problem with Emerson's poetry is how to read it.[3]

From one point of view Emerson invited such a response. Near the end of "The Poet" the narrator confides, with more than a touch of disappointment, "I look in vain for the poet whom I describe" (*W*, III, 37). Critics have tended to look elsewhere and into the future, as Emerson seems to do, for the kind of poet and poetry envisioned in "The Poet." The completion of the essay, however, was followed by a two-year period of intense and extensive poetry writing and revision that culminated in the appearance of his first volume of poems in 1847. In his journals, letters, and comments to friends he was modest about his verse, but the concentration on poetry in 1845–46 is a characteristic Emersonian venture to enact his vision as life and to enact both in the literary genre he admired above all others and in forms that, he hoped, would help to redefine poetry. The poetic function, as he formulated it in "The Poet," is to create the logos or new word by receiving and translating images of one's environment into a form of forms that surpasses the images only to give them context. Or, to paraphrase a key passage in the essay, poets must learn to find their world and, having done that, find in that world another world, indeed worlds, without ends.

In 1844 Emerson failed to find in his generation poets "capable of a new energy" (*W*, III, 26). The same was true of the poetry of old England: the artful thunder of the logos was largely absent; what poetry featured was conventional dialogos. In his own poetry, which at times embarrassed and exasperated him, his expectations can be thrown into intelligible relief if we examine "The Snow-Storm," "The Sphinx," and "Days," three representative poems from his early, middle, and later career.

Seen from the comparative and historical vantage points, Emerson's definition of poetry as transformation into higher forms is neither new nor unorthodox. Plato through Augustine, we are inclined to say. We are inclined to follow the tendency through Sidney through Shakespeare through the English metaphysicals through Milton through Kant through Coleridge through Emerson. And we can trace an American succession down to our day and to a number of our contemporary poets. The principle governing this tradition is transformation or, as Emerson called it, the "law of metamorphosis." Like "a temple whose walls are covered with emblems" (*W*, III, 17), or like a numbing snowstorm, a sulking sphinx, or the processional spectacle of "Days," the poet's world presents splendid possibilities that are also his sternest tests: "We stand before the secret of the world, there where Being passes into Appearance and Unity into Variety" (*W*, III, 14). Whether the search for the poet is in vain depends on whether his poems manage to transform the images they receive, an action sufficient "to reach the quick and compel the reproduction" and one that becomes, at the same time, a primary act—"a whole new experience" (*W*, III, 6, 10). In the words of Jamblichus, quoted in "The Poet," " 'Things more excellent than every image . . . are expressed through images' " (*W*, III, 13).

In this context Kant and Coleridge deserve additional comment. It is no secret that initially Emerson got much of his Kant and Coleridge from James Marsh's 1829 American edition of *Aids to Reflection,* then from Frederic Hedge's essay "Coleridge" in 1833, the main subject of which is Kant rather than Coleridge. After Coleridge's death in 1834, Emerson returned to his writings, studying *The Friend* with care and also taking up again the *Biographia Literaria.* Just as Coleridge had mapped Kant to fit his own system, Emerson refashioned Coleridge's Kant as well as Coleridge according to the emerging Emersonian design.

One of the results of rereading Coleridge in the mid-1830s was a greater appreciation of Wordsworth, whose poems approached the kind of achievement warranted and justified by Emerson's version of Kant and Coleridge: in the transformation of environmental images into a metaphoric construct, the poet achieved a reconciliation of *Verstand* and *Vernunft,* experience and the law of experience, objective and subjective, parts and whole, individual and universal. In his quasi-philosophical comments about poetry at this stage he seems to have anticipated the view that a successful poem achieved a convergence, mutual interpenetration, and re-conciliation of one's subjectively experienced world with transcendent law or objective form. At this early stage of his literary career, however, this standpoint was sought in a context that within a few years would strike him as archaic, a context with strong affinities to Swedenborg, from whom he drew inferences that corresponded to his understanding of Coleridge.[4]

Emerson's high regard in the 1830s for Coleridge's theories and Wordsworth's poems helps to explain his preference in Coleridge's poetry for pieces such as the conversation-poems over the better-known "Ancient Mariner" and "Christabel." The former are closer in mode to Wordsworth's poems and Emerson's assumptions and practice. In *Nature* he described the creation of works of art as a marriage of environment and imagination-as-builder. In the "Language" chapter he proposed that the environment furnishes the images with which the true poet creates metaphors. This action of taking hold of one's experience of nature and translating it is, for the poet, a unified one, combining what has been described as the two nucleii of Emerson's inclination as artist—the downward and the upward thrusts.[5] Central to the poet's achievement is the metamorphosis produced by way of the metaphor, that is, by the images transformed into a symbolic form, a metaphysical act in the strict sense of transcending physical images, albeit entirely by means of those images. A poet is a god in ruins if he fails to transform "each" of the images into the "all" of the poem with its new governance.

In the mid-1830s Emerson's formula for such transformation of natural facts into the higher form of the poem is clearly laid out in his finest poem of this period, "The Snow-Storm" (*W*, IX, 41–42), a poem that represents a rich and complex technique in its enactment of transformation even while standing back from itself to comment on the achievement. Nature provides the materials: storm-clouds, wind, fields, hills, woods, river, blizzard, farmhouse, housemates, the wind's snow sculptures. The first section paints the scene with strong sensory images infused with possibilities beyond themselves even while limited strictly to sensuous facts. In august (and for the moment Augustan) fashion the snow is announced by "all the trumpets of the sky," those winds that eventually will be more than their own clarion call. With the arrival of the snow, space is framed and time is frozen. The inherent world of the storm and poem is hidden, imprisoned beneath the cover of a white mist that crystallizes the air. Made captives within this expanse of whiteness, the traveler is unable to continue along his path and the courier is delayed in delivering his message. Indeed, this storm, which holds everything outside the veiled farmhouse in its power, imprisons the housemates as well. Huddling about the fireplace, they are "enclosed / In a tumultuous privacy of storm."

Both "enclosed" and "privacy" suggest shelter, but they also signal a double imprisonment here: prisoners of the farmhouse and of their own sensibilities. Like the traveler and courier, the housemates have stopped, shut in by their private refuge, shut out from the "mad wind's night-work." Thus enclosed, they have no prospects other than their condition. For them, it appears, the poem ends here; nothing more is possible or desired. In "The Poet" Emerson describes a somewhat similar condition, although the individual described is trapped outside by the blizzard:

The fate of the poor shepherd, who, blinded and lost in the snow-storm, perishes in a drift within a few feet of his cottage door, is an emblem of the state of man. On the brink of the waters of life and truth, we are miserably dying. The inaccessibleness of every thought but that we are in, is wonderful. . . . Every thought is also a prison; every heaven is also a prison. Therefore we love the poet, the inventor, who in any form . . . has yielded us a new thought. He unlocks our chains and admits us to a new scene. (*W*, III, 33)

The process of nature, however—the agency of wind and snow—is transforming the world of the housemates and the poem. Whether the poet can respond in kind with the "new thought" that frees images and poem from their prison and serves as transforming agent and passport "to a new scene"

148

is the crucial factor in extending both the poem and its vision.

Within the privacy of his storm, the poet-speaker labors to "ascend into a higher form" (*W*, III, 20). The prelude to his accomplishment is a friendly Frostian cajoling of both imagination and reader: "Come see the north wind's masonry." That invitation is also the start of the poet's liberating work and the poem's transformation. Even as the poem has turned in like an hourglass as the wide sweep of the storm narrows to farmhouse, traveler, courier, and private enclosure, the narrowness widens, the perspective moves far outward, and the transformation of the world (as far as the poetic eye can behold) into a panoramic work of art begins. In short, the images of the storm are not trapped in the narrow enclosure; rather, we witness the "passage of the world into the soul of [the poet-speaker], to suffer there a change and reappear a new and higher fact" (*W*, III, 21). The world unfolds its beauty in a panoply of the snow-storm's delicate artistry. But then, if the reader's ear has recorded well, the shift does not come unannounced. The prevailing iambic pentameter of the poem is suspended in the last line of the first part, and the two strong spondees in the opening line of the second reinforce the shift and the reader's awareness of it.

From this point on, through the eyes of the poet and the metamorphosis of images in the poem, the reader beholds, as it were, another world. As seer and sayer the poet infuses the scene with impressive form by lifting images beyond themselves while pushing perception well beyond the limits of the housemates. Sky, storm, and poem become "an unseen quarry," the snow is the "tile" with which the wind, "the fierce artificer," re-forms the world by molding his fortresses around every stake, tree, and door. Protean in his demonstrations, the personified north wind sculptures wreaths of what seem to be white marble around coop and kennel, transfigures the thorn bush or tree into a swan-like form, and erects a tower over the graceful curves of the gate's new drapery. With the simplicity called for in "The Poet," each image reports the wind's invisible yet dynamic power to transform the image and thus the world it helps to constitute. The image also enacts and thereby confirms a kindred energy in the poet and his language. Within each is an unseen force whose presence and efficacy, however, are evident. The kindred energy reminds us that metaphoric action has occurred unannounced, unostentatiously, naturally. Language has translated narrow and private perception into liberated perception, image into thought, north wind into poet, nature's beauty into the power and form of art, words into logos. For the true poet and poem such words are, in Emerson's view, "modes of the divine energy"—actions that become a "second nature, grown out of the first, as a leaf out of a tree" (*W*, III, 8, 22).[6] Or, we might add, the second part out of the first.

Or Emerson's "The Snow-Storm" out of the prose version as recorded in his journals, for that matter (*JMN*, VI, 246). Seen from one point of view, the poem is virtually identical to the journal entry: except for a few changes here and there the same words, phrases, and sequencing. Seen from another point, the poem is a transformed version of the original prose passage, the wild work of the storm having been begun in prose but completed in verse. The poem marshals the iambics into a blank verse organization and conjugates the lines evenly and regularly except for the crucial turn at the conclusion of the first section and the beginning of the second, where the metric pattern aptly shifts as the poem apparently seals its closure only to transcend it with "Come." Equally notable is the introduction of numerous commas, four periods, three semi-colons, and a colon to slow cadences and lines, measure them with pauses, and throughout the poem maintain a reserve of expectation. The most impressive transformation of the journal passage is achieved through shaping. Whereas the prose version consists of a rambling paragraph and a brief, coda-like reflection, the poem's two sections, by way of contrast to each other and to the astonishing shift in part two, chart the achievement of wind as artist and Emerson as poet of transformation. "The Snow-Storm" is a twice-told record of unfolding, the unfolding of one imaginative-verbal order into another and a prior exfoliation of journal notation into formal verse.

We can say, then, that for the reader of poetry familiar with literary history and persisting poetic conventions, Emerson's poem "The Snow-Storm" meets at least two expectations. First, and foremost only in terms of the sequential development of the poem, it makes unmistakably present to the reader a particular world with tightly limited time, space, verbal and intellectual-emotional possibilities. This limitation is achieved by locating the reader in a field of particular images even while closely harnessing poem and reader by them. Second, through the transformational formula the harness is loosened, time and space open out, resonances widen and deepen, and the transformed verbal order establishes a new intellectual-emotional reverberation. Understood in these terms, the transformational formula bears some striking resemblances to the mode of a typical Wordsworth lyric as defined by Geoffrey Hartman in "The Halted Traveler," the opening chapter of his study of Wordsworth's poetry.[7] The poem does not depart from itself but literally stops to report the transformation of a nature, speaker, and language already introduced.

Were "The Snow-Storm" the only kind of poem in Emerson's inventory, then surely he would have waited in vain at least until the appearance of Whitman's *Leaves of Grass* for the type of poet he had described. His journals noted that method in thought, language, and poetry meant progressive arrangement, and his comments on Wordsworth and Coleridge implied that these two represented one such kind of arrangement. By the end of the 1830s, however, these poets had largely been replaced in his center of admiration and theoretical speculations by Goethe, who in the next decade would figure more prominently in his journals than Homer, Jesus, Plutarch, Dante, and Milton.

In the 1840s Emerson's journals and his essay on Goethe identify several reasons for Goethe's importance to him: not as a "corroboration of Coleridge's method"—a claim recently made[8]—but, among the principal reasons, that Goethe represented a modern application of Heraclitus's flowing philosophy to nature, perception, language, art, and the individual and collective human history. Of similar stature and important for some of the same reasons was Montaigne, whose restively skeptical law of change in creeds, social institutions, and history of ideas corresponded to Goethe's theory and practice of literary art. Emerson's poem "The Sphinx," composed six years after "The Snow-Storm" and placed in lead-off position in the 1847 volume of poems (no doubt using its position to emphasize its claim to the kind of achievement he now identified with the poet), helps to disclose through its artistic enactment and implication why Goethe and Montaigne had essentially replaced Wordsworth and Kant-Coleridge in his pantheon. The most succinct explanation, however, can be inferred from a key passage in "The Poet," which in its evocations and rationalizations supports the mode of "The Sphinx." Not surprisingly, Emerson placed "The Poet" at the beginning of his *Essays: Second Series,* where its function has affinity to that of "The Sphinx" in the book of poems.[9]

It is in the nature of the transformation, not the fact of transformation, that "The Sphinx" goes well beyond the achievement in "The Snow-Storm." When we read in "The Poet" that "The metamorphosis excites in the beholder an emotion of joy . . . of emancipation and exhilaration" and that "This is the effect on us of tropes . . . and all poetic forms," we are reminded of "The Snow-Storm." When we read on that "Men have really got a new sense, and found within their world another world, or nest of worlds" (*W,* III, 30), that codicil—"or nest of worlds"—recalls "The Sphinx" and suggests a key to it. The conclusion of the sentence cited here is more apropos: "for, the metamorphosis once seen" ("The Snow-Storm," Wordsworth, Coleridge), "we divine that it does not stop" ("The Sphinx," Goethe, Montaigne, and eventually Hegel).

Goethe, in Emerson's *Representative Men* a philosopher of multiplicity who detected "the old cunning Proteus, nestling close beside us" (*W,* IV, 271, 273), represented an important correction to any thought, thinker, science, or art unallied to or only superficially given to the entelechy and flowing law of endless permutation. For his revised text of *Nature,* published in 1849, Emerson chose as his new motto a poetic litany on the unceasing "spires of form," a litany that begins "A subtle chain of countless rings / The next unto the farthest brings," and that recalls *Wilhelm Meister's Lehrjahre* and *Faust* more than Goethe's late nature writings. In the words of the Chorus mysticus at the final curtain of Faust, Part II—which at one point Emerson declared to be the grandest literature since *Paradise Lost* (*JMN,* IX, 43–44)—"Alles Vergängliche / Ist nur ein Gleichnis." A Gleichnis (analogy) of what? Of flowing law, the nest of worlds with its teleological transience. Although Goethe's word "Vergängliche" is customarily translated as "transitory," a term whose associations recall both the Plato-to-Coleridge tradition and orthodox theological views, Emerson's reading appears to have been "transient," which would turn the adverb "nur" into a reminder that in the world of endless permutation and art of ceaseless transformation we need to distinguish between means and ends, the individual transformation and the law it signals.

Emerson's doctrine of flux, as applied to art, extends beyond recent attempts to characterize it, such as that the "American Muse is a *daimon* of disorder, whose whispered counsel in the dark is: 'Evade and multiply,' "[10] or that "Emerson was trying to bring his poetry closer to the actual processes of thought, to create what we today might see as a rudimentary 'stream of consciousness' technique."[11] In the words of the journals, "The method of advance in nature is perpetual transformation" (*JMN,* VII, 524), an appropriate characterization of "The Sphinx" and an even apter explanation of the catalogue that concludes the poem without reaching a point of conclusion. Experience, thought, and poetry are not exempt from the method of nature: "As the bird alights on the bough, then plunes into the air again, so the thoughts of God pause but for a moment in any form" (*W*, VIII, 15). As for dilettantes, whether poets or critics, "Dull people think they have traced the matter far enough if they have reached the history of one of these temporary forms, which they describe as fixed & final" (*JMN*, IX, 301)—an oracle accepted as "the revealed word of truth" (*JMN*, VII, 32). The "poetic eye" sees man, life, and art in constant metamorphosis (*JMN*, VII, 539).

It is true poets, then, who "advance with every word" (*JMN*, VII, 386). According to "The Poet" every word was once a poem. Elsewhere Emerson stipulates that "Every poem must be made up of lines that are poems" (*JMN*, XI, 18), a view subscribed to by Whitman and modern American poets partial to enumerative logic, catalogue rhetoric, parataxis, and the use of syntax, punctuation, stanza, and in some cases larger structural units to turn ends into beginnings by poising the moment of transition. Each advance within the poem, or the poem as a whole for that matter, if seen as end or ens, is false. Hence the paradox that in Wallace Stevens becomes the core of his ars poetica. The poet tells the truth through ever-changing fictions, which is to say, one apprehends and comprehends through an incessantly mutational truth-making wherein no single transformation is normative and no self and world can be made intelligible except within and through metamorphosis. The greatest believer is also the greatest infidel, and the truest muse is the "giant of nothingness," who is "ever changing, living in change." The language and assumptions here lead us into the most commanding tradition in American poetry. From Emerson the genealogy proceeds to Whitman, includes as lateral descendant Hart Crane's mode in *The Bridge*, finds a more direct descendant in Williams in *Paterson* V, and recognizes its most authoritative scion in Stevens.[12]

Underlying this tradition are Emerson's epistemological base and linguistic-artistic assumptions. Over this tradition stands "The Sphinx" (*W*, IX, 20–25). To quote one of the briefest yet most trenchant commentaries on the poem, "nature tests man's affirmations by requiring him to find them in her. She is his 'eyebeam.' . . . Abstract statement is not enough; there is no such thing as naked truth. . . . The poem itself achieves the infiniteness of nature, although not by solving the Sphinx's riddle but by stating it adequately."[13] This statement is made not through the brooding lament of the Theban monster or the bald declarations of the poet but through the mode of structural progression culminating in the catalogue that concludes the poem. Stephen Whicher's prejudices against Emerson's poetry notwithstanding, "The Sphinx" must have been one of the poems on his mind when he wrote that seen from one point of view Emerson's poems "ask the reader to share as equal and friend in a process of invention, rather than invite his admiration for the completed work of a master."[14]

"The Sphinx" is of three parts or stages, the sphinx and her dirge possessing the first, the poet and his doctrines featured in the second, and the sphinx, poet, and a new poetry inhabiting the third. The defeatist admission at the outset is one of the poem's ploys to invite speakers and reader into a series of transformations. As major protagonist in the poem, the sphinx also owns the title.

Like "The Snow-Storm," "The Sphinx" opens in the present tense to an event overshadowed by a problematical situation. In this case the divine monster broods and nods her way through a protracted complaint over oafish man's condition, a complaint that recalls the particulars, although not the tone, of the orphic poet at the end of *Nature*. In this opening scene, three related yet distinct prospects for transformation stir into presence like sleeping resources. Can the dirge of the sphinx be transformed by and according to the dynamic elements that flicker on and off in her imagery; can the sphinx and the poem transcend the fixedness and private enclosure of the beast; and will the actions of a man make the sphinx's words a lie even as they have been the truth? In short, will the lethean dullness of the poem's opening stanza be overcome by an Emersonian poetry? Insofar as that will be realized, and everything will be drawn into the protean dynamism, "The Sphinx" is a paradigm of Emerson's view of poet and poetic process.

But in the early stanzas such prospects are dim. Apparently the sphinx, like the speaker in "The Poet," has been looking "in vain for the poet I describe":

> "Who'll tell my secret,
>   The ages have kept?—
> I awaited the seer
>   While they slumbered and slept:—

Although "The Poet" will argue that each age needs its own confession, the sphinx grieves that for ages upon ages (the Greek definition of "everlasting" or "forever") there has been no real age because there has been no "seer" to make history, that is, to put his stamp on his sleeping age and thus claim and transform it. The poignancy of the plaint comes home to the reader in stanzas two to six, a protean series of vital images that, in the plenum of a seer, would be the means to individual acts of transformation and a dynamic ascent of definition and creation through a procession of transitive forms. Even in her drowsiness mixed strongly with pessimism the sphinx seems to have the ability to find a new world in and through the image, and beyond that a nest of worlds.

These stanzas, however, which in some of their particulars recall passages from *Nature,* "The American Scholar," "The Divinity School Address," and "Circles" and look forward to "The Poet," the latter part of "Experience," and much of the poem "Uriel," are at once the strongest anticipation of the conclusion of "The Sphinx" and the paradigm of the problem at the heart of the lament. The poetry has no immediate promise. Not only is its potential unrealized over the span of these stanzas and those that immediately follow; it is also quashed and nullified by the subtractive conjunction "But," which marks a crucial disjunction rather than connection between expectation and fulfillment. The problem is "man," who "Absconds and conceals" (literally: hides away and keeps out of sight, an apt description of what has just happened with the vital possibilities of stanzas two to six). The failure is criminal, one wants to say; man is both criminal and accomplice, the sphinx declares.

Notes of anxiety and pity, but not consolation, conclude the dirge as the sphinx quotes the troubled queries of the "great mother" nature, questions that through the early desolate pages of "Experience" are foremost in the language of the text and the mind of the reader. Like the essay, the poem appears to be in the power of the Fury despair. Sphinx and nature, or sphinx-nature, can only wait.

The "world seems always waiting for its poet," observes the speaker in "The Poet" (*W*, III, 10). However many millennia the sphinx has been waiting, poem and reader do not wait long: "I heard a poet answer / Aloud and cheerfully." In this second stage of the poem, most of the poet's rejoinder is a declaration in verse form of Emerson's doctrines of poetry. The poet's assertions not only counter the dirge but cavalierly minimize all that the sphinx has spoken. The strategy is simple: to insist on a new vantage point from which to invoke the doctrines that have been hinted at through the negative dialectic of the sphinx's complaint.

Before he actually launches into his trumpet-tongued manifesto, the answering poet welcomes the sphinx's words and encourages her to "Say on," for he has caught in her "pictures of time" not the dirge but "Their meaning sublime." As if tutoring a potential writer in the classroom, he exclaims that he has recognized the extraordinary possibilities in the sphinx's flow of images. Under the failure, we must infer, stirs a principle that promises success. In his mind, as it were, he has already written the stanzas as the sphinx might have written them and almost did.

The principle that the poet identifies as "Deep love" calls to mind Goethe's *Faust,* Part II, especially its program of transience, its passages through spires of form, and its cul-

minating exemplar of the law of the drama and its protagonist in the Gretchen-madonna metamorphosis. Inherent in all of these is a continual invoking of the entelechy
of the metamorphic urge ("das ewig Weibliche"). The urge
onward through spires of form is also an urge to dive deeply, and to accept deep beneath deep. In Emerson's poem,
"Love" is love of the dynamic, changing, growing, becoming, in short, life and art according to the law of progressive
metamorphosis:

> To vision profounder,
>   Man's spirit must dive;
> His aye-rolling orb
>   At no goal will arrive;

Another name for love (other namings are in keeping with
the mode and vision of the poem) is "Eterne alternation."
Love's antitheses are "Lethe," final "goal," "heaven" in the
singular rather than plural, and, inherent in and the cause
of all of these, "Pride." Because they imperiously insisted on
conformity and consistency, pride has "ruined the angels"
of mythology and of American culture, pride has
threatened to ruin this poem by opposing metamorphosis,
and, we can add today, pride did ruin the poem for Emerson's editors (including his son Edward) and, stylistic
shortcomings aside, for a number of Emerson scholars
down to the present.

No stern old war gods shake their heads at the poet's
pronouncement. The sphinx does bite "her thick lip," however, when addressed in his concluding salvo as "Dull
Sphinx," the shift from "sweet Sphinx" indicating to her the
extent to which the poet's enthusiasm and boldness have
shaded into fleering. The poet is right, of course; the real
issue is "sight," or seeing and interpreting adequately. Consequently the sphinx does not contest any of his declarations. Instead, she offers a conclusion in keeping with his
assumptions and culminating his argument. In so doing, she
turns the tables on a poet too ready to take full credit for his
vision, as though it were exclusively his or had originated

with him. Without answering questions, sphinxian or other, she arises as his double, or, better said, original, and so his perfect clarification. Yet nature's language and hers have been one. She, nature, the poet, and the poem are linked in a mutual order and purpose that she will embody in the life of nature and he must enact in the nature of his words—a fusion of mode and achievement confirming a single dynamic law as in "Brahma." Nature and sphinx are their own hymn, both subject and object, but the poet will sing that hymn, confirming that he is a "yoke-fellow" whose spirit and eyebeam belong to the sphinx. She has mastered him even as he has mastered her nature. Poet and sphinx are writing the same poem; his mode is hers and his lines are suggested entirely by her. The possibilities of stanzas two to six are being realized; the failure was only temporary (that is, as in "Threnody," another "answer" that "is a lie"), nature has not stopped, the sphinx has not really been crouching in stony fixation, and poet and poem are ready to "Ask on." However the poem has written itself and will write itself to its last word, the sphinx, not the poet, has drafted it first.

The poet's enterprise, we now recognize, is to catch her if he can. This is what she has waited for—to show her real nature and to find in the poet an adequate partner. The final stage of "The Sphinx" begins auspiciously with "Uprose the merry Sphinx / And crouched no more in stone." Those words introduce one of the most memorable passages in Emerson's poetry, characterized as "symbolic" catalogue rheotric,[15] a repeated enactment of "the genesis of symbolism,"[16] and "the essential statement and act of all the other poems that accompanied 'The Sphinx,' "[17] Each new image or statement is a point of no return to the previous order, recomposing the previous order and its context and thereby establishing the new truth only to have that truth made a "lie" by further advance. Poetry as enacted by the sphinx and "The Sphinx" is a voyage of perpetual discovery and definition whose center is on the move. Inherent in the multiform advance is continual redefinition of the apparent order in behalf of the prospective order or, in Emerson's view, transcendence.[18] Such poetry "never rests or repeats itself, but casts its old garb, and reappears, another creature: the old energy in a new form, with all the vigor of the earth" (*W,* XII, 71). The true poet

shows us all things in their right series and procession. For through that better perception he stands one step nearer to things, and sees the flowing or metamorphosis; perceives that thought is multiform; that within the form of every creature is a force impelling it to ascend into a higher form; and following with his eyes the life, uses the forms which express that life, and so his speech flows with the flowing of nature. (*W,* III, 20–21)

Just as Emerson's transformation of the prose version of "The Snow-Storm" into an achievement answerable to the night wind's architecture corresponds to the kind of transformation that occurs within the poem itself, so the changes he made to the first published version of "The Sphinx" (*The Dial,* January, 1841) correspond to the kind of transformation inherent in this poem and strengthen the dialectic of transitive forms. Changes in spelling in stanza ten, minor as they may seem, introduce a subtle shift in emphasis: "best" is raised to "Best" whereas "Perfect" is downgraded to "perfect," a proper adjustment given the declaration in the next stanza that "His aye-rolling orb / At no goal will arrive." Apparently in the interest of stressing the partnership of sphinx and poet, Emerson substitutes "yoke-fellow" for "Manchild" and connects the word with the assertion that follows it rather than perhaps with the question that precedes it, perhaps with neither. The first version reads "Who taught thee me to name? / Manchild! I am thy spirit." As for the crucial stanza beginning "Uprose the merry Sphinx," despite Feidelson's belief that Emerson "was seemingly undisturbed by any resistance to metaphoric fusion" and that, as far as Emerson was concerned, "any image will do,"[19] Emerson did not think so, for he cancelled two lines that allowed too much discontinuity into the tone and poetic logic. "She melted into purple cloud, / She silvered in the moon" originally read, "She hopped into the baby's eyes, / She hopped into the moon."

By any standard, however, the major changes have to do with punctuation. Although revision of this kind is too extensive to be accounted for in detail here, the intention is suggested by the chief alteration, affecting primarily the sphinx's dirge and the final stanzas. Extensive substitution of semicolons for commas (or comma-dashes) and periods strategically creates the pause in which the next advance is poised against the one just completed—a stop used as connective, departure without rupture, end transformed into beginning, vital change without discontinuity. To quote the journals: "A wise man is not deceived by the pause: he knows that it is momentary: he already foresees the new departure, and departure after departure, in long series" (*JMN*, IX, 301). The idea in this journal entry, as in many of Emerson's poems, is largely a function of syntax, punctuation, and construction through continual reconstruction.

Whereas "The Sphinx" seizes the opportunity to offer such a series and thereby feature a poet "without impediment, who sees and handles that which others dream of" (*W*, III, 6), in the poem "Days" (1851), "Such is the hope, but the fruition is postponed" (*W*, III, 12). The ironies of the poem remind the reader, however, that the failure does not apply to the poem as such but is limited strictly to the speaker, who, we discover step by step, is victim rather than master of the processional flow. The fact that the nest of worlds so strongly and repeatedly invoked in the 1840s is here somehow tied to a poet-speaker's failure suggests an author who recognizes that not every would-be poet can work under the law of metamorphosis, and that even the artist with the best of intentions can fail. More important, it suggests a reexamination of the art of ceaseless permutation and the recognition of potential hazards.

Both journals and essays reveal such reexamination and shift in emphasis. In the year that Emerson composed "The Sphinx" he wrote of nature, "O protean Nature whose energy is change evermore" (*JMN*, VIII, 4), of the soul's method with nature as "a geometry of sunbeams" (*JMN*,

VII, 413), and of genius as "always new, subtle, frolicsome, musical, unpredictable" (*JMN*, VII, 442). In short, "motion or change is [nature's] mode of existence. The poetic eye sees in Man the Brother of the River. . . . Heroes . . . invent a resource for every moment" (*JMN*, VII, 539–40). The only stability and continuity in all the metamorphoses is the "I" established by, yet always transcending, the poetic eye: "Through all the running sea of forms I am truth, I am love and immutable, I transcend form as I do time & space" (*JMN*, VII, 429). This is an "I" or persona as assured, subjective, and heady in his pronouncements and creations as the poet in "The Sphinx." Only a few years later Emerson remapped the equator, suggesting in "Experience" that a proper proportion must be maintained between the power of the protean artist and the form of his expression. By this time Swedenborg was regularly chided for his simplistic view of metamorphosis. By the end of the decade Hegel had replaced Montaigne as the philosopher of flux and Goethe continued to elicit admiration because of his mature understanding of metamorphosis; indeed, in "Fate" (written early in the '50s) Goethe and Hegel lead off a brief list of "profound persons and a few active persons who epitomize the times" (*W*, VI, 39).

The practical implications of Emerson's rethinking of metamorphosis are hinted at in a journal entry on the protagonist in prose fiction, an analogue of sorts to the image in the poem and the persona in the essays: "If I wrote a novel, my hero should begin a soldier & rise out of that to such degrees of wisdom & virtue as we could paint; for that is the order of nature" (*JMN*, XI, 13). If we extend the statement to any literary art, including poetry, we have art under the governance not of metamorphosis but of a teleological progression or leitmotif in the metamorphosis. To borrow an analogy from musical composition, the work does not simply proceed through a series of changes in keys but progresses through a free yet necessary and teleological modulation of keys. This is essentially what Emerson calls for in a journal entry in 1851: "As Vishnu in the Vedas pursues Maya in all forms, when, to avoid him, she changes herself into a cow, then he into a bull; she into a doe, he into a buck; she into a mare, he into a stallion; she into a hen, he into a cock, & so forth; so our metaphysics should be able to follow the flying force through all the transformations, & name the new pair, identical thro' all variety. For Memory, imagination, Reason, sense, are only masks of one power" (*JMN*, XI, 417). The power to follow the flying force and so to cope with our world of "physical & spiritual" limitations is the great "Necessity" in the essay "Fate"; three times the conclusion invites the reader to build altars to "the Beautiful Necessity."

As slight as the shift in Emerson's thinking appears to be—after all, he continues to insist on the law of metamorphosis—his new emphasis is important to his own writing as well as to the history of subsequent practice and theory in American literature. The Coleridgean transformation in "The Snow-Storm" is both limited and expertly balanced. The dilation of the poem's circle, a synchronic activity, is matched by a linear step forward. Awareness is deepened even as we witness a modest advance in time and space, a balance between vertical sonority and horizontal progression, to borrow another analogy from music. Once poetry comes under the law of perpetual transformations, however, the series of departures in the poem can easily incline it one way or the other, toward an astonishing accumulation of simultaneous melodies and effects (a complicated sonority-turned-dissonance) or to an endless series of steps (the phalanx of individual advances crowding out an intelligible leitmotif). Composed and seen as vertical or dilational achievement, the poem may present seemingly unlimited linguistic layers and a mounting clutter of images, a stratigraphy betraying separateness even under its own pressure. Written and read as a horizontal progression, the catalogue of advances suggests either discontinuity or non-directed, uninterpretable flow. In either case the progression appears to be a sequence without a recognizable genealogy and the "flying force" of the poet.

Whether "The Sphinx" is finally graspable, that is, whether its conclusion is a free yet intelligible modulation, is questionable. No matter what our answer, the question comes after the fact in Emerson's development, and is refracted in some of his central observations about poetry after the appearance of "The Poet." The spires-of-form epigraph for the 1849 edition of *Nature* suggests the possibility of extending the renovation of language, recognition, and sensibility, as witnessed in "The Snow-Storm," into a nest of worlds by means of self-evolving circles as well as a "long series" of advance, the conflation of the two implicit in the helix-like progression. For the poet, the ambition of Emerson's desire is appealing and formidable: both the poetic eye and the rationally drilled mind are bound to live many of their days under the same roof with failure.

"Days" (*W*, IX, 228) is a poem about such a failure and, beyond that, about the hazards with which the poet of metamorphosis must live. The "meaning sublime" of the "pictures of time" in "The Sphinx" does not become present with and through the "Daughters of Time" in "Days." Nor does the speaker perceive the principle and principals[20] behind "the hypocritic Days," which are "muffled and dumb" like the ritual masked figures in Greek drama or the participants in an English court masque. Since they are also as muffled and dumb as the frozen snowscape of "The Snow-Storm" and the sphinx in her narco-drowsiness, the speaker's response is the obverse of the culminating pronouncement in *Nature*, "Know then that the world exists for you." The negation in "Days" follows hard on the heels of a sequence of images in line six that is reminiscent of the progression in *Nature* from "Commodity" to "Discipline" to "Idealism" to "Spirit." Standing aside in the enclosure of his "pleachéd garden," the speaker is left empty-handed and empty-minded after watching the "pomp," and he settles for a few herbs and apples from his own garden, the procession essentially lost on him as though it had not occurred.

Just how far short the speaker in "Days" stops from the prospects strongly suggested by the first six lines is obvious from the condemnation that concludes the poem. Not as obvious is whether the speaker or the ungraspable nature of the transitive world is the cardinal factor in the failure. A recent study notes that "the passive man in the bower is the failed poet," yet argues in a preceding chapter that " 'Days' takes account of untranslatable realities brought into Emerson's poetry."[21] Both, according to another recent study, lead to the same result: "nature seems to become a succession of fleeting surfaces and the observer disintegrates into a jumble of moods."[22] According to "The Poet," however, such a condition is largely the poet's responsibility: "Day and night, house and garden, a few books, a few actions, serve us as well as would all trades and all spectacles. We are far from having exhausted the significance of the few symbols we use" (*W,* III, 18).

Although explicators of "Days" have speculated on the ironies in the poem, its negative dialectic has somehow been ignored, notwithstanding the fact that the technique is the structuring principle for major parts of essays like "Experience," "Montaigne," "Fate," and "Fortune of the Republic," and is the means whereby Vergil unmistakably clarifies the meaning and mission of one of Emerson's heroes, Aeneas, the builder of a city, culture, and history, whose destiny Emerson identified with his own when he moved to Concord in 1834. As in Book IX of *The Aeneid* and in a number of the essays of Emerson's middle and late career, so in "Days" the necessary presence is defined in terms of its absence, desired success by failure, discipline through its lack, flying law through anarchic succession. It is words without the word, spectral procession inducing failure of nerve. Although the first six lines of "Days" are rich with the prospects in the sphinx's opening speech, the poem shifts abruptly into a denial of its own transitive forms and their possibilities. Unlike "The Sphinx," "Days" does not rise above its negative definition to positive enactment. Through the negative dialectic, however, we understand exactly what is required.

Just as many of the memorable statements in "The Poet" can stand as subtitles for "The Snow-Storm" and "The

Sphinx," the same statements apply as well to "Days" if a simple negative is inserted. The speaker does *not* re-attach "even artificial things . . . to nature, by a deeper insight" (*W*, III, 18); the fluxional scene is *not* "put under the mind for verb and noun" (p. 20); the poet does *not* give the vehicular and transitive lines "a power which makes their old use forgotten," thus putting "eyes and a tongue into every dumb and inanimate object"; he does *not* perceive "that within the form of every creature is a force impelling it to ascend into a higher form" (p. 20); "new passages" are *not* "opened for us into nature" and "the metamorphosis is [*not*] possible" (p. 27). "You must be a day yourself," Emerson had written in his journals several years earlier, "and not interrogate life like a college professor. Every thing in the Universe goes by indirection" (*JMN*, X, 380). The speaker in "Days" is like that unyielding professor, or like the imprisoned housemates in "The Snow-Storm" or the dull sphinx of the early stanzas. At the poem's end the world is still "waiting for its poet," whose mission has become as clear as his inability to follow and connect the series of departures. The Day establishes her authority of presence in the act of absenting herself, departing in silence, leaving behind an astringent "scorn" where she herself might and should have been, and was (and is) for Emerson and the reader. There is a double meaning, then, in a notably personal observation in "The Poet": "The poet has a new thought; he has a whole new experience to unfold; he will tell us how it was with him, and all men will be the richer in his fortune" (*W*, III, 10).

That double meaning—success and failure, positive and negative, the positive through its negation—is absent from the rudimentary journal version out of which came "Days." On May 24, 1847, Emerson entered in his notebook, "The Days come & go like muffled & veiled figures sent from a distant friendly party, but they say nothing, & if we do not use the gifts they bring, they carry them as silently away" (*JMN*, X, 61). The one-dimensional language here turns on the conditional, establishing simply an equation of forfeiture if the vaguely-stated condition (to "use the gifts") is not met. Even in a poem whose subject is failure, Emerson achieves a transformation that signifies the true poetic function.

"The Snow-Storm," "The Sphinx," and "Days" come close to establishing something normative in Emerson's poetry because of the weight and distribution of emphasis they provide the corpus. Of these three, "The Sphinx" is clearly the most significant. In the category of "The Snow-Storm" and its single impressive act of transformation belong poems such as "Each and All," "Concord Hymn," "The Apology," and "Two Rivers." Poems much closer to "Days" in tone, mode, and implication are "Eros," "Blight," and "The World-Soul," the latter a delicate balancing act between positive prospects and the failure in "Days."

Far and away the largest category of poems, and most characteristically Emersonian, is the poetry for which "The Sphinx" stands at the center. Notwithstanding the fact that none of Emerson's poems before the late 1830s belongs to this category, it claims more than half of his poetry, including titles such as: "Woodnotes," "Ode to Beauty," "Uriel," "Threnody," "Hamatreya," "Merlin," "Seashore," "Brahma," "Waldeinsamkeit," "Illusions," "Music," "The Titmouse," "Terminus," and the original version of "Woodnotes II." Few are as interesting and complex as "The Sphinx"; some, however, reveal a maturer understanding and poetic grasp of perpetual metamorphosis, the "old energy" forever reappearing "in a new form."

Of these poems "The Titmouse" (*W*, IX, 233–36) is the most notable for its achievement. As in "The Sphinx," the implications of the poem and its conclusion proceed from several stages or types of transformation. In the first half, winter frozenness, inwardness, and repose are changed note by note to "gymnastic play" until the speaker burns with the fire of the bird and stands ready to ape "thy daredevil array" (reminiscent of the north wind and poet in "The Snow-Storm"), once having acquired "the titmouse dimension." The "dare-devil array" is also the beginning of another stage in the poem, in which the speaker comes to understand the bird's song to mean essentially what the final stanza of "The Sphinx" implies. The titmouse, too, is the master of mutations, of the flowing law of perpetual transformation. Appropriately, in the next-to-last stanza the speaker becomes master of the catalogue as he seeks to be the perfect partner, through his power and form to "follow the flying force through all the transformations." Recognizing where his chief loyalty must be, he makes a promise we expect him to keep:

> Doubt not, so long as earth has bread,
> Thou first and foremost shalt be fed;

The declaration reveals both ambition and humility; the poet of metamorphosis is eager to follow the changes, to remain in flight, beat for wingbeat, with the bird. He and the poem have proceeded through a number of transformations and are moving toward others. With "the titmouse dimension" the poem will not fail or confuse. The transformations are disclosing their law: forward is also outward, and the unmistakable advances, not fully fathomable, are intelligibly reported through a medley-melody of transformations. In the event that the reader misconstrue or underestimate the speaker's promise to the bird, he announces as boldly as the speaker of "The Poet": "I will write our annals new."

•7•

Tendencies, Forms, & Personae in *Nature*

To return to *Nature* at this stage of the discussion is not to find the reading easier or the meanings simpler. Knowing Emerson well can also mean not knowing him at all or knowing him only in part—that part that reminds us how small the Emerson text has remained for most of the scholars over the years and, with notable exceptions, how repetitious the scholarship has been. The student of Emerson cannot help but be familiar with the commonly-repeated assertion that the impulse in *Nature* was to devise "a little manual of pantheism" under "the common aegis of Lamarck and Plotinus."[1] One hopes that as the student struggles to understand the speaker of "The Titmouse" in his declaration "I will write our annals new," the student will allow the remark concerning the "little manual of pantheism" its inconsequentiality. Writing our annals new is susceptible to a range of definitions provided by Emerson's poems and essays and, as this chapter will discuss, by *Nature*.

Much of the notable scholarship on *Nature,* beginning with Vivian Hopkins's *Spires of Form* and Sherman Paul's *Emerson's Angle of Vision,* has contributed implicitly to a recognition that for Emerson nature's principal function is to admit man into the lessons of metamorphosis and that the central motif of *Nature* is to proceed from the untransformed to the transformed by way of rather than away from the untransformed. Whitman was one of the few nineteenth-century American readers to understand Emerson's rites of passage from the "apparition" surrounding man to man thinking (Whitman's SELF-turned-POET). Seen with an

169

eye for general tendency, *Nature* is a repetitive catalogue of transformation. Viewed more closely, this outline and surface discloses, under the aegis of the central motif, a range of transformations that in turn establish the motif by exploring its manifold versions: question to answer, negation to affirmation, interrogation to clarification, possibility to realization, old to new, present to future, nature's stimuli to man's constructive initiatives, non-reflexive identity with things and events to a maturer relatedness, image to metaphor, one metaphoric concentration to another, rhetorical urgency to complex formal achievement, parts to whole, one version of persona to another, and individual wealth to commonwealth.

We may now return to the epistemological problems and the inimitable structure and style of *Nature* with an expanded sense of philosophy as literary process, process as trope and metamorphosis of trope, metamorphic advance as the adumbrating, clarifying, and redefining of a self-as-persona, and persona (Emerson's most important trope) as the literary creation and enactment of man thinking.

To set the focus on *Nature* and the at once delightful and exasperating difficulty of recognizing and describing its tendencies, one might cite the chapters "Idealism" and "Spirit." The latter challenges not only the dualistic assumptions of Platonism but Platonic idealism itself. The obvious response to the problem created by "Idealism" is a contrary vector. And so "Spirit," the briefest chapter of *Nature,* counters "Idealism" with the self-evident insight "that spirit creates; that behind nature, throughout nature, spirit is present; one and not compound; that spirit does not act upon us from without, that is, in space and time, but spiritually, or through ourselves." Having identified man as a crucial presence in the Plotinian continuum that has replaced the Platonic hierarchy (Plotinus is means to Emerson's ends), the chapter shifts without the slightest philosophical qualms or grammatical or rhetorical transition to an organic metaphor of exfoliation in which "the bosom of God" and "the earth" are, for the moment, one and the same rather than opposite ends of the continuum. Aware of a growing inclination in his essay and of the inclination of Christian theology and of his age to depreciate the world of natural fact in favor of a spiritual order, Emerson seeks to arrive at natural fact just as surely and authoritatively as at spirit. In this respect we can speak of at least two vectors or inclinations in *Nature*—an attempt to substantiate a heaven of vital mind and an earth of natural fact. One needs to take these inclinations farther, of course, and observe how the essay encourages each of them but does so in a context of reciprocal metaphoric definition in which man is central. This further clarification becomes all the more crucial as one discovers that *Nature* accommodates more than two inclinations.

Both the multiple vectors in *Nature* (*CW,* I, 1–45) and the failure to recognize their mutual and reciprocal significance in the unfolding of the essay are factors in the lack of scholarly agreement on the work and the moderately bewildering range of models and sources attributed to it by critics over the last one hundred years. Probably with *Nature* uppermost in his mind, John Macy suggested that Emerson "gathers the wisdom of twenty sages into one discourse"[2]—a safe, if uninformative, number. As for specific models, sources, and affinities attributed to *Nature,* the list has attracted almost every wind of doctrine: Plato, Plotinus, Jesus, St. Paul, Plutarch, Augustine, Bacon, Milton, Cudworth, Jonathan Edwards, Swedenborg, Rousseau, Dougald Stewart, Goethe, Kant, Fichte, Schelling, Coleridge, Wordsworth, Hegel, Kierkegaard, Nietzsche, William James, Dewey, Whitehead, Wallace Stevens, Tillich, Merleau-Ponty, Heidegger, Hinduism, Brahminism, Zoroastrianism, Zen Buddhism, Quakerism, Puritan mysticism, classic Christian idealism, romantic Unitarianism, American nationalism, Nazism, and virtually all American poetry since Whitman, to name the most notable examples. Trying to bag the winds of Aeolus, George Williamson suggested some years ago a reduction of Emerson to four

171

types: the Yankee, the Romantic, the Platonist, and the Oriental.[3]

The number of tendencies Williamson identifies (the categories as such aside) strikes me as the proper figure for the most generative and definitional vectors in *Nature,* which I see to be the Platonist-Christian legacy, a Plotinian alternative or counter-current, the naturalist (lover of natural fact), and, in alliance with the sequence of personae in *Nature,* the poet of metamorphosis (truth-maker and world-builder). The metamorphosis of nature and man, as understood and envisioned in *Nature,* is, finally, the essay's rationale and thus answers the key question asked early on, "to what end is nature?" All else in the essay is means to the end, by which I suggest that we need to distinguish carefully between means and ends when throwing into relief the so-called ideas of the essay or examining its form or structuring principles. For instance, by the time we arrive at "Prospects," and even before, it is clear that Emerson's end is not to develop a system of correspondences or to formulate a doctrine of correspondences. Cudworth's, Swedenborg's, Schelling's, or any similar system offered Emerson promising metaphors that, in their suggestiveness, could help to restore to nature her rightful status and account for the "occult relation between man and the vegetable." Nor does *Nature* offer a philosophical program of reconciling perceiver and the object-world perceived. For that, one must search the entire Emerson canon and himself become the philosopher of the many parts. Nor is it advisable to extrapolate from *Nature* in order to formulate the "complete cosmogony" diagrammed in a recent commentary.[4] The most instructive discussions continue to be the dialectical approaches, and for good reason: given *Nature*'s several different vectors, the critic is faced with the problem of accounting for these and the manner in which they are all somehow accommodated as means to Emerson's ends.[5]

The four inclinations of *Nature* already identified come under this observation. Emerson's Platonism has been documented many times over, but seldom in the light of the assertions in "The American Scholar" that "I had better never see a book than to be warped by its attraction clean out of my own orbit, and made a satellite instead of a system," and that whenever "the mind is braced by labor and invention, the page of whatever book we read becomes luminous with manifold allusion" (*CW*, I, 56, 58). Platonic ideas, then, like so many others, served Emerson as tropes to center and concentrate his own thinking—the kind of plagiarism we note in Coleridge and T. S. Eliot rather than in their disciples. To underscore Emerson's metaphoric use of Plato is not to ignore but rather to clarify an important aspect of his training. A thorough steeping in Christian idealism, a major component of which in Europe, young America, and Harvard Divinity School had always been a Christianized version of Platonism, inculcated in Emerson and his age certain models and values associated with its major emphases. Platonic tropes affected Emerson's consciousness not by laying doctrinal siege to it but by furnishing analogies for thinking of world and man very much in the way that metaphors from technology have invaded our thinking and language about nature and the nature of man. It should be noted here that although the philosophical succession from Plato down to Emerson's age is not monolithic in preserving original Platonic assumptions and formulations, I use the term Platonism out of a lack of finding better terms, recognizing in Plato a persistently suggestive force in the history and assumptions of Christian idealism, especially in Protestantism.

The dualism inherent in the cosmology-epistemology of Christian Platonism (and the concomitant inclination to regard nature merely as man's means of transcending it), repeatedly discloses itself in the language of *Nature*. Rather than compile an inventory of such disclosures, I shall note their presence in several of the chapters preceding "Idealism" and the Platonism at the heart of it. In the "Introduction" the philosophical reduction of the universe to "Nature" and "the Soul" and the ranking implicit in the paragraph is the first such presence, but here, as in

"Beauty," vaguely informed by Kant. The three-tiered argument of "Beauty" begins with eighteenth-century sensationalism, proceeds to an essentially Kantian-Coleridgean aesthetic, and culminates in a Platonic-Christian language. This language flickers on and off in the chapter "Language" until its third stage, where Emerson's metaphors to explain the nature of metaphor are strongly informed by Platonic views. As though the progress of the argument depends to an increasing extent on Platonic tropes, parts 2 and 3 of "Discipline" are replete with echoes of Plato and traditional Christian depreciation of natural fact. "Idealism," the apparent culmination of all preceding parts of *Nature,* is in many respects an exercise in conventional homiletic form designed to convince the reader-listener of the efficacy of the "Ideal Philosophy" in explaining all existence and being. According to the summation of "Idealism" in the first paragraph of "Spirit":

all the uses of nature admit of being summed in one, which yields the activity of man an infinite scope. Through all its kingdoms . . . it is faithful to the cause whence it had its origin. It always speaks of Spirit. It suggests the absolute. It is a perpetual effect. It is a great shadow pointing always to the sun behind us. (*CW,* I, 37)

As the reader of *Nature* knows, this summation is also a transition to a counter-argument of sorts, since the Platonic hypothesis fails to "satisfy the demands of the spirit." Platonic idealism, in which Emerson was well read, conceives of forms as objective, that is, not identified with the cause but divorced from creative spirit. Although the divine spirit itself is seen as self-moved and dynamic, it is the efficient cause of static and immutable forms above and quite different from nature. Man's world, in contrast, is characterized by constant motion and metamorphosis, but these are illusions, mere fictions vaguely shadowing the perfectly consistent and immutable ideal world. Such a dualism, the persona of "Spirit" protests, "leaves God out of me" and leaves man in nature and as part of nature "to wander without end" in "the splendid labyrinth of my perceptions." The counter-motion throughout the essay and most obviously in "Spirit" is a Plotinian inclination. Although as much a philosophical idealist as Plato, Plotinus sought with his theory of eternal and unbroken emanation or externalization of spirit to reconcile aspects of pre-Socratics like Heraclitus and his doctrine of flux, Plato's self-moved and dynamic cause, Aristotle's view of nature as a world of generation and becoming, and his own model of emanation outward from the self-moving transcendent cause through the evolving-creative force of a world soul to the forms of man and nature. Emanation means, among other things, a striving toward further creation, or an endless reproduction and extension. In this model all existence and being could be plotted on a concentric continuum from divine idea (spirit) to natural fact. The Plotinian conception, which apparently came to Emerson primarily through Cudworth's *The True Intellectual System of the Universe,* offered a diagram compatible with Emerson's nascent organicist thinking in the three years following his visit to the Jardin des Plantes in Paris, where he received memorable instruction in the importance of natural fact.

Whereas Platonic idealism begins with the delusionary fictions of natural fact in order to find another world—a realm of eternal forms and a wholly other creative spirit—Plotinus begins with spirit and ends with non-reflexive action, or natural fact. Natural fact to spirit, spirit to natural fact, this is how the Platonic and Plotinian schemes worked as tropes for Emerson in 1836. Both of these schemes as tropes, and the opposite inclinations they generate and report in *Nature,* have created problems for the readers of *Nature* even as they create potential problems in the essay. The overstatement in the following observation notwithstanding, it assists in explaining the problem of the Platonism or of the reader who recognizes the Platonism at the expense of all other tendencies: "Emerson's books are about general ideas; in most of the essays the infinite gets the last word, the external world having been left far behind."[6] Henry James, Sr.'s " 'Oh you man without a handle!' " was for Henry James, Jr. "a remarkably felicitous expression, as it strikes me, of that difficulty often felt by the passionately-living of the earlier time, as they may be called, to draw down their noble philosopher's great overhanging heaven of universal and ethereal answers to the plane of their comparatively terrestrial and personal questions."[7] And yet even Henry James, Sr. recognized quite another tendency in *Nature,* so strong a concentration on natural fact that he complained of a "police-spy upon it" who engenders in the reader not a love of natural fact but a love of imitating Emerson. This was James in his old age, however, when he chided Emerson for "his ignorance of everything above the senses"[8] and thereby admitted a preference for the overhanging heaven of universal forms, even the one in *Nature.*

The reciprocal Platonist-Plotinian tendency is really Emerson's attempt to reconcile two tendencies and thus avoid the customary idealist mistake of leaving the external world far behind. Aside from the motto of the 1836 text of *Nature,* the location of the extended Plotinian passages in *Nature* confirm this. In part 3 of "Beauty" the metaphysics of beauty and the interpretation of the highest kind of beauty are a conflation of Plato and Plotinus culminating in a formula that accommodates the two tendencies and the desire for reciprocal dependence: "The beauty of nature reforms itself in the mind [Platonic], and not for barren contemplation, but for new creation [Plotinian]." If one remembers that for Emerson art is a second nature equivalent to nature, the nature-to-spirit, spirit-to-nature doubleness is instructive. "Language" features the same doubleness, albeit in somewhat different format. Whereas Emerson's metaphysics of language recall Plotinus, his interpretation of the nature of language is reminiscent of Plato's "The Cratylus." Moreover, the chapter begins with natural fact, defining it as the passport to a higher and more authoritative order, then proceeds through Platonic transformations, only to conclude with Plotinian allusions in order to return us to "Fact," the "terminus . . . of the invisible world," and to reinforce this emphasis by citing Oegger.

"Discipline" begins where "Language" leaves off—with the "objects of nature" waiting to become "a part of the domain of knowledge," thereby augmenting man's "magazine of power." The tedious training of "sensible objects" provides a basic degree of proficiency in the act of living. Higher degrees of proficiency are evocatively discussed in the second part of the chapter, where the speaker shifts from "understanding" to "Reason." Since the discussion proceeds from the lower to the higher degrees ("to spiritual nature"), we anticipate and get a considerable quantum of Platonist vocabulary and allusion. Also meeting expectations, based on the pattern established in earlier chapters, is the periodic and habitual intervention of Plotinianism, always radiating back to the circumference of natural fact as though—and by now the assumption is clear—Emerson cannot assent to the one without the other. The essay will offer its best credentials to the realm of idea ("the mind") and must, as a consequence, celebrate that which is at once the raw material and "publication" of thought: "In fact, the eye,—the mind,—is always accompanied by these forms, male and female; and these are incomparably the richest informations of the power and order that lie at the heart of things." The concentrated Platonic exercise of "Idealism" and the deft reversal of "Spirit" culminate this dialectic. Understood in this context, an observation by Lawrence Buell becomes informative in a new way: "Both the tactic of veering away from an initial statement and then working back to it, and the tactic of fanning out from a statement with a barrage of apothegms (to be brought back abruptly, often-times, at the start of a new paragraph) are . . . typical of Emerson."[9]

No matter how frequent or extensive the veering away from the external world, *Nature* never fails to return to nature. The essay reminds us not only of an author whose examination of the Jardin des Plantes during his otherwise tedious four weeks in Paris stimulated new interests, but of the Emerson who since that visit had been searching his mind for an answer to the question "to what end is nature" even while bringing his new enthusiasm for natural facts to the nature of Concord. In his first lecture after returning from Europe to America he noted in words of unusual intensity:

The limits of the possible are enlarged, and the real is stranger than the imaginary. The universe is a more amazing puzzle than ever, as you look along this bewildering series of animated forms, the hazy butterflies, the carved shells, the birds, beasts, snakes, fish, and the upheaving principle of life every where incipient. . . . We feel that there is an occult relation between the very worm, the crawling scorpions, and man. I am moved by great sympathies. I say I will listen to this invitation. I will be a naturalist. (*EL*, I, 10)

A more telling confirmation of Emerson's increasing assent to the invitation of the naturalist than the early lectures on nature is his lecture "Martin Luther," given in February of 1835. While paying tribute to a revolutionary, Emerson challenged the foundation of Luther's protest. This fundamental difference between Luther's Protestantism and Emerson's protesting indicates that Luther was removed relatively early from Emerson's changing lists of representative men. In a passage of considerable indirect self-revelation Emerson declared:

Luther's singular position in history is that of a scholar or spiritual man leading a great revolution, and from first to last faithful to his position. He achieved a spiritual revolution by spiritual arms alone. . . . He had such an unbounded confidence in the might of spiritual weapons that he would not degrade his cause by calling in the aid of flesh and blood. He believed a single truth was of strength to put to flight all the armies, all the kingdoms of the world. His ministry (to which he esteemed himself called by special impulses from heaven) was to communicate the truths which he received. . . . He thought like Plato, "that the soul is unwillingly deprived of truth." . . . He scorned the use of outward force because it distrusted this divine force. (*EL*, I, 127–28)

Later in the lecture, after characterizing Luther as the last of those to proclaim an unmediated, unaligned divine spirit to the world (all great religious men since "have joined Nature to Revelation"), Emerson notes that Luther was a

poet who "walked in a charmed world. Everything to his eye
assumed a symbolical aspect. All occurrences, all institutions, all persons seemed to him only occasions for the
activity of supernatural agents. . . . All objects, all events are
transparent" (*EL*, I, 132). Emerson's marrying of Christianity (in this case original Protestantism) with Plato is instructive. In fact, Plato and Isaiah are mentioned virtually in the
same connection, as though Plato forms a natural bridge
between the Jewish prophets and Jesus and his apostles, a
view common among the Patristics and some of the Reformers. What is most fascinating because enigmatic about the
lecture is the ambiguous characterization of this Renaissance world-shaker's ministry. Are the divine truth and
energy Luther invoked real? Despite the fact that when
Emerson returned from Europe in 1833 he had pretty
much abandoned revealed theology, the answer appears to
be yes. But are they Emerson's ultimate reality? Divorced
from nature, no. Luther is faulted on his estrangement from
and rejection of the natural environment. Was Luther's
transmitting of "divine force" to the world of men an attempt to lift man out of his broken world or to redeem the
world? The former, Emerson seems to think. Apparently
Luther shared the contempti mundi of his pessimistic age.
In other words, Luther distinguished between the an-
thropological and the natural world, looking toward the
redemption of the former and the destruction of the latter.
Luther's conviction that "the kingdom of this world" is
destined to become "the kingdom of our Lord and his
Christ" supported rather than challenged his view of
nature—human nature must be divinely restored and as a
new nature must find its true sanctuary only in an order
above and beyond this world of nature, human institutions,
and finite endeavors.

What is most attractive about Luther is his Isaiah-like role,
lips touched by the pure fire of the divine spirit and pleading
with man to return to the spiritual kingdom. From the first
journal entry Emerson made in his new home of Concord at
the onset of his literary vocation, it appears that he invoked

179

both the spiritual vision and weapons of Luther ("divine force" and the natural world (the "outward force" that Luther "scorned"). The impact of the new calling and the magnificent natural setting of Concord is implied in the entry, which begins with the prayer of the divinely commissioned Aeneas as he stands before his beached boats and looks out over the land of the Latins:

Concord, 15 November, 1834. Hail to the quiet fields of my fathers! Not wholly unattended by supernatural friendship & favor let me come hither. Bless my purposes as they are simple & virtuous. . . . Henceforth I design not to utter any speech, poem, or book that is not entirely & peculiarly my work. (*JMN*, IV, 335)

Although the vigorous promise recalls Luther's theses on the cathedral door and his new theologico-pastoral line, the model here is Vergil's epic hero, whose mission and achievements are compounded of divine force and outward force. Like Aeneas, Emerson looks to build a city and world in accord with the designs of Providence, yet whose foundation is here, in "the quiet fields of my fathers," at once a formal literary citation and a hymn to Concord's natural beauty. Both fields and fathers promise a homecoming. Emerson's journals of the next year are replete with reports of delightful exploratory walks to the fields, rivers, ponds, woods, and hills of the area. On the other hand, in the summer of 1835 he used the occasion of his keynote address at Concord's Bicentennial to remind his townsmen that he was the youngest in a succession of energetic and divinely encouraged representatives of a new land and new thoughts, and with none of the timidities of the times.[10]

This love of natural fact, as Emerson noted in the last chapter of *Nature*, satisfies the demands of the spirit as much as "perception" does, and "love" and "perception" are the equally important credentials of the "naturalist." At the risk of belaboring the obvious, then, it should be noted that delight in natural fact as revealed by the personae of *Nature* is represented as primarily personal and spontaneous although it is philosophically important. The much-discussed bare common passage sets the tone early on for the chapters and personae that follow. Repeatedly the persona comes alive in his being by making contact with the life around him. He is built up through nature, however, only to discover that nature is also his building material. To quote "Prospects," "when a faithful thinker, resolute to detach every object from personal relations . . . shall, at the same time, kindle science with the fire of the holiest affections, then will God go forth anew into the creation" ("creation" referring to both the world of nature and creations of man). Earlier in this paragraph the persona dissociates himself on the one hand from those whose devotion to God and the "tradition of their fathers" alienates them from nature, on the other hand from the naturalist whose "wintry light" freezes his subject, estranging him as well from nature. Even in "Idealism," where "Spirit" receives the five-fold last word, an autobiographical speaker interjects, "I have no hostility to nature, but a child's love to it. I expand and live in the warm day like corn and melons. Let us speak her fair. I do not wish to fling stones at my beautiful mother, nor soil my gentle nest."[11]

The metaphor of expansion and exfoliation is the implied answer, before the fact, to the rhetorical statement that follows: "I only wish to indicate the true position in regard to man . . . as the ground which to attain is the object of human life, that is, man's connexion with nature." (One suspects a deliberate pun in "ground.") Or, in the words of the first paragraph of "Spirit": "It is essential to a true theory of nature and of man, that it should contain somewhat progressive. . . . And all the uses of nature admit of being summed in one, which yields the activity of man an infinite scope." The life of man in nature has as its principal end a metamorphosis of exfoliation that the Platonic and Plotinian can help to support in theory and trope and that a healthy transaction with nature insures in practice. This transformation, although not the sole answer, is the ultimate answer to the question "to what end is nature,"—a question not to be confused with, To what end is *Nature*?

The transformations initiated already in the first paragraph are many: the "retrospective" of the first sentence to the prospective of the latter part of the paragraph and the concluding chapter, "sepulchres" to uterine-like "floods of life," "dry bones" and "faded wardrobe" to "new land, new men, new thoughts." At the outset the metamorphosis is limited to contrastive images and grammatical-rhetorical flourish alone, but these set the precedent for the next four chapters, each of which begins with the objects of nature (image) and proceeds to spiritual perception (the ultimate language or grammar). To put it another way, "nature is already, in its forms and tendencies, describing its own design" (second paragraph); what is needed is for man to "interrogate" those forms and designs. The result is manifold: the modest epiphany on the bare common, the lessons in commodity that make man a craftsman, the emergence of the artist, the development of the speaker and writer, in short, the education of the understanding and the Reason. As a critic has noted, the early paragraphs of *Nature* are paradigms for the mode of each chapter and of the entire book.[12]

The view expressed in *Nature* had clarified itself in Emerson since 1833. Until then, traditional moral philosophy and natural theology governed his hazy reflections on "external nature." A journal entry in 1826 is typical: "The changes of external nature are continually suggesting to us the changes in the condition of man" (*JMN*, III, 50–51). Eight months after the publication of *Nature*, Emerson summarized the levels and dimensions of metamorphosis as follows:

There are three degrees of proficiency in this lesson of life. The one class live to the utility of the symbol as the majority of men do. . . . Another class live above this mark, to the beauty of the symbol; as the poet & artist, and the Sensual school in philosophy. A third class live above the beauty of the symbol, to the beauty of the thing signified; and these are wise men. The first class have common sense; the second, taste; and the third spiritual perception. (*JMN*, V, 326)

Although not an outline of *Nature,* this journal entry outlines the range of metamorphoses possible with natural fact—from the utilitarian to what in this journal passage and in *Nature* is characterized as "spiritual," elsewhere as "transcendental." Implicit in that journal passage is Emerson's definition of transcendentalist: the individual who understands the range of metamorphoses and enacts transformation at each and all of the levels between pure fact and pure idea.

Understanding the range of metamorphoses is not to be equated with understanding their full range. Emerson's various observations and shifting opinions on *Nature* suggest that his views of the essay underwent some of the metamorphosis enacted in the essay. To Carlyle he announced the publication of *Nature* with confidence and determination; it was "an entering wedge, I hope, for something more worthy and significant" (*CEC,* 149). Although the first yield was largely pride, it also included misgivings. "There is, as always, one crack in it not easily soldered or welded" (*RL,* II, 32), he wrote shortly before completing the work, perhaps recalling an earlier journal entry that pronounced "a crack in every thing God has made except Reason" (*JMN,* IV, 262). Eight months later he reflected:

It ought to have been more distinctly stated in "Nature" than it is that life is our inexhaustible treasure of language for thought. Years are well spent in the country in country labors, in towns, in the insight into trades & manufactures, in intimate intercourse with many men & women, in science, in art, to the one end of mastering in all their facts a language by which to illustrate & speak out our emotions and perceptions. . . . ⟨Nature⟩ My garden is my dictionary. (*JMN,* V, 325–26)

The doubts registered in these passages should not be exaggerated. Still, Emerson suspects and then is convinced that his intentions, whether or not these had been clear to him, had not been clearly conveyed in *Nature;* the intentions he now attributes to the essay are at least in part the product of reflection on the work since publication and the subsequent clarifications in his own mind. Were he to rewrite *Nature* or compose it with the benefit of hindsight, he would reinforce the naturalist tendency, expand the meaning of nature to include towns, trades, manufacturing, science, and art, and underscore the importance of a language that truly reports and illustrates man thinking.

These reconsiderations and redefinitions of *Nature* continued for more than a decade. In 1841 Emerson lectured in Maine at Colby College (then called Waterville) on "The Method of Nature," a lecture as much on the method of experience, language, thought, and the principle of growth in man as on the method of nature. A year later he wrote in his journals, "The Poet should not only be able to use nature as his hieroglyphic, but he should have a still higher power, namely, an adequate message to communicate; a vision fit for such a faculty" (*JMN*, VIII, 229). The following year he drafted "Nature" (*W*, III), and during the next few years wrote revealingly but not consistently about the scope and significance of nature. "Like the efforts to define the role of the Scholar," writes Richard Francis, "these attempts at redefining nature were characterized by ambivalences."[13] Shortly after Emerson had revised *Nature* for the 1849 publication of *Nature, Addresses, and Lectures* (the revisions revealing still another reconsideration of the 1836 text), he noted in less ambiguous and ambivalent language the three eras of interpreting nature: *"the Greek,"* which combined animism and pantheism, *"the Christian,"* which "craved a heaven out of nature & above it,—looking on nature now as evil,—the world was a mere stage & school, a snare," and *"the Modern;* when the too idealistic tendencies of the Christian period running into the diseases of cant, monachism, and a church, demonstrating the impossibility of Christianity, have forced men to retrace their steps, & rally again on Nature; but now the tendency is to marry mind to nature, to put nature under the mind" (*JMN*, XI, 201). Whether the Emerson of 1849 endorses the subjugation of nature to the mind and, if so, what he means by this dominion, is not clear. In any event, the evidence calls into question an assertion in an excellent critical discussion of Emerson's *Nature:* "What Emerson envisioned from the beginning (as he later expressed it while preparing the essay for republication in 1849) was a rebirth of Nature freed from the excesses both of pagan and Christian assumptions."[14] After the fact, in 1849, yes; in 1836, perhaps. The structure and several vectors of the 1836 *Nature* suggest otherwise: that at this time Emerson's formulations were compounded of several inclinations, some of these not entirely reconcilable and subject to more than one version of reconciliation. Herein, perhaps, is Emerson's meaning when he referred to the crack in his essay that resisted the solder iron.

The question "to what end is nature" called forth *Nature* for Emerson, and the reader's question as to what end is *Nature* is visited by a series of related answers in the essay: nature, that is, man's use of nature and delight in her, that is, man in his world, a relation that restores to nature a high status, which invites a more precise explanation of man's complex transactions with nature, which is to identify man's possibilities and awesome responsibilities. What appears at first to be a mere conjugation of the uses of nature by means of archaic scientific and philosophic classifications is transformed into an on-going metamorphosis—of nature heretofore ignored or distrusted, of penny-wise man, of equally penny-wise language, art, "retrospective" present, and prospectless future.

In keeping with the Platonic-Plotinian efflux-influx and the treatment of the past in the "Historical Discourse," composed the previous year, Emerson spans the desultory present by arcing from a prospective past (the "foregoing generations") to future prospects, when the present generation will recover the "new relation" of "the fathers" and thus become a new generation.[15] The trajectory is always from an original connection with natural facts that has already made history to one that will become history, the two adumbrating the new dispensation by which the present is to be governed. Characteristically, the personae are identified with both the prospective facts of a usable past and the facts of the future. These facts are always central in the dialectic ranging from fact to symbol, to significance of symbol, to fact, without end.

Let me focus on the autobiographical elements in *Nature* to define less abstractly what has just been proposed. Merton Sealts's tabulation of journal passages used in *Nature*[16] reveals not only that Emerson mined his journals prolifically but also that a number of items he culled were autobiographical. Although the case can be made, and has recently been argued, that Emerson's reworking of these notations was an attempt to increase the illusion of the highly personal and particular that we associate with the romantic and post-romantic use of the autobiographical,[17] Emerson can also be seen doing precisely the opposite, translating the personal into a more representative and public illustration. The bare common passage is perhaps the most striking example of transformation from a rather general, impersonal, and non-temporal observation into a report of an immediate, powerfully felt, private experience. On the other hand, much of the rest of the paragraph following this report reveals the obverse—a tendency to transform personal, private, and temporally specific notations into representative and general insights. This dual tendency, at work in scores of instances from the beginning to the end of *Nature,* is consonant with the Platonic-Plotinian oscillation and serves as the earnest of metamorphosis by both transforming individual fact and always recovering it. By the same token, and with the same results, Emerson reworks journal sources to increase and decrease the illusion of specificity and the degree of the presence of natural fact as natural fact. One might say, then, that the Platonic and Plotinian tendencies in the transformations of the essay and in its many parts have their equivalencies in Emerson's use of his principal source of materials, his journals. In an essay seeking no less than the participation of the readers in a life of transformation, Emerson's autobiographical interest centers on rich

186

personal considerations that can be translated into the representative ones without losing their capacity to reach the individual reader as individual statement. A journal entry made a few years later reminds us that these reciprocally dependent aims continued to claim his attention. The voice is that of the writer in relation to his material:

That which is individual & remains individual in my experience is of no value. What is fit to engage me & so engage others permanently, is what has put off its weeds of time & place & personal relation. Therefore all that befals me in the way of criticism & extreme blame & praise drawing me out of equilibrium,—putting me for a time in false position to people, & disallowing the spontaneous sentiments . . . shuts me up within poor personal considerations. (*JMN*, VII, 65)

The extensive culling of autobiographical elements in the journals, a practice first noticeable in Emerson's poetry of the mid 1830's and the "Historical Discourse," also helps to clarify the relation of time, tense, and metamorphosis in *Nature*. Intrinsically, each metamorphosis translates something out of the present and into its future, that is, into a new presence as new present. Likewise, all the metamorphoses of *Nature* combined into a symphonic metamorphosis achieve the same end of transforming the present into a new kind of age. For *Nature* and the self to be part and parcel of metamorphosis, however, each must discover and continually recover the condition for metamorphosis—both the "face to face" relation to natural fact and the readiness to be remade by this relation even as one builds with natural fact and well beyond it. The language of chapter one repeatedly gropes toward suggestive definitions of this condition: "perpetual presence of the sublime," "a certain reverence" awakened, the "kindred impression" of natural facts "when the mind is open to their influence," "curiosity," a "wise spirit," a "distinct but most poetical sense in the mind," the "integrity of impression," the true adjustment of "inward and outward senses," the sense that there is something within oneself that "corresponds" with nature, and, as a culminating definition, a description of crossing the bare common on a cloudy evening when, instead of feeling the cold dampness of the season seep into his shoes, the speaker enjoys "a perfect exhilaration."

The numerous autobiographical elements culled from the journals for use in chapter one become Emerson's version of what Coleridge referred to as preserving the vitality of a usable past in the present for the future.[18] In the first two-thirds of this chapter, relatively impersonal and non-temporal generalizations in the journals have been reworked into more personal and autobiographical reports, a concomitant of which is a strong present tense and a sense of immediacy. In the latter third of the chapter, the reworking of highly personal journal notations to less personal and more representative generalizations consistently reveals a change from the preterit of the journals (past experiences and past tense) to the present of the essay. In short, both non-temporal and preterit elements are changed and admitted into a world of present conjugation. Yet this present is not the present of the culture or even of the author. The new present is, clearly, that condition that makes the future possible and that places *Nature* and its personae on the threshold of the future. Significantly, the warranty for this condition is never merely an actual present; rather, the inspirations and illustrations of the past conspire with the readiness of the personae to admit the new generation and to participate in creating it. The son joins the fathers, and the adult becomes a party to his personal past, which reaches from childhood to recent spots of time, in an on-going dispensation. *Nature* invokes the fathers but rejects their sepulchers, works with a usable past but repudiates dry-bone retrospection.

By way of summary we can say, then, that the subject of *Nature* is only ostensibly nature or, for that matter, man. Nor does *Nature* seek to affirm a chain of being or hierarchy of reality. To see Emerson's subject as the method of nature is to approach the work more closely, since metamorphosis is at the heart of nature's method. To the extent that *Nature* creates the conditions of metamorphosis and enacts trans-

formations as the means toward new prospects that counter
yet include and transform the retrospective present age, the
essay develops its own "forms and tendencies" in contrast to
derivative models.

At first glance, for instance, the structure of *Nature* appears pretty much in keeping with Hugh Blair's division of
the essay: introduction, definition and division of subject,
narration or explication, reasoning within these divisions,
the pathetic or emotional crescendo, and the conclusion.
This initial impression also suggests adherence to Blair's
prescriptions of symmetry, rising action in sentence and
paragraph, and the importance of illustration and analogy.[19] Yet Blair's retrospective and closed system belongs
to the retrospective present that *Nature* transforms. In behalf of transformation Blair is used against Blair, subver-
sively, in the "classification" of *Nature,* which is designed to lift the "gymnastics of the understanding" to a
higher perception. In the words of a journal entry dated a
few months prior to the time Emerson began to compose
Nature: "All this polemics, syllogism, & definition is so much
wastepaper & Montaigne is almost the only man who has
never lost sight of this fact" (*JMN,* V, 57). This passage is
directed at those who propose to fight with the "Weapons of
the Understanding." Understandably, Hugh Blair would
not have agreed with the recent observation that Emerson
"was far more in control than at first appears."[20]

The hope latent in Emerson's strategy is the new reader.
Undoubtedly such a reader would appreciate Richard
Poirier's instructive comment that Emerson's projected
presence in the rhythms and vocabularies of his prose "often
reveals . . . an allegiance to the very forms and conventions which are at the same time being attacked."[21] He
would probably recognize, also, that Poirier stops one step
short of Emerson, whose inclination to use conventions and
familiar definitions and tropes against themselves and their
customary context is at the heart of his method in *Nature,* as
it is in an essay like "The Divinity School Address." His
properly-attired subversion is the primary reason for the

angry reaction of the Harvard Divinity School's small faculty and their like-minded colleagues, who were threatened because they understood, not because they failed to understand, Emerson's ends.

The scholar's obligation, it would appear, is no less than to follow *Nature* to its end (in both senses of that word) and to understand not only the prospects arcing its conclusion but the fact that these prospects preside over the entire essay to such an extent that having arrived at the end of "Prospects" one is finally prepared to understand the language of the opening paragraphs of *Nature*. In this respect the essay creates its own audience, preparing the reader by reorganizing his "eye" to where he can recognize the "forms and tendencies" of the essay and, having reached the end and recognized its ends, is ready to read *Nature* for the first time. The many kinds and degrees of metamorphosis in the chapters of *Nature* notwithstanding, the culmination of personae in the final and thoroughly knowledgeable voice of "Prospects" and the metamorphosis of the reader into an Emersonian reader produce a transformed *Nature* and preside over it. All other transformations anticipate and serve this principal one. In this regard Whitman's *Song of Myself* implicitly follows the design of *Nature*. The poet-visionary's concluding stanza about "Failing to fetch me at first" points the sympathetic and translating "You" back to the beginning of what, by now, has become a new poem.[22]

The readiness to read *Nature* includes an ear for tone and both eye and ear for persona. Emerson himself declared, "It is not the proposition but the tone that signifies" (*JMN*, VIII, 58). His characterization of the lecture room as "the true church of today" (*JMN*, VII, 277) is as much a literary admonition as a theological statement, reminding us that the essayist was also a lecturer who used techniques important to public discourse in *Nature* in order to sound "the persuasion, that by its very melody imparadises my heart" (*CW*, I, 85). On hearing his first Emerson lecture, Bronson Alcott was surprised by the strange and compelling language.[23] Alcott, of course, was a reassuring audience, and Emerson was not beyond the need for reassurance in his ambitious literary endeavor. "I am to invite men drenched in time to recover themselves & come out of time, & taste their native immortal air" reads a journal entry weighted with tiredness (*JMN*, VII, 271). This tiredness is absent from *Nature* except in the descriptions of the "gymnastics of the understanding" and penny-wise, imbruted man. The personae and vocabularies of *Nature* remind us of an enthusiastic and energetic lecturer skilled in his craft, a point made by George Willis Cooke in his early and important treatise on Emerson: "The essayist needs to be interpreted by the lecturer; for his voice and manner become a fine commentary on his written thought, giving to it new and unexpected meanings and a rich suggestiveness not otherwise to be had."[24] The role of lecturer was not always welcome to Emerson, whose anxieties over the possibility of a small deficit were often unfounded and always betrayed a comfortable standard of living.[25] His economic reasons for lecturing were not known to the audience, however, the most astute of whom were impressed with his ability to act out his personae.

Recently the subjects of voice and personae in Emerson's art have begun to attract scholarly attention.[26] Despite Emerson's warnings, however, the so-called propositions of his essays have tended to define him and continue to do so. These propositions, it is commonly assumed, are delivered by a voice as obvious and unchanging as that of Yahweh on Sinai. A recent essay has it that the tone in Emerson is "sober, sincere, austere, and straightforward" and that his essays speak "directly and forcefully,"[27] an apt characterization of the scholarly essay in question but not of Emerson or *Nature*.

It is through the tone of *Nature* and by means of the personae that Emerson discloses important aspects of his purpose. These are also the means whereby the essay confirms and clarifies both the degree and kind of metamorphosis at the center of the action. When Poirier complains

191

that *Nature* features "no speaking 'I' for the seeing 'eye' "[28] he is conceding, with some unwillingness, an assumption such as Buell's, "that in respect to the persona Emerson *is* an abstraction and wished to be taken as such."[29] Emerson's voice in *Nature* can be defined, but it does not call attention to itself or readily define itself because it operates under numerous guises. Different personae adopt each a certain voice posture, perspective, and matrix of interest and images. Furthermore, when the individual persona shifts away from exposition in order to exhort, mimic, parody, sigh, repeat, pay tribute, blame, celebrate, or modulate in any other manner, such a shift, crucial to change and therefore to transformations, comes through less in the statements and vocabulary as such than in the voice. For Emerson the sentence in the essays is not primarily a grammatical arrangement of words from a set Emersonian vocabulary but a "sound" posture and a centering metaphor appropriate to the persona. "Why not write as variously as we dress & think" is one of those richly suggestive entries one learns to expect in Emerson's journals, the rhetorical question noting the importance to the written work of variety in trope, persona, and thought (*JMN,* VII, 224).

Herein lies the chief explanation for Emerson's dissatisfaction with the novel. His objection was not as much to prose (although he regarded poetry as the finest of all the arts) or to novels as it was to the prose fiction of his era. Fielding merely reflected his culture rather than transcending it by exploring through a multitude of voices alternative arts of the possible; Scott's characters "brave each other with smart epigrammatic speeches, but . . . [he] does not please on the second reading" (*W,* III, 148); and "Like Cooper & Hawthorne," Dickens "has no dramatic talent" (*JMN,* VII, 244–45). "If I wrote a novel," Emerson reflected, "my hero should begin a soldier & rise out of that to such degrees of wisdom & virtue as we could paint; for that is the order of nature" (*JMN,* XI, 13). Emerson's insistence on a persona developed as naturally as the life of nature and his view that collectively the personae illustrate through dramatic anal-

ogy the law of metamorphosis in nature lie behind his disappointment over the relatively low ambition and achievements in the novel and help to explain his purpose in *Nature*.

Early in chapter one he distinguishes between the impressions made by natural objects on different perceivers. The
standing tree is timber to the woodcutter, another and better kind of property to the artist and the poet. (Emerson had
not as yet purchased his woodlot at Walden Pond.) The
range moves from "superficial seeing" to the proper adjustment of "inward and outward senses." The personae of
Nature fill out this range by enacting varying degrees of
understanding and Reason. Principally they are used toward another end, however, which is to arrive at the highest
possible ends given the means (materials and designs) of
each persona. The initial persona, impatient with the defi-
ciencies of "our age" and ready to ask the right kinds of
questions, modulates into a somewhat more personal "I"
who through general argument and personal autobiographical touches is established as the informed "eye," one
that not only sees with "the integrity of impression" but
recognizes that most of the readers have a superficial seeing.
The gap between what is seen (what is seeing) and what
ought to be seen (what seeing should be) creates the problem and opportunity for the chapters that follow, which, in
various ways and to varying degrees, bridge that gap by
transforming superficial seeing to what the seeing should
be. The economist of "Commodity" is not unlike the narra-
tors in Thoreau's "Bean-Field" and Carlyle's *Sartor Resartus*.
The gospeler of work yields to the artist of "Beauty," a
persona closer in temperament to the speaker of chapter
one. His poetic images and classical allusions serve him
throughout as his eye converts emotional delight into
aesthetic sensibility, which in turn is transformed into "spiritual perception." This progression in the chapter is concur-
rent with a depersonalizing of the voice.

The speaker in "Language" is less personal, individual,
and familiar but not less distinctive or human in his syllogiz-
ing and scholarly disquisition. On him, especially, lies the

burden, to quote William James, that "our fields of experience" are limited by "our fields of view."[30] We are told, for instance, that we can judge the power of a person's mind by the richness or poverty of his language, that is, the extent to which natural fact surpasses itself in anyone's language. The personal and familiar voice of Yankee know-how in "Commodity" now becomes more philosophic and metaphoric, the chapter makes its point both by argument and enactment: a man is fed that he may work, and the highest order of work is language that truly works. The only warranty of new weapons "in the magazine of power" is a language perpetually transforming itself.

The modulation in earlier chapters of "I," "you," "he," "one," and "a man" and of personal observation, scholarly argument through the editorial "we," and examples (some of them personal) in the third person now shifts to the impersonal and tutorial "we," the preeminent mode of dress and address in "Language." Although the language of metamorphosis returns at strategic moments to the "visible world" to recover "natural fact," the impersonal and abstract personae are less apt to return to the specific, personal, and autobiographical. This dissociation of natural fact-to-spirit modulation from a correspondingly specific and autobiographical-to-disembodied voice-of-truth modulation presents a problem to the reader. It is easy enough for the "I" to be responsive to the variety of metamorphoses in nature, but the observation in "Spiritual Laws" that "The wild fertility of nature is felt in comparing our rigid names and reputations with our fluid consciousness" (*CW*, II, 81) helps to account for the primacy of the "we" in "Language"—the disembodied voice of fluid consciousness is disclosing itself in action while also philosophically accounting for itself. Eventually Emerson will solve this dilemma of "Language" (which is perpetuated in "Discipline"). Pronouns and personae will add up to a composite identity that articulates particular and general, concrete and abstract, personal and impersonal, individual and collective. In "Language," however, there is a discontinuity between the claims made for consciousness and the resources of voice available, a problem somewhat less apparent in the vocabulary and hardly evident in the imagery and metaphoric action. The vision possesses the language more expertly than the persona, a problem Whitman was able to surmount, by and large, in the writing of *Song of Myself*.

In "Discipline," finding a persona to "illustrate and embody our perceptions" (*CW*, I, 61) results in less dissociation of imagery and persona, but only because abstract terminology is in the saddle, disembodying and generalizing the sememes to where they correspond with the universal orientation and voice of the persona. Now "the things we aim at and converse with" (*W*, III, 48) are articulated as authoritatively as is allowed by language, a limited and unreliable medium. The price appears to be a momentary unhitching from the means that make it possible for us to take our aim. The only vestiges of a lively existence in the visible world of natural fact are the discussion of understanding, which is condescendingly ironic and impatient to transcend itself, and the Plotinian reminders near the end of the chapter.

The depersonalizing and universalizing of the persona culminates in the Platonic "Idealism," where the universal oracle and the voice of the human soul are one and the same. Any authority, selected almost at random, can be appealed to for "proof" that the highest results in transformation consistently confirm the ideal vision. Less particular, limited, and *human* than any previous persona, this one can turn to the evidence of perceptual relativity, poetry, philosophy, science, religion and ethics, analytic subdivisions, syllogisms, multiple allusions, and the testimony of anyone and everyone to create an illusion of an all-inclusive, comprehensive persona-become-principle, a transparent eyeball identified with spirit. The "finite organs" basic to the law of metamorphosis have grown transparent and have vanished; the persona "respects the end too much, to immerse itself in the means."

And yet, as already noted, a sudden intervention of a particular and autobiographical "I" reminiscent of the speaker in the early chapters establishes a counter-emphasis, and the universal voice yields for the moment to natural fact and a distinctively human voice. The latter, in particular, is significant as a signal of what to expect in "Spirit," where "Idealism" is found wanting because it denies "substantive being to men and women" or, to put it another way, "It leaves God out of me." That "me" marks the most crucial shift in *Nature*. In the remainder of "Spirit" and in "Prospects," we return to the complex and unostentatiously easy modulation between "I," "we," "man," "he," the "poet," "a certain poet," "every bard," a "wise writer," "faithful thinker," "Every spirit," and "you" (both singular and plural). The voice is many and one, monotypic yet rich with variety, particular and representative, individual and collective, personal as well as impersonal and suprapersonal, utilitarian, aesthetic, literary, philosophical, political, religious, benignly meditative, dramatic, privately musing, openly proselytizing. All personae in *Nature* are subsumed by the final one, who represents the range of Emerson's aims and the readers' experiences. Multiple accommodation to the audience is but a means of accommodating a multifarious audience to the Emersonian vision.

Lest the inference be drawn that in its conclusion *Nature* comes full circle (to its old beginning), it should be noted that the comprehensive and compelling persona of "Prospects" represents a considerable advance beyond the personal yet inclusive voice at the beginning. The speaker of "Prospects" is richer and more complex by sheer accumulation and major modulations through a succession of chapters. Nor should we overlook the fact that he has earned his right to speak personally and representatively for the times, prophetically to the times, and vatically free of time. As for the first, "in the thick darkness, there are not wanting gleams of a better light,—occasional examples of the action of man upon nature with his entire force." As for the second, "Every spirit builds itself a house; and beyond its house a world. . . . Know then that the world exists for you." As for the third, "As when the summer comes from the south

196

. . . so shall the advancing spirit create its ornaments along its path . . . ; it shall draw beautiful faces, and warm hearts, and wise discourse, and heroic acts, around its way, until evil is no more seen." These declarations belong un- mistakably in the final chapter; none properly fits the state- ments or befits the voice of the first chapter. To restate this in a slightly different context, the most dramatic meta- morphosis in *Nature* is in the persona. To the extent that the persona of "Prospects" has conspired successfully with the "you" addressed in the concluding paragraphs, "we come to look at the world" and the world of *Nature* "with new eyes." It is a *Nature* transformed, and approached by a reader now ready and able to accept the implications of the orphic poet's pronouncement, "Nature is not fixed but fluid." In coming to *Nature* with new eyes, the reader recognizes man thinking and the invitational aspect of the persona's rhetorical ques- tion, "why should we grope among the dry bones of the past, or put the living generation into masquerade out of its faded wardrobe? . . . There are new lands, new men, new thoughts."

The reminder in *Nature* that "Nothing is quite beautiful alone: nothing but is beautiful in the whole" (*CW*, I, 17) applies equally to *Nature* and our reading of it and to aes- thetics in general. And it applies to the persona as much as to the images, metaphors, and chapter organizations. In other words, the journal statement "Who can make a good sentence can make a good book" (*JMN*, V, 79) implies a correlative in dramatic terms—that the artist who can create an effective persona is able to compose a lecture or essay. Whether he will write the essay depends on the greatness of eye, ear, and soul, for the "foolish consistency" of pinched minds will insist on one good sentence, repeated or re- fracted and raised to the level of safe moral vision, and in a single, clearly identified, and straightforward persona. If a sentence is a mirror that "causes us to see ourselves" (*JMN*, V, 278), another sentence will allow us to see another aspect of ourselves, or to see the old aspect in a new way. Not surprisingly, Emerson referred to great literature as the result "of trials & a thousand rejections"—"a poem made that shall thrill the world by the mere juxtaposition & interaction of lines & sentences that singly would have been of little worth & short date" (*JMN*, V, 39).

The reader is here explicitly cautioned by Emerson that individual passages, personae, or pronouncements may seem silly, trite, or worthless by themselves, and are read as single and final effects to the detriment of both the work and the mind of the reader. It is tempting to oversimplify an Emerson pronouncement such as "Who can make a good sentence can make a good book." The statement actually establishes a correspondence between the orchestration of elements required in an effective sentence and the integration of parts in an enduring book. No part of the sentence is judged by itself, no sentence stands alone, no chapter is the quintessential whole, and no persona is in and by himself *the* persona in Emerson or the essential Emerson.

To hold up individual passages for the purpose of admiring Emerson's successful artistic moments plays mischief with Emerson's vision even while raising personal taste to critical premise. To lift these favorite passages above supposedly bathetic ones nearby in order to epitomize Emerson and make him permanently suggestive and appealing to subscribers of a particular twentieth-century poetic[31] is less fatal to *Nature* than to the later essays, in which, as the next chapter will argue, Emerson's use of personae is increasingly complex and diverse. Even in *Nature,* however, such an approach leads us away from Emerson as much as bringing us very close to aspects of him. As was noted in a recent essay, Emerson's familiar manifesto "The soul's emphasis is always right" (*CW*, II, 84) has its equally instructive counter that "The individual is always mistaken" (*W*, III, 69).[32]

What Emerson means by "mistaken" is clear enough in its context and throughout the Emerson canon—the partial, fragmentary, unallied, out-of-context. When the reader engages a vatic voice at the end of *Nature* rhapsodizing about the disappearance of "disagreeable appearances," the temptation to hear merely an analytical judgment in the future tense is also an inclination to be mistaken in the Emersonian sense of the word. The naïve vulnerability frequently charged to Emerson is not without indirect self-revelation. By himself every persona is vulnerable, and by itself the conclusion of *Nature* is as disagreeable as the appearances "Prospects" appears to be sweeping rhetorically out of existence. Read by itself, the chapter raises any number of possibilities as nagging questions. Is the purpose of nature and *Nature* to introduce a paradise without? Or perhaps within? Or is it to induce a special kind of seeing' (which may also be a form of blindness)? Or is the conclusion a rhetorical and metaphoric lapse of the kind attributed by more than one critic to the author of the transparent eyeball passage? Is Emerson perhaps aiming above the mark in order to hit it, a strategy both he and Thoreau recommended from time to time? Or are we to believe that through the foolishness of the speaker the wisdom of many readers, not to mention those specialists he referred to as "thinkers" in contrast to man thinking, is put to nought?

Presiding over the evocative language of the conclusion is the reference to "educated Will," a terminology understood if the reader has heard each persona and witnessed the gradual transformation of eye and will through the retinue of voices. To the extent that one has been educated by the essay to read *Nature* "with new eyes," one is ready to witness a "correspondent revolution in things," that is, to believe in transformation because one has observed Emerson bring it about and has participated in the transformation. From the evidence of the journals Emerson kept during and shortly after the time that he drafted and published *Nature,* we have to conclude that the coterie of readers and listeners addressed in *Nature* was so small in Emerson's opinion that he often despaired of Concord and young America even as he exulted in the law of metamorphosis and invoked transformation as the end of his art.

•8•

Personae & Vision
in Later Essays

As Emerson matured in his art and began to earn his reputation as a skilled lecturer, his interest grew in poetic-dramatic identities that enact a range of tone, mood, decorum, and assumption. The voice of a veteran speaker is evident in the journal directive, "fix your eye on the audience, & the fit word will utter itself as when the eye seeks the person in the remote corner of the house the voice accomodates [*sic*] itself to the area to be filled"(*JMN*, V, 223). Several years later he recommended an oratory that surpasses mere exhibition and eloquence: "There are . . . persons who are not actors, not speakers, but influences; persons too great for fame, for display; who disdain eloquence; to whom all we call art and artist, seems too nearly allied to show and by-ends" (*CW*, I, 91).[1] Together, these two passages help to define Emerson the actor, creator of personae, and to distinguish the lower and higher role of the *hypokrites* in literary art.

It is both fascinating and instructive for the reader of Emerson's essays to consult contemporary accounts of Emerson as lecturer, the best of these by acquaintances who heard him in his middle and late years. Henry James, Sr., a wary and reluctant admirer, wrote the following:

his weird monotone began to reverberate in your bosom's depths, and his words flowed on, now with a river's volume, grand, majestic, free, and anon diminished themselves to the fitful cadence of a brook, impeded in its course, and returning in melodious coquetry upon itself, and you saw the clear eye . . . and beheld the musing countenance turned within.[2]

201

Moncure Conway, a more enthusiastic and unreserved admirer, reported much the same:

There was no attempt at effect in Emerson's descriptions—no gestures—yet the subtlest actor could not more have moved the vast audience. On his face was seen that face of the friar in which every eye read perfect sincerity and courage. We saw the friar, frank and fearless, kneeling to confess his wrong, and, pleading in justification, ask pardon of those he had deprived of a brother. We saw his victory through humiliation . . . and finally, when Fra Cristoforo had departed through the company, kneeling for the blessing of him who had knelt, we saw the bewildered nobleman saying, "That devil of a monk, if he had knelt there longer, I believe I should have asked his pardon for killing my own brother." A smile beamed on the face of the speaker and played on the faces before him, at these his last words.[3]

There are signs aplenty that Emerson understood and cultivated his role as the actor whose persona or personae commanded the audience in the lyceum and the readers in their study. In fact, Emerson himself furnishes perhaps the best description of his aim: "That which he wishes, that which eloquence ought to reach, is not a particular skill in telling a story, or neatly summing up evidence, or arguing logically, or dexterously addressing the prejudice of the company,—no, but a taking sovereign possession of the audience." To what end? To "alter in a pair of hours, perhaps in a half hour's discourse, the convictions and habits of years." Many different audiences "greet the variety of style and topic" in the lecture or essay; "sometimes the same individual will take active part in them all, in turn" (*W*, VII, 65, 64, 67).

Almost too simple, one objects, and too contrived, power-conscious, and cynically manipulative. Emerson was aware of the objection, which he regarded as an appropriate criticism of much of the commanding oratory in America, a brigandage of cynical power exploiting the naïveté and ignorance of the powerless. Nor are total self-possession (often confused by scholars with Emersonian self-reliance) and the earned confidence of the audience sufficient justification: "A supreme commander over all his passions and affections; but the secret of his ruling is higher than that. It is the power of Nature running without impediment from the brain and will into the hands" (*W*, VII, 79). The poetic language here evokes man thinking, who in league with nature's method is building a world. The key to "Eloquence," then, is the key to "The Sphinx." Not all will understand this, and many who do understand will be inclined to resist. The power and method of nature, Emerson insisted over a lifetime, have always invited resistance from all quarters of society. But this inevitable rivalry between the artist and his audience is his greatest opportunity. Those of the same turn of mind, but with an eye that falls short of the artist's, will perhaps be ruled by a larger perception; those who lack facts are offered a guide (often more playful than importunate); and those who lack method or whose methods are non-functional are encouraged to join in organizing their world.

Behind and above the ploys of the artist—"imagery, selection, tenacity of memory, power of dealing with facts, of illuminating them, of sinking them by ridicule or by diversion of the mind, rapid generalization, humor, pathos" (a "charming" weaponry with the "power to ensnare and mislead" both us and Emerson)—is the "reinforcing of man from events" (*W*, VII, 90, 91, 92). Such an organizing and reorganizing, which correspond to his environment, to nature itself, are what the literary artist finds along the way as he conspires with nature, in the manner of the poet in "The Sphinx," to know and follow nature's method. With a perfect "concentration," "regnant calmness," and ultimate rather than immediate purpose, he offers this method to his audience by artistic enactment. "The possession the subject has of his mind is so entire that it insures an order of expression which is the order of Nature itself" (*W*, VII, 93, 92–93). Persona and the processive, transitive method of nature converge in Emerson's art. The range of speakers, tone, and point of view in "The Sphinx" is entirely fitting in a poem on the riddle of nature and its relation to art.

Shifts in Emerson's understanding of the method of nature—and by extension, the method of art—as documented in the analysis of "The Snow-Storm," "The Sphinx," and "Days" correspond to developments in his use of personae in his essays. Although moving beyond "The Snow-Storm" in its view of metamorphosis, *Nature* is allied as much to this early poem in mode and vision as to "The Sphinx." In *Nature,* as in the poem, "The catalogue is endless, and the examples so obvious, that I shall leave them to the reader's reflection" (*CW*, I, 12). Here the endless catalogue is not an external chain of generation and redefinition but a set of particular perceptions and generalizations awaiting transformation. Until the mid-1830s, Emerson had kept encyclopedic journals that sought to define his world by accumulating all extant definitions of the world and combining these, somehow, into a master diagram. The more he accumulated, the less complete was his definition (see *JMN*, VII, 302–3). His recognition of this problem accounts for his decision artfully to miniaturize both in his journals and his early essays, that is, to perceive, think, and declare in terms of representative situations and personae, each one a new version of essentially the same truth, the many testifying of the one. In so doing, he could fill out that truth even while always transcending the partial, or "mistaken." The accumulative impulse was replaced, in essays such as *Nature,* "The American Scholar," and "The Divinity School Address," by a desire to work by means of salient personae and centering metaphors. In these works, voices and dress function somewhat as they do in Eliot's *The Waste Land,* where they repeat, reinforce, and extend each other as they appear in new guises and claim additional aspects of the culture for the poem. All voices serve the same master and master vision. In this respect the modes of "The Snow-Storm" and *Nature* inform "History," an essay written about the same time, which declares:

Genius watches the monad through all his masks as he performs the metempsychosis of nature. Genius detects . . . through the egg, *the constant individual;* through countless individuals the fixed species; through many species the genus; through all genera *the steadfast type;* through all the kingdoms of organized life the eternal unity. Nature is a mutable cloud, which is *always and never the same.* (*CW,* II, 8; italics mine)

The emphasis in the fluid change is on "always . . . the same." To describe this emphasis in terms of *Nature,* one might say that the continuing predicative composition is prescribed by the several personae conspiring toward the same end. Or toward the same center, we might say. Personae are means to the end, which is a persona identified with the master vision. Both recurring and new patterns of voice, image, allusion, and vector supply an integument of sorts while acting as a cooperative body of radii to the center eventually recognized and then recognized to have been implied throughout. The roll-call finds all personae necessary and present in the persona of "Prospects."

In this respect it is useful to contrast "Circles" to *Nature,* which sends us back to the beginning and in which the end is a new beginning in the sense that we understand the old beginning in a new way. Although all of Emerson's essays unfold themselves by educating the reader to read them well, "Circles" (a reading of which will be offered later in this chapter) reveals a grammatical, rhetorical, and structural progression different from that in *Nature.* If one recalls the statement in "Art" about mutable nature "which is always and never the same," the emphasis now falls somewhat more on "never" than on "always." In "Circles" the procession of images, the contrastive and elided shifts between the sentences of the concluding paragraphs, and the curious momentum of the latter part of the essay created by the additions, departures, and each apparent conclusion (which refuses to be one but anticipates a conclusion that, in turn, is an occasion for further development) urges the movement outward into openness and to a new reverberation[4] not yet spoken. Syntactically speaking, numerous sentences are characterized by a closure that finishes them and seems to end the essay without at all finishing the movement of the essay. As in the latter part of "The Sphinx," image and predication are extended syntactically, visually, and rhythmically beyond each terminus. "Circles" concludes on a threshold that resembles the beginning only because the beginning, too, was a threshold. The kind of extension and openness we observe in "Circles" and the dramatic illusion of a shifting and changing persona associated with these characteristics are Emerson's patent on his prose of the 1840s and '50s, the flying force of his writing, and the flying buttresses of his imagination.

In essays like "The Method of Nature" and "Experience" (both of which will be discussed in this chapter), voices undercut each other and the persona is capable of radical change. In each the vision is created by the unfolding of the persona, by his variety of tones, changing perceptions, and shifts in opinion, and by the continual dialectic in which he is caught. In summarizing the "threads on the loom of time" the speaker of "Experience" does "not assume to give their order, but I name them as I find them in my way. . . . I can very confidently announce one or another law, which throws itself into relief and form, but I am too young yet by some ages to compile a code" (*W,* III, 83). The irony is perfectly timed, for the passage is directed at novices, who would demand of this essay, and of their world, much more and much less than this essay allows. Swedenborg, Emerson had come to recognize, was such a novice, whose "design of exhibiting correspondences," and thus creating "the poem of the world," was defeated by his monistic unity and reductiveness, which tethered "every symbol to a several ecclesiastic sense. The slippery Proteus is not so easily caught. . . . In the transmission of the heavenly waters, every hose fits every hydrant. Nature avenges herself speedily on the hard pedantry that would chain her waves. . . . Every thing must be taken genially, and we must be at the top of our condition to understand any thing rightly" (*W,* IV, 120–21).[5] Only the true poet of metamorphosis can hope to write "the poem of the world."

Being "at the top of our condition" is as important to the reader of Emerson's later essays with their slippery persona as it is for the artist profoundly aware of the "slippery Proteus" of his world. Sometimes Emerson's persona affirms without check because he is an exaggerator, at other times because he is naîve or foolish. More often we observe a persona who pauses to answer objections to his position in the form of a dramatic monologue, on occasions deftly modifying his position thereby. More frequently than critics have allowed, we must assume a reader-listener who refuses to go along with everything (sometimes with anything) that is being declared. It is as though Emerson is now educating the persona, now the reader, both of whom range from remarkably astute to stupid, both of whom sometimes deserve the final word, sometimes an enlightenment (momentary or continual and progressive), sometimes a polite, rational non-answer to real or imagined objections.

One should never want to underestimate the students of Waterville College; it is patently safer to blame the incomprehensibility of Emerson's discourse of August 11, 1841, on his overestimation of the students. They were mystified and thus unimpressed by "The Method of Nature" (*CW*, I, 117–37). Their lack of enthusiasm is shared by the editors of the new *Collected Works of Ralph Waldo Emerson,* whose editorial preamble to this lecture-essay notes that Emerson "seems to have lost the balanced clarity of view which gave so much conviction and power to his earlier addresses, for he had been struggling since 1839 with emotional and intellectual problems that left him temporarily uncertain in his attitudes toward both people and ideas" (*CW*, I, 117). The accuracy of the biographical note notwithstanding, its pertinence in explaining either the reception of the lecture or the structure of the essay is less than self-evident. They have overlooked, for instance, the extent to which "The Method of Nature" anticipates the vision of "The Sphinx," "Circles," and "Experience" and is closely allied to an emerging phase—the major phase—in Emerson's development. On the other hand, the shifts at this stage of Emerson's life are not ignored or discounted as they are by another Emerson editor, who has suggested recently that the years 1838–42 were for Emerson "a period of consolidation and application rather than expansion."[6]

"The Method of Nature" opens with strong signals of impatience over crude and grasping behavior, impoverished thinking, and conformity. Unlike the poetic evocations early in "The Divinity School Address," which forcefully sang their rebellion into the hearts of the listeners, the tone of "Self-Reliance," "Friendship," "Heroism," and "The Method of Nature" manifests an intolerance with the degrading aims and desponding doctrines of the many, including many in his audience. In the small "charmed circle" of scholars, however, "a new order of ideas" presides. "Nothing solid is secure; everything tilts and rocks. Even the scholar is not safe; he too is searched and revised." The words are searching in more than one respect. They are confrontational, challenging the listener to separate himself from the company of the ignorant, fearful, and vicious. They search, moreover, for desirable tendencies in the "puny and fickle." And they search out an audience of individuals who are alienated by their love for the better rather than for the worse. Once this community is established, their conspiracy is quickly translated into an act of religious devotion, and the paean of joyful worship inaugurates "The festival of the intellect," Emerson's theme in this essay. The almost truculent persona who shamed the audience for its enmity to the mind becomes the divine brother encouraging his fellows to join fully in the festival of the vital mind, an unsettling celebration for him and them because the first forceful reminders of the intellect show man to be a golden impossibility, who in his quests is always haunted by the "poor and pinched result." The NOT ME cannot adequately change those results, for the mind finds nature to be a slippery Proteus. This routing of all false starting-points reduces the now-troubled festival to its lowest denominator in the sense of irreducible and undeniable term, the method of nature. In finding this point the speaker-now-as-artist recognizes the possibility that "it is transferable to the literary life." At the same time he reveals how difficult the scholar's pledge is. It would have been much easier not to have joined the festival.

The remainder of the discourse is essentially a gloss on "The Sphinx" sans the poet's cocksure ebullience. No longer do Platonist and Plotinian allusions report diverse tendencies seeking accommodation. Defining the method of nature gets under way with the image of the rushing stream, which initiates a flow of image permutation in which the term "emanation" serves as the transitive force from one image to another. Attuned to his language, the persona is as importunate as the stream: "If anything could stand still, it would be crushed and dissipated by the torrent it resisted, and if it were a mind, would be crazed; as insane persons are those who hold fast to one thought, and do not flow with the course of nature."

From "penny-wisdom" in *Nature* to "hobgoblin of little minds" in "Self-Reliance" to "insane persons" in "The Method of Nature." This Uriel-like persona, in his series of mounting clauses, seems bent on searching and trying even his most loyal and receptive listeners.[7] He has arrived where only nature, poet, and vital mind dare to be, and to conjoin in a sobering symphony—the recognition of the "simultaneous life throughout the whole body, the equal serving of innumerable ends without the least emphasis or preference to any," yet a life best represented by a "circular movement. . . . Each effect strengthens every other." Despite his celebrations Whitman, too, understood how formidable the demands of such a democracy are in a world of words as well as in a community of scholars and artists.

Just how far beyond *Nature* the assumptions of this essay have proceeded is clear from a cautionary reminder near the midpoint. "That no single end may be selected and nature judged thereby, appears from this," declares the lecturing voice to allies and attentive listeners of other parties, "that if man himself be considered as the end, and it be assumed that the final cause of the world is to make holy or wise or beautiful men, we see that it has not succeeded."

According to this persona the purpose of nature for man is not realized in his lordship, who with new eyes builds an imperial house, world, and heaven commensurate with his true being and destiny. In a world where men lay traps for each other and glut the innocent spaces of the planet with ruin and defects, nature teaches the elementary and profound truth of her method—constant growth and "rapid metamorphosis." This impression of nature "does not exist to any one or to any number of particular ends, but to numberless and endless benefit, that there is in it no private will, no rebel leaf or limb, but the whole is oppressed by one superincumbent tendency, obeys that redundancy or excess of life which in conscious beings we call *ecstasy*." In underscoring the word "ecstasy" Emerson sends it back to its original meaning—to stand outside of oneself and in relation to a larger context or economy.

Having proceeded from vantage point to other vantage points and through a series of tonal shifts, positive and negative dialectic, and varying degrees of disclosure, the persona finally establishes himself as someone above and beyond particular ends and partial or isolated interests. His wealth is the commonwealth, nothing exists in isolation, the partial and unallied are unknown to nature, private will and individual effect are alien to art married to nature. The protean play of metamorphosis inheres in both nature and true art as the law of permutation with its democratic implications. "O rich and various Man! thou palace of sight and sound, carrying in thy senses the morning and the night and the unfathomable galaxy; in thy brain, the geometry of the City of God. . . . An individual man is a fruit which it cost all the foregoing ages to form and ripen." To the extent of his ripeness he will strive "to lead things from disorder into order"; to the extent that he works in unison with the method of nature he will succeed in his striving. What the essay calls for is far from relinquishing the active soul and submitting with resignation to general tendencies outside of us and foreign to the personal energy.[8] Philosophically we are in the world of "The Sphinx" and "Circles"; poetically the view is that of Whitman in his "Preface" to the 1855 *Leaves of Grass*. In contrast, to insist on private will, personal ends, and arbitrary self-created reality will eventually embitter, disgust, and tire the individual until he "hates the enterprise which lately seemed so fair" and is tempted to cast "himself into the arms of that society and manner of life which he had newly abandoned with so much pride and hope." "Love" and vital mind are the same; "it is all abandonment." "When thought is best" it is in series, in continual expansion. It "knows so deeply and speaks so musically because it is itself a mutation of the thing it describes. It is sun and moon and wave and fire in music."

The essay concludes with this perspective and tone. The persona has done his work, adopting several tones and frequently readjusting the angle of vision in the interest of the trinity of "intellect," "assembly of the learned," and "the sequent Revolution," the counterpart in this essay to the house-world-heaven progression in *Nature*. Appropriately, the essay is characterized by networks of associationism, catalogues, altering rhythms, dialectical progression, and shifting stances of the persona.

"Spiritual Laws" (*CW*, II, 75–96), also written early in the decade of the 1840s, is more affirmative and less fretful than "The Method of Nature," in part, no doubt, because Emerson wrote the essay for his book of *Essays* rather than for a lecture audience. Certainly the persona has changed. Gracefulness of style and graciousness of tone, combined with the theme of laws not made by men but liberating if observed by men, lend the essay the aura of religious meditation and spirit of worship. Sorties of definition, illustration, and association at the outset are summed up thus: "The lesson is forcibly taught by these observations that our life might be much easier and simpler than we make it; that the world might be a happier place than it is; that there is no need of struggles, convulsions, and despairs, of the wringing of the hands and the gnashing of the teeth; that we miscreate our own evils."

This persona is as subtle and subversive as any that can be

found in Emerson, for with only the slightest of transitions he slyly identifies some of the convulsions, despairs, and hand wringing as "Sunday schools and churches and pauper-societies," three of many examples of artificial contrivances contrary to the laws and method of nature. "A little consideration of what takes place around us every day would show us, that a higher law than that of our will regulates events," he declares, the first three words continuing the understatement and graciously arrogant chiding. "Belief and love,—a believing love will relieve us of a vast load of care." The warm, brotherly, and devout associations of these words encircle readers who hold dear their associations. That these readers are loyal to a view he intends to undercut is obvious to Emerson, who does not allow the persona levity or sarcasm. What is the true and loving believer to be relieved of? All of his derivative and orthodox views concerning "society, letters, arts, science, religion." Setting aside, for the moment, necessary distinctions between Emerson and his persona—as most of Emerson's listeners and readers were wont to do because of the immediate power of the man and his reputation—one can appreciate Oliver Wendell Holmes's observation that a "few generations ago this preacher of a new gospel would have been burned; a little later he would have been tried and imprisoned; less than fifty years ago he was called infidel and atheist." The numerous public attacks on Emerson fail to support Holmes's assertion, however, that it was "next to impossible to quarrel with the gentle image-breaker."[9] Still, in this essay iconoclasm is tantamount to pure and quiet devotion; the speaker transforms dismantling of altars into an act of worship. True virtue is to "make habitually a new estimate," to anticipate the "condition and society whose poetry is not yet written," to be joined to the next step not yet taken and know one's affinity to the next series of expansion about to begin. These acts are their own future because they create it, and with it the momentum of faith.

Typical of the subversion in this essay is the fourth paragraph, which develops a permutational retinue from God or

212

God's presence to the human character to Timoleon to Homer and Plutarch to soul in action to thanksgiving to God for the active soul. A progression that at first invites association with orthodox Christian theological teaching on natural revelation in which the most concrete and human elements are the reflectors from deity back to deity becomes instead a revelation of man at his best, "whose acts are all regal, graceful and pleasant."[10] The presence of God is linked to characters (the pun allows both great men and fresh, spontaneous images), to a hero, to those who write about the hero and thus re-create him (literary artist), to the soul as "regal, graceful and pleasant" action, to gratitude toward such action for being God's presence. Self-consciousness and self-congratulations are undesirable in this soul-become-God enterprise. Of far- and deep-sighted heroes the speaker notes, "Their success lay in their parallelism to the course of thought, which found in them an unobstructed channel; and the wonders of which they were the visible conductors, seemed to the eye their deed." The end of this argument is not God, nor divine man, for that matter, but the kind of action poeticized in "Circles," in which a traditional definition of God becomes Emerson's emblem for the exploring-creating mind. Appropriately, the remainder of "Spiritual Laws" is devoted to the building of new altars to replace those that the persona has been commissioned to dismantle. Once the soul is free of the iron collar of a false god and linked to the method of nature, "The soul's emphasis is always right," and individual man, not nature, is the image of "all the beauty and worth he sees." Yet "We can love nothing but nature," for any series of demonstrations of genius "show the direction of the stream."

In any series of demonstrations of man thinking we behold "the direction of the stream," or, as the presiding metaphor of Emerson's "Circles" argues, the metamorphic succession of the expanding circle. "Our globe seen by God, is a transparent law," declares the persona at the beginning of "Circles" (*CW*, II, 177–90), after which he assumes the authority to identify and explicate this law to the readers and, as circular philosopher, to do Uriel one better by arguing good out of evil and heaven out of hell. Similarities to Satan's argument in the first book of *Paradise Lost* are deceiving, for the good-evil and heaven-hell categories are themselves swallowed by the "equivalence and indifferency of all actions," the kind of perception one attributes to a god or *Übermensch* beyond human categories of good and evil. What complicates the reader's task of discerning Emerson's intention is that the persona is addressing an imagined reader by quoting that reader's protest to the "circular philosopher" of "Circles" and, by extension, of numerous other works, including "The Method of Nature" and "Spiritual Laws."

Does the law of metamorphosis ultimately mean what the protesting reader pronounces it to mean—Pyrrhonism? If so, is the speaker a tutor for someone like Nietzsche? "I am not careful to justify myself," he replies with a touch of superciliousness, playing on "careful" ("anxious" or "concerned" as well as "heedful" or "circumspect") and "justify" ("to make right" or to "acknowledge as true" as well as "to confirm" or "support"). If this persona is unconcerned to make his view right or true, are we being addressed by someone so superior in vision that any justification would be lost on little minds? Or is his argument so obviously correct that protestors immediately withdraw their protests? Or is he a charlatan or fool who does not deserve our approval and does not have Emerson's? A recent characterization of "Circles" as a vague use of motifs more clearly developed in "The Over-Soul"[11] suggests that the obfuscations of an essay unclear in its purpose are a more serious problem than its apparent Pyrrhonism.

As several scholars have shown, however, structurally "Circles" is a sophisticated justification of circular philosophy.[12] The essay affirms and structurally illustrates "that there is no end in nature," that the end or purpose of nature is not fixation but unceasing permutation, and that all life can be pictured by the "self-evolving circle." Their discussions help to answer several of the questions and protests registered in the preceding paragraph. Yet they do not confront the issue of Pyrrhonism. "Circles" itself examines the principle of the self-evolving circle, however, to where the "Pyrrhonism" of the persona's statements becomes apparent. In so doing, it confronts the disturbing implications that the persona so cavalierly dismisses. The vision is essentially that of "The Sphinx"; nonetheless, the persona's moments of self-mockery and imperious treatment of protestors and the changing degree of ironic distance between him and Emerson remind us of the Emerson who in his journals was beginning to express concern over the possibility that continual modulation in a series or evolving circles might lack continuity, definition, intelligibility, and flying force.

Does incessant movement and progression make obsolete all moral, aesthetic, and intellectual judgments? Traditional judgments are clearly rejected. The act of making such judgments, however, is not. A particularly instructive analysis of "Circles" notes that "The rigid moralist who mistakes the meliorism of 'Circles' for Pyrrhonism is doubtless also the kind of man likely to worry about his heavenly prerogatives—the kind of man who, historically speaking, was decidedly *not* gladdened at the news that hell possessed 'extreme satisfactions.' " On the other hand, "Emerson is attempting a discrimination of relativisms. He wishes to make clear that *his* brand of relativism has nothing to do with pyrrhonism, which does indeed posit 'an equivalence and indifferency of all actions,' but resembles instead the relativism of St. Paul, which teaches that what appears virtuous to a worldly observer may appear vicious to one of the faithful."[13] The persona is not always faithful.

This position, with its reversal of true believer and infidel, is established only through careful justification. Old forms crumble in "Circles," as they do in most of Emerson's works, early and late. Fixity or permanence is the most obsolete form of all. The other side of belief is skepticism, as is always

215

the case in Emerson. New affirmation depends for its life on denial; justifying and unsettling are reciprocally related. But such a view is qualified by the recognition that in superficial minds and irresponsible hands it becomes careless and unjustifiable. Not every evil will produce good. The darkest evil is the repose of superficial and settled opinion and belief. In "Circles," as elsewhere, repose is the enemy of truth and therefore of life itself. A number of other unredeemable evils are noted or implied, among them the habit of viewing nature as "stable and secular," a soul without "force and truth," the crime of forging iron empires and keeping them intact with an iron sway, rules empowered to govern art rather than being regulated and justified by the process of art, the refusal to live at the "abyss of skepticism," the unwillingness to lose a friend, the worship of literary or other reputations, a belief in one's own reputation.

Viewed from this vantage point, even the doubts about the catalogue rhetoric of a poem like "The Sphinx" are answered. Not any poet will do, and not every catalogue of images is acceptable. In the trust of a poet who cannot or will not understand Emerson's view, poetry cannot be trusted. Emerson's trust, after all, implies a commitment to the future. Whitman could be trusted, at least until his public-relations stratagems embarrassed Emerson, for he understood why the genetic chain of images was crucial to his work and to American poetry, and why "Nothing out of its place is good." There have been many imitators since Emerson and Whitman who would not have gotten Emerson's endorsement.

The affirmations of the persona in the first two-thirds of "Circles" appear to have Emerson's endorsement. Ironies, mockery, playfulness, and exhortation are not designed to disqualify the persona but to qualify the reader, that is, to instruct him by unsettling him. Whether the charge of Pyrrhonism is leveled by a reader aware of the problem in the argument or by one who is himself the problem is unclear and probably unimportant. Emerson's aim quickly becomes clear: to use this serious protest as an opportunity to recon-

sider the persona's affirmations in a trustworthy way, in
other words, to make the persona vulnerable so as to justify
his arguments more carefully. The essay studies and edu-
cates the persona while tutoring the reader. Once the vantage point is the true one, now "for the first time, seem I to
know any thing rightly." Those who "have outlived their
hope" will find the concluding paragraphs absurd; those too
naïve, intemperate, or egotistical to hold the true vantage
point will be made absurd by their false enthusiasm for these
paragraphs. When Emerson allows the persona a statement
from his journal of several years before, "Nothing great was
ever achieved without enthusiasm" (see *JMN*, V, 15), he also
gives him enough etymological insight into "enthusiasm" to
understand the relation of perpetual transformation to possessing God.

In the world of the essay, then, as in the reader's changing
spectacle of time and space and his participation in them,
"no evil is pure" and no good is absolute. "Do not set the least
value on what I do, or the least discredit on what I do not,"
cautions the speaker as he draws yet another circle for the
essay, "as if I pretended to settle anything as true and false. I
unsettle all things. . . . I simply experiment, an endless
seeker, with no Past at my back." Emerson has unsettled
even this essay and all the circles drawn thus far. Whether
the persona is aware of the implications is hard to tell. Quite
possibly he overlooks the important "end" of the "endless"
seeking. Yet he seems to share much of Emerson's understanding; in the next paragraph he points to a principle of
stability, a "central life" or leitmotif in the "incessant movement and progression," as if "that which is made, instructs
how to make a better." This progression to the better, which
welcomes the next perception and generalization, sentence
and stanza, essay and paradigm, is "better" because, in going
beyond what is already there, it subsumes everything by its
new energy and functions. "It carries in its bosom all the
energies of the past, yet is itself an exhalation of the morning."

The reference to "central life" is perhaps the most significant transitional point in the essay. It becomes the most careful qualification and hence justification of the persona, who has admitted too casually and cavalierly that he does not or does not need to justify himself or his argument. The reference also becomes the leitmotif or centering metaphor for the rest of the essay. Here the world is not the dancer discussed in the second chapter but "incessant movement and progression." Although syntactically, rhetorically, and logically the language of the concluding paragraphs enacts the incessant movement and progression (creating the illusion that the essay could have been concluded with the fifth-from-last paragraph or with any of the paragraphs that follow it), the very movement and progression and the surer definition of life thus furnished become the central life in the somewhat repetitive yet always expanding circles. In terms of the individual, "central life" returns us to the notion of man thinking, in terms of the individual in a culture we are reminded of commonwealth and representative man. Central life and "way of life" cannot, finally, be separated, just as the vision of "Circles" cannot be divorced from the mode of the essay. But discriminations can be made: movement and progression are central to "building up our being" and fortifying "all the company."

"Circles" is limited to but not limited by a single persona as teacher-student, who joins the reader in learning even though he is doing much of the teaching, and who repeatedly appears to have adjourned the essay only to draw another circle, enlarge the prospect, and so more closely approach or act out the central life.

Since the 1950s the scholarly commonplace has it that Emerson's essays of 1836–39 are more fresh, vigorous, revolutionary, and visionary than the essays of the 1840s and considerably more so than the essays of the '50s, a development in the essays usually tied to some version of what Stephen Whicher charts as the shift from freedom to fate and of what Jonathan Bishop characterizes as a shift from transcendental faith to skepticism and despair to Victorian accommodation and vapid generalization. Indirectly and unwittingly Emerson in "Eloquence" prophesied such a reaction when he chided Americans for their fascination with oratory of rhetorical flourish, "small-pot-soon-hot" argument, overt dramatic effect, and the emotional despotism of visionary fervor. "There are degrees of power," the essay warns, after which it repeats with approval the observation of an American statesman that the "curse of this country is eloquent men. . . . We believe there may be a man who is a match for events, one who never found his match, against whom other men being dashed are broken, . . . who can give you any odds and beat you" (*W*, VII, 74–76). Because the immediate power of early discourses and essays wins hands down, even over the divinity professors staring stonily at the floor of the chancel stage, this Emerson still excites us, most of us joining in the response of the Harvard Divinity students of 1838. It is easier to poke fun at the divinity professors than the students, who responded well to powerful oratory and to what some of us, at least, regard as a humanely liberating point of view. A century and a half later, however, Emerson survives as literature, and his warning against being mesmerized by the great and immediate force of oratory is doubly pertinent. Both the history of Emerson's maturation as a writer of essays and the record of his revisions of earlier published pieces for new volumes or editions reveal the efficient choices of an increasingly skillful artist. Even his lectures changed, increasingly resembling his essays. This is the Emerson least attended to today, when scholars continue to endorse the commandeering tone and energetic rhetoric of the early work, in which Emerson has not yet resigned from the pulpit.

"Experience" (*W*, III, 43–86), completed in 1844, is consistently exempted, however, from the practice of devaluing later essays. Although reasons as such are rarely specified, as though they were self-evident, I would like to suggest, beyond the obvious fact that the essay is one of Emerson's most skillful and forceful compositions, several reasons for the centrality of "Experience" in most of the treatises on Emerson in the last three decades. These are: the overtly auto-biographical mode of the essay and the critical attraction to biographical provenance; the Childe Harold syndrome among students of American romanticism (which celebrates the youthful vision even as it insists on the martyrdom of this vision in a hostile environment); the high fashion of suffering, despair, and defeat among today's thematically-poised students of literature; the equation of modernity in literature with some post-Spenglerian version of what to make of a diminished thing; and the currency of aesthetic and philosophical assumptions that lift up dispossession and loss as the purest and most basic gain.

In support of his anti-transcendental interpretation of "Experience," Stephen Whicher contends that five of its seven lords of life are principles of weakness.[14] His moving and doubly autobiographical reading, which has in its way become a lord of literary life, finds its most impressive reconfirmation in Jonathan Bishop's analysis. According to Bishop, the essay opens to a frozen landscape of the soul after tragedy, like a killing winter, has swept Emerson's life. The speaker, a transparent disguise for Emerson, has stopped somewhere in the midst of endless stairs, awakening from Lethe to find himself lost and his accomplishments futile. In his new and dark ruminations the metaphor of the expanding circle has suffered a pessimistic devaluation. According to Bishop, the speaker nonetheless refuses to retreat to some sleepy hollow, choosing, rather, to face the exigencies of life with greater caution, skepticism, and emotional repression. As the self yields "adroitly before a world that is not apt to alter under a reformer's eye," the horrible truth that life "is a bubble and a skepticism, and a sleep within a sleep," is something he can live with even though it puts all divinity to rout. If he can learn to skate well, he will be able to salvage a little power while submitting to the demands of form, and will enjoy, from time to time, serendipitous moments of epiphany with their reaffirmation of spirit.[15]

Looked at through the eyes of the persona, and with the

attention bounded by the first four lords of life, "Experience" is an essay about what to make of a diminished thing. In this respect the loss and resignation are as thoroughgoing as Bishop suggests. On the other hand, the essay's evocation of loss and lostness culminates in the treatise on "surface," the lord of life whose definition serves to summarize the discussion of the first four lords. Although the persona is slow to show awareness of the implications, the reader is apprised of deeper structures beneath this surface etched by the artful skater. Once the persona is made mindful of these structures by reminding himself that they exist, that from time to time he has penetrated to them, he can proceed to other lords of life with a perspective now essentially normative in the essay. Accordingly, the persona is less and more than an Emerson surrogate and the essay is much more than naked confession. Indeed, the persona and the movement of the essay are Emerson's version of Carlyle's *Sartor Resartus,* specifically "The Everlasting No," "The Centre of Indifference," and "The Everlasting Yea." We are reminded of Emerson's enormous admiration for this work[16] as well as his habit of borrowing and stealing materials from other sources only to fashion an essay with assumptions, terms, technique, and speaker belonging to the essay and so to himself. For example, instead of the fiery furnace of doubt, death-songs, and defiance in "The Everlasting No," "Experience" strides through expanding circles of illusoriness, alienation, and the gathering blankness of unbelief. Moreover, the center of the essay, "indifferency," resembles a state of affairs in "Circles" rather than Carlyle's "Centre." To cite a similarity to "Circles," however, can also mislead; "indifferency" has come to characterize the temperament and belief of the persona of "Experience" and is the brooding problem of the essay.

Strategically located as preamble to the announcing of "indifferency," the principle that wisdom infers from all sides, is the trenchant comment on the times, one of several signals of socio-cultural resonances in the essay. "Our young people have thought and written much on labor and reform," the persona tiredly declares, "and for all that they have written, neither the world nor themselves have got on a step." Culture "ends in headache. Unspeakably sad and barren does life look to those who a few months ago were dazzled with the splendor of the promise of the times." This statement has immediate and specific reference to the age, especially to the early 1840s, as the journals for these years bear out. The essay is not an elegy for young Waldo or for a dead faith; on the other hand, the absence of an "affirmative principle," or its denial, is very much at issue. The persona, as much a literary creation as Carlyle's Teufelsdröckh, slows and steadies his restless pilgrimage through the illusions of the phenomenal world and restrains his specter-fighting desires. Even the fact that "the splendor of the promise of the times" is merely a principal in the litany of illusoriness elicits no protest in this monologic drama. "Objections and criticism we have had our fill of. There are objections to every course of life and action, and the practical wisdom infers an indifferency, from the omnipresence of objection."

Instead of protesting, the persona is inclined to lecture the reader with a number of supposed truisms, many of these alien to the weight of emphasis in other Emerson essays of these years. The declaration in "Experience" that "There is now no longer any right course of action" is made by a voice more emphatically Pyrrhonist than the speaker of "Circles." Advice such as "Do not craze yourself with thinking. . . . Life is not intellectual or critical" is diametrically opposite to an emphasis in Emerson from *Nature* and "The American Scholar" to his post–Civil War lectures on the intellect. If we assume Emerson agrees with the persona's potentially absurd credo that "We live amid surfaces, and the true art of life is to skate well on them," then we will either be embarrassed by the rest of the essay or will dispose of the remainder as an embarrassingly weak, contrived, and unconvincing coda. To distinguish between persona and author is not to deny or ignore Emerson's accurate and poignant use of autobiographical matters such as the death of Waldo, his wary impatience with the age, and his pessimism over the masses in America. It is merely a reminder of where Emerson is in relation to these matters. The metaphor of skating well on the surface does not mean to be superficial.

Since the persona has set his heart on honesty, he qualifies, already within the discussion of "indifferency" but especially thereafter, much of what he pronounces in this section. "Life is not dialectics" appears at the outset of the dialectical discussion of "surface," in which the persona eventually concedes, "I accept the clangor and jangle of contrary tendencies." These antithetical statements occur in an essay frequently cited as compelling evidence of dialectical structure in Emerson's essays. The assertion that life's "chief good is for well-mixed people who can enjoy what they find, without question," has implications quite different from those in the observation four paragraphs later that "Man lives by pulses; our organic movements are such . . . and the mind goes antagonizing on, and never prospers but by fits." It is as though every statement in this section is potentially "noxious if unmixed." To announce that "Intellectual tasting of life will not supersede muscular activity" is to introduce an element "in excess" that "makes a mischief as hurtful as its defect." But then this section also endorses "genius" and "moral sentiment," and arrives at a point where "The ardors of piety agree at last with the coldest scepticism." The latter characterizes the conclusion that "A man is a golden impossibility," which, in its denial, anticipates the ardor of a related pronouncement in the next paragraph: "Every man is an impossibility until he is born; everything impossible until we see a success."

The extent of shifts and transformations is even more apparent if we contrast declarations in the discussion of "surface" with radically different versions in the latter parts of the essay. According to the persona in the "surface" passage, "Five minutes of to-day are worth as much to me as five minutes in the next millennium. . . . [The] only ballast I know is a respect to the present hour." In his meditation on

223

"reality," in contrast, the persona suggests that "Our life seems not present so much as prospective; not for the affairs on which it is wasted, but as a hint of this vast-flowing vigor." Similarly, the recommended attitude of "accepting our actual companions and circumstances," assured in our mind that "their contentment, which is the last victory of justice, is a more satisfying echo to the heart than the voice of poets," is pointedly undercut by the concluding paragraph of the essay, in which the persona knows "that the world I converse with in the city and in the farms, is not the world I *think*." At the end of this passage the language of the heart is also the voice of the poet: "Never mind the ridicule, never mind the defeat; up again, old heart!—it seems to say,—there is victory yet for all justice." The reader's lesson is not to slip back and forth on the surface of the argumentation, but to be surprised by the pattern that emerges in the argumentation, a gradual but unmistakable change in persona and essay.

Let me return from these comparisons to the movement of the essay as a whole. Like "Circles," "Experience" involves the application of circular philosophy. The affirmative figure of evolving circles becomes here a sea of illusions, a succession of moods, and the slipperiness of change. Nothing is stable or fixed except, perhaps, contemporary man, which makes his plight in this world even worse than the unstable speaker's. In the first four sections of the essay the outward expansion of circles, then, is used pessimistically not only to reject a cheap faith but, at this stage, also to deny any faith. These sections belong to rebellious and self-exiled outcasts who totally "lack the affirmative principle.[17] Provisionally one of these outcasts, the persona speaks from personal experiences, many of which are autobiographically Emerson's. The use of autobiographical material is not at all unusual, but Emerson's use of unpromising material in so unpromising a fashion is. For the unfixed and unstable self there is only the advice of rejecting even temporary anchorages, for the fixed self there is loneliness at the center of a world that rushes away with its secrets. The lords of life offer little hope in this processive drama, and "Our friends early appear to us as representatives of certain ideas which they never pass or succeed." Bitter complaint and grief are the shallowest of responses to such a condition, mere "plays about the surface" rather than contact with it. To quote the introductory paragraph of "Spiritual Laws," "No man ever stated his griefs as lightly as he might."[18]

As for the persona's insistence that "I have set my heart on honesty," the discussion of "temperament" sets the limits of honesty. The implications of the tonal modulation might be summarized by the observation in "Nominalist and Realist," which belongs to the same period, "I am always insincere, as always knowing there are other moods" (*W,* III, 247). Honesty, in fact, acknowledges this kind of insincerity as necessary. Whereas the persona may be trapped by his desire for total sincerity, the wry ironies and wit of this section hint of where and what Emerson's temperament is in "Experience." In the midst of the persona's cheerless and hopeless sentiments Emerson introduces an anecdote that seems to illustrate the persona's argument but, in fact, treats both Calvinists and Unitarians satirically and places the persona and his argument close to the company of the former, for whom Emerson rarely showed any respect: "I knew a witty physician who found the creed in the biliary duct, and used to affirm that if there was disease in the liver, the man became a Calvinist, and if that organ was sound, he became a Unitarian." Hence we are entertained more than surprised by the punning in the complaint, "Temperament puts all divinity to rout. . . . Spirit is matter reduced to an extreme thinness: O *so* thin!" The most is made of the opportunity to complement the persona's doubts and confusion with cynicism while registering uncomplimentary observations of the age. "Shall I preclude my future by taking a high seat and kindly adapting my conversation to the shape of heads?" is the persona's humorous version of a sincere desire to break out of his dilemma.

Recanting is not the answer, the persona confides in the discussion of succession. "This onward trick of nature is too strong for us: *Pero si muove.*" The words "too strong for us" play their own tricks, suggesting defeat for the one who cannot stay abreast of change as well as the one who moves, against his conservative will, with nature. Yet Galileo's words also suggest a modest victory for sanity and enlightened conviction in a culture that insanely seeks to silence talk of metamorphosis. This doubleness is maintained throughout the section. The prospects do not appear to be those of the poet and his poetry in "The Sphinx." "Life is not worth the taking, to do tricks in." Especially if the tricks are all on man and they are all that one can take of life. On the other hand, "The plays of children are nonsense, but very educative nonsense. So it is with the largest and solemnest things."

Pedantically to harp on any of these points, or dismiss them all as rubbish, is noxious, the Pyrrhonist persona concludes as he presses the principle of "indifference." Even those statements that seem to lift momentarily beyond indifferency are not spared. "The mid-world is best. Nature, as we know her, is no saint," is one of several notable lessons tethered with a short rope in the mid-world. Not much can be gained from "Nature, as we know her," when we know very little and when any set of beliefs tends to be an excess of wisdom and any particular knowledge pressed too hard makes a fool of man. "The line he must walk is a hair's breadth" is the generalization of the persona, who in his epigrammatic wisdom is almost the fool. As his qualifications and alterations reveal, he, too, is forced to walk a hair's-breadth line, and thus is finally not the fool.

Required to hold that line without slipping, he disengages himself from Pyrrhonism and admits, at first with discomfiture and then with considerable delight, the "angel-whispering" factor in our success—"surprise." Significantly, Emerson conflates much of the discussion of surprise with his discourse on surface, an intermingling that has occurred to some extent in the discussion of each of the lords of life but is most extensive here. One of the most rigorous explications of "Experience" observes that "various lords seem so closely interrelated that they become on occasion mistakable for one another."[19] Emerson's point is obvious: we live on

226

the surface of surprise, and we must be willing to etch that surface often and well if we hope to be surprised by structures and insights beneath and beyond the superficial. The directive to skate the surface well is foolish only if we see the essay ending here or if we become literalists with the metaphor of skating. Seen in the context of the dialectic at work, succession and surface are close kinsmen, both of which imply the action of "The Sphinx" and each of which promises surprise. In fact, the procession of curiously related lords in "Experience" and the logic of permutation they establish are Emerson's most convincing evocation of succession and surface.

With the introduction of "surprise" the essay turns toward the renovation that has flickered here and there as feeble anticipations in the early sections. Persona and essay move outward into affirmation, a marked contrast to the first three sections. In the words of the critic cited in the preceding paragraph, "Experience" is "a purposeful pilgrimage of redemption."[20] The principal turn in the essay is best characterized by Emerson's own words, in a journal entry: "Poetry seems to begin in the slightest change of name, or, detecting identity under variety of surface" (*JMN*, XIII, 60). Poetry, the highest expression of vital mind, is both cause and effect in our contacting and conversing with the real or deeper structures, which Emerson names "reality" and poetically describes as "the Ideal journeying always with us, the heaven without rent or seam." The sentiment that repeatedly renovates the one who truly masters surfaces goes by many names, all of them too quaint and imprecise to do it justice. In *Nature* Emerson called it "Reason." In "Experience" it is the cause "which refuses to be named" but before which the "intellect must still kneel." Named or unnamed, it advocates and confirms subjectiveness, but subjectiveness free of the errors of particular excess and "private sympathy." These two errors belong to Emerson's definition of "the Fall of Man," as they do to the unreliable persona of the early sections.

"Suffice it for the joy of the universe," exclaims the transformed persona, "that we have not arrived at a wall [and the words of doom written large on the wall], but at interminable oceans." This sea opens to new navigation and strong navigators in contrast to the "unnavigable sea" that the persona had described in the opening section as washing "with silent waves between us and the things we aim at and converse with." The prospect of "Experience" can now be identified—to realize one's world by translating the "genius" of "reality" into "practical power."[21] As usual, but without the usual associations, Emerson has chosen his terms with care. The progression from the "practical wisdom" of "indifference" to the "practical power" of the conclusion is crucial, and the latter and higher principle puts to nought the wisdom of the wise. Had "indifference" been the persona's final word, the foolishness of preaching that necessary principle would have been the preaching of foolishness.

Practical power, however, is a prospect that hovers over the effort to "realize your own world." For one thing, it is not practical in the sense that "manipular attempts" and "many eager persons" demand. For another, like art it is not deceived by "the element of time," as reformers, polemicists, and (Emerson believed) most of his contemporaries were. It is the nature of the age, but not of man thinking, to postpone indefinitely by ignoring and resisting the genius that can be translated into practical power. Mere secularism (being caught up totally in the particular moment and the succession of immediate events) encourages what the journals call "thinking for the market," which they contrast to "what is private, & yours, & essential" (*JMN*, XIII, 141). "Experience" not only saves but honors the "private fruit," a harvest that acknowledges genius and maintains sanity in what Emerson saw as a frenetic and anti-intellectual age.

In part, then, this essay is Emerson's response to the attitudes, assumptions, and actions of reformers and polemicists who sought to capture the age with a web of hopes he regarded as fragile and brief. The essay helps us to understand his hatred of slavery and opposition to political compromise on this "destitution" while he doggedly refused to join any of the abolitionist crusades.[22] "Experience" also helps to clarify and increase one's appreciation of a poem such as the "Ode (Inscribed to W. H. Channing)." At the beginning and end of "Experience," and repeatedly throughout, the reader is carefully instructed that this essay is burdened by Emerson's America and by the slim prospects of his vision and commitments in a superficial, nervous, and passionate age that out of a "paltry empiricism" ridiculed or unconsciously quarantined the scholar and the poet. Initially the persona appears to be one of those disillusioned survivors of Fruitlands, or Brook Farm, or religious revivalism, or the all-out battles of abolitionism or some other social crusade, or a Horace Mann political campaign, or Congress: in any event, someone who has come back less than innocent and thoroughly soured. Eventually he and Emerson join in transcending ridicule and defeat and refusing to "ask for a rash effect from meditations, counsels and the hiving of truths."

In the light of the transformation enacted in the essay, the conclusion, with its invocation of "private fruit" and its rejection of "rash effect," accords with Emerson's essays of the late 1830s and early '40s and with the evidence of his journals and letters of the early and mid '40s. Occasionally his writings of these years lead one to wonder whether the allowance he makes for the recovery and building up of the individual wealth is limited to the individual. Does the conclusion of "Experience," for instance, deny as premature or immature the desire to build the commonwealth? The context of the reference to "private fruit" implies an environment hostile for the present to any kind of fruition. A recalcitrant and shallow age is impicated in the tyranny of illusion, temperament, succession, and surface. Once again we are made aware that Emerson's philosophizing has cultural—some might prefer the term "ideological"—resonances. The perilous adventure of management in "Experience" begins with an exhibit, if not admission, of personal defects and limitation and an unpromising foray into a culture marked by defects and strewn with wrecks. To

229

allow oneself to become entrapped in one's world of negative inner and outer circumstances requires little effort. The school of experience, however, has taught the persona that much of the right kind of effort is required to escape such entrapment and thereby to discover or recover vision and power. Conclusions such as these correspond to the emphasis in the journals and letters in suggesting that Emerson demanded considerably more of himself than of his age and more of the artist in his America than did most of his contemporaries.

The doubleness of the persona in "Experience" and the ambivalence of his situation can be summarized in two Emerson passages that are at once synonymous and antonymous. If we focus on the persona's rhetorical dance, lack of commitment to positions just established, logical dialectic, and sheer constructive ability, an exclamation in "Resources" is strikingly apt: "Ah! what a plastic little creature he is! so shifty, so adaptive! his body a chest of tools, and he making himself comfortable in every climate, in every condition" (*W*, VIII, 141). The oppressive force of a number of lords of life, on the other hand, reminds us that all too frequently the poet's condition makes the effort "to escape . . . that jailyard of individual relations in which he is enclosed" (*W*, III, 28) a stringent urgency, an urgency remembered too late and felt too slightly by the persona of "Days," yet present in the design of the poem and flashing in the scornful eye of "the Day."

Critical commentary on "Experience" has for the most part identified the "private fruit" this essay settles for with paltry results such as the few herbs and apples of "Days," and has suggested that the evidence points to a remarkable shift in Emerson's vision. An objection needs to be raised, as implied in the preceding pages, by way of keeping central to the critical act both the literary art and its context. The private harvest alluded to in the essay includes the essay itself, with its remarkable modulations and final relations, which in the prisonyard of tyrannical lords and their trustees transforms tone, imagery, persona, and vision. If Emerson lost faith, as he did from time to time and was tempted to do much of the time, it was in a culture and age he saw as faithless. The irony of his dilemma was not lost on him, as he revealed in essays as early as "The American Scholar," "The Divinity School Address," and "Self-Reliance." In his essays of the 1850s, particularly those in *The Conduct of Life,* the dilemma informs virtually every essay and the role of each persona. According to the essays of *The Conduct of Life,* freedom from the prison of relations enclosing man must be won repeatedly, with each new organization and construction. Emerson's view of what this means for the literary artist is pretty much in agreement with the implications of an essay by Roland Barthes when he notes that

writing is an ambiguous reality; on the one hand it unquestionably arises from a confrontation of the writer with the society of his time; on the other hand, from this social finality, it refers the writer back, by a sort of tragic reversal, to the sources, that is to say, the instruments of creation. Failing the power to supply him with a freely consumed language, History suggests to him the demand for one freely produced. . . . It is under the pressure of History and Tradition that the possible modes of writing for a given writer are established.[23]

The Conduct of Life is framed by the essays "Fate" and "Illusions," in both of which the coercive yet indifferent lords of circumstances threaten personal performance. This similarity to "Experience" extends also to the persona, who in each case is given to autobiographical confidences and illustrations. Once again the leading question is "What to do?" or how to survive those conundrums of forces and conditions that intervene between the persona and the transformation of vision and desire into practical power. "Illusions" examines the fateful lords of individual consciousness, those portly and grim faces whose omnipresence condemns the persona of "Experience" to puzzlement and denial. "Fate," on the other hand, deals with "the Times"— specifically, culture and nature. Together these two promote a centrifugal entropy that seems to dissipate any concentration of personal initiative. Although not ignoring the problem of illusoriness and limitation in private perception and interpretation, "Fate," ca. 1853–54 (*W,* VI, 1–49), analyzes the "social situations from the perspective of Fate"[24] and fate from the vantage point of nature.

These contemporary and outer manifestations of fate barely adumbrate fate, but they clearly identify a number of examples of what one cannot do given a particular context. To address fate is to address the times as experienced; to confront the times is to see the shadowy presence of fortuna, the context for individual texts of fortune and misfortune. In the first half of the essay any paltry life and hope that survive the persona's concessions are conclusive evidence of the massive omnipresence of fate. The only countermotion to this emphasis is a persistent penchant for sarcasm, understatement, and wry irreverence, stratagems too defensive, it would appear, to steer the fragile life through the lines of fate.[25]

Yet the ironies make a difference. The third paragraph, which abstractly balances liberty and fate more conclusively than any paragraph or argument later in the essay or in the conclusion, turns with only the slightest transition to an observation that undercuts the entire paragraph: "Our America has a bad name for superficialness. Great men, great nations, have not been boasters or buffoons, but perceivers of the terrors of life." An inventory of unsentimental and death-dealing nature is punctuated by a reference to "an amiable parson" who "believes in a pistareen-Providence" and again by the mischievous understatement, "The way of Providence is a little rude." Once again they help to identify the persona as well as his relation to subject and readers. In this essay the ironies are not used to expose a dubious or duped persona, exasperatingly superficial reader, or imbruted age, although such a reader and age are implied throughout. Rather, irony serves mainly as the inspector of the construction taking shape and of the house of fate eventually raised. In the formidable presence of the structure of fate the reader is surprised and amused by a persona who builds the house of fate because he must but who insists on building it right. He is both builder and shrewd investigator. The construction must conform to two expectations, fate's and his. Without the ironic intrusions, these expectations would coincide. Irritability expressed from time to time over still another diagram of fate merely reinforces in his mind the aching question of what to do, that is, exactly how to proceed. What seems to be befuddling and intimidating evidence sharpens his awareness of an omnipresent yet purposeless fate that will destroy not only man's faith but man himself. Consequently he purposes to study carefully the house of purposeless fate. A tough-minded builder yet kindly pedagogue leads the reader to the next paragraph, argument, and illustration not simply to build the house of fate but to inspect it closely and, above all, to observe himself, and to invite us to observe him, building. Not until late in the essay does the reader recognize that to raise the house of fate so convincingly is, in a sense, to raze it.

One must have the mind of fate to profile it. At the outset we are not aware that being equal to the task makes the persona the equal of fate. Skillfully he encourages doubts about fate, only to raise serious doubts as to whether the book of life has any proprietor but fate. He also waits out those doubts. In this schooling of the mind blind to fate, non-reflective and tranquil credulity is routed by a compelling advocacy of necessitarianism and fatalism. But these, in turn, are allowed only a temporary authority as blueprints, for they are philosophically immature. Like nature, the persona deliberately turns "the gigantic pages" in "the book of Fate"—"leaf after leaf,—never re-turning one."

Ironically, the models and methods of boldly enterprising man reveal the power of fate, these pages seem to confirm. The most telling confirmation, perhaps, is the illustration of genetic engineering used to rekindle our hope of reforming man. Reformation, which envisions greater freedom and positive power, is entrusted to its philosophical opposite, a deterministic engineering. But according to the persona such a confusion is hardly an anomaly in a nation that cannot as yet perceive "the terror of life," or in Western civilizations that "quickly narrowed to village theologies" the ethics of Jesus, or in a Protestantism that, in the name of reform, produced the doctrine of election and its politico-cultural counterpart, the American doctrine of exceptionalism. In his invocations of freedom man has confirmed, gesture upon gesture, the tyranny of fate.

If society is a thoroughgoing manifestation of fate and thus part of the persona's building material, nature is also. This further turn in the argument exonerates the reader, who had been assumed to be superficial. First, the reader no longer is able unconsciously to confirm fate while consciously affirming freedom; as he has watched the persona turn the pages, the conscious has come to coincide with the unconscious. Second, through an accumulation of illustration and analogy the reader learns that the truth about himself in relation to fate is in keeping with the evidence of nature. The method of nature is, in fact, the law of fate, and the book of fate is but another title for the book of nature.

Desultorily within almost every proof of fate cited from the book of nature and cumulatively through the series of proofs as a whole (a method reminiscent of the proofs of "Idealism" in *Nature*), the persona establishes the equation between nature and human nature, then pointedly underscores this immediately after the series. Like the times, the individual manifests the fatedness of nature. Even philosophical-political belief and ethical behavior are physiologically based, that is, written into those of us who seek to write our own confessions: "conservatives are such from personal defects." Fate is a major factor in the making of a conservative, a conservative is a victim of that fate, and "conservative" in Emerson's own dictionary characterized most fellow Americans and fellowmen.

A notable feature in this profiling of fate, the climactic opening and the conclusiveness of the early part, is a common feature in Emerson's essays as well as some of his poems but is more noticeable here than in any other essay except perhaps "Experience." Were it not for the persona's ironies, the tabernacle raised to fate would be a permanent temple—the beginning would be its own end, with no other prospects. Conversely, the conclusion is open and initiative. This reversal of what one usually expects and finds in beginnings and endings is entirely in keeping with Emerson's vision in "Fate." In its predicatives, reversals, repeated use of "but" to open new paragraphs or change the direction within the paragraph,[26] reciprocal definitions, and tonal shifts, the essay moves away from its beginning-as-end toward its end-as-beginning.[27]

Building up fate so as to create the condition for another structure also recalls Emerson's technique in "Experience," in which inherent in the structuring of oppressive lords of life is the very principle of challenging the oppression. Constructing the house of experience temporarily conceals and, it would seem, repudiates the principle that makes possible the argumentation and, by extension, the drafting and revising of the essay. In "Fate" both the dilemma and the opportunity are more obviously developed. Fate is the given, the undeniable pressure under which everyone, including artist and reformer, must work. The unquestioned decrees of fate are challenged not by pitting "Fate against Fate" but by building the structure of freedom with its altar to Necessity as centerpiece. Whatever structure is raised, man constructs under the pressure of fate; in both cases the persona is the builder and works with essentially the same building materials. The acts of building the argument for fate, raising an altar to Necessity, and composing an essay like "Fate" disclose the relation of man to fate. The persona, for instance, is free to work with his fated material, to reinforce or transform it. By instructive words and especially by example he seeks to establish that how one organizes the undeniable elements of his world in order to survive and work well in his world of fate depends every moment on thought and action that take "man out of servitude into freedom."

On the *quality* of thought and action, one should add. To

suggest that the philosophical and existential problems of "Fate" are resolved by recognizing and affirming merely the act of building or merely the building of a privately-enclosed and self-reflexive structure is to ignore much of the question at issue in favor of a solipsistic escape. The world of words built by Emerson is never disengaged from his idea of commonwealth. Since the "common catastrophe" memorably documented in the first half of the essay is not denied or even questioned in the second half, the real issue is victimization. The apparent reversal in the essay has to do with transforming an impression of victimization into one of survival and success. If one ignores the persona's ironies and pedagogical manner, we are left with the impression in the first half of the essay of a journeyman draftsman and builder for fate who is skeptical about the possibility of better designs and superior employment and cynical about constructions nature has discredited and he himself has forsaken. A bolder soul would prefer to be the martyr, not the votary, of omnipotent fate. Yet how does one struggle against a fate that lacks design and purpose? Although the structure of fate confirms man as builder—after all, the design does not originate with fate but with man in nature—the act of building this structure is not a rallying point but proof, for the moment, of "one victim more in the common catastrophe."

The passage just quoted also defines the catastrophe in terms of negatives: "no divinity, or wise and instructed soul." Implied are both the possibility and desirability of an instructed soul. In other words, the lessons of fate have been preliminary instruction. And the laborious effort to build a monumental fate by piecing together the materials of fate is but an interpretation, and an inadequately instructed one at that. Hence the persona is free to shift his perspective and argue a new one as forcefully as he argued in behalf of fate. The "tyrannous circumstance" that defines what we may do by prescribing what we may not do meets its match in the "fatal courage" of personal power, "which composes and decomposes nature" as much as fate composes and decomposes man. Before the reader has had sufficient opportunity to adjust to the abrupt shift and locate persona and new viewpoint, the forceful new argument is itself abandoned as "only parrying and defence." Such a parrying, described recently in another context as the "working of internal and external pressures against each other,"[28] merely pits self against culture, courageous resistance against resignation, faith against unbelief, and freedom against fate. If the critic is on the side of metaphysical philosophy, he can perhaps insist on the talismanic paradox of the mutual dependence of fate and freedom.

The latter part of "Fate" offers no such resolution. Sisyphus is mistaken: neither being nor resistance is enough. Nor is mere accumulation of evidence to counter the claim of fate. "We are not Manicheans not believers in two hostile principles" (*JMN*, VIII, 137). What the persona relies on is the reader's recognition that arguments are being constructed and visions fashioned. Just as the power of fate comes home through the power of words, the affirmation of freedom is given proportionate words. In each case a builder has fashioned a monument, both of these a personal choice yet each proposed by conditions. Here the persona arrives at the height of Emerson's argument. The condition of man thinking, as Emerson sees it, must be recovered repeatedly, with each act of building. The literary artist, for instance, writes his way to freedom with each new and vital advance in his work. Here is not only a veteran Emerson argument but a thoroughly experienced voice sounding like an Emerson who looks back on two decades of writing and lecturing since he resigned from the Second Church of Boston. "We rightly say of ourselves, we were born and afterward we were born again, and many times." Even the act of raising the structure of fate has not been exempt from this truth, although the structure itself, a "pictorial impression," denies that the power of the mind "is of the maker, not of what is made."

Perhaps the most illuminating gloss on the designs of "Fate" can be found in the poetry of Wallace Stevens, whose vision shares the suppositions of Emerson's mature essays. Because we readily admit that Stevens is both his own dictionary and a genuinely modern writer, we do not underestimate as platitudinous or naïvely affirmative the tricky opening lines of "The Well Dressed Man With a Beard": "After the final no there comes a yes / And on that yes the future world depends." The persona of "Fate" has many surrogates in Stevens: to name a few, the narrator in "Sunday Morning," who goes beyond what the woman hears; the poet-painter whose words give dominion to the striding black of fate; the prince of the peacocks, who creates just the right kind and degree of pressure for the poet; the irreverent lecturer of the high-toned old Christian woman who responds to her church-fated construction with another construction; the eye that records the sea surface full of clouds; the interpreter of the woman's song on the shore at Key West; the medley-minded man with the blue guitar; the indefatigable man on the dump; the artist who puts a pineapple together. Not the early Emerson but the Emerson of "Fate," then, can be regarded as the spiritual father of Stevens, who liked to depict the initiatives of the artist as the necessary angel doing his necessary and willful work under the pressure of reality. As builder, Stevens would say, we are connoisseurs of fate, chaos, and freedom, with the courage and satisfactions of an irrepressible dissatisfaction that keeps us building and rebuilding.

The will to continue, which Emerson calls the "moral sentiment," implies in "Fate" as in "The Divinity School Address" and "Spiritual Laws" the courage to pull down altars and fashion new ones, without end. The poet of "The Sphinx" is bristling with such a courage, but his courageous work meets with little resistance in a poem that does not focus darkly on the "jet of chaos which threatens to exterminate us," a key statement in "Fate." In "Experience" this chaos belongs to the world of succession and surface, those precursors of surprise and reality. In "Fate" the negative forces of fate are characterized as impersonal, pointless in individual human terms, and chaotic. It is this chaos that is the given: fate simply is, it does not have particular designs with us nor does it have its own coherent profile or organization. Chaos, then, is a principal element in unstructured fate and in the literary construction of this terror. If "Fate is ore and quarry," man is the artificer, and "limitation is power that shall be." "Nature and Thought" jostle each other enough in this essay to produce two designs, one of these a sketching of the lineaments of amorphous fate, the other a documenting and giving some tangible shape to man's creative and designing thought. Since Emerson's persona, like Stevens's in "A High-Toned Old Christian Woman," recognizes both of these contenders as acts of construction that live in change and grow out of a terrible yet fertile chaos, he wins his argument without being forced to prove his second design superior to the first. The second design is implied in the first and is, in fact, the flying force of the essay, the artist, and man thinking.

"Fate" is the builder's daring aesthetics of control, mere child's play (often with fatal results) for the one who fails to recognize the risks of building, a dangerous presumption for someone who resigns to fate because it has become his sole reality or who seeks salvation in the comfort of a single and fixed position or who seeks release from obligations of building still other altars. In "this vagabond life" the necessary hazard of building and rebuilding the materials of fate is man's supreme game and truest ordeal. The persona, Emerson's apologist (somewhat like Plato's Socrates) throughout the essay, harnesses the chaos of fate neither by attacking fate nor by declaring an abstract freedom to end all fate but by returning us to the heart of Emerson's argument. That argument acknowledges the transforming power of the mind awake and loyal to its chief necessity, metamorphosis—"a Law which is not intelligent but intelligence." The first three sentences of "Fate" raise the omens of chance, coincidence, and random happening repectively, a remarkably organized way of introducing chaos. The persona responds to the implications of a capricious cosmos with a question that invites both an honest admission of the terror of life and a shaping of it. Deliberately he dips into blacker and blacker ink, quite aware, as we realize later, that he will not fall into the inkpot.

The Emerson of the 1840s and '50s continues to draw remarkably diverse responses from the scholars. "Having abandoned the ministry in 1832," writes Richard Poirier, "Emerson invented the ideal type of self-expressive man who supplies the titles of some of his essays—The Scholar, Representative Man, The Poet. . . . Rejecting as explicitly as he does all institutionalized allegiances, he is forced to claim a place and function for himself almost wholly through his style."[29] On this the major Emerson scholars since the late 1950s have agreed. Disagreements concern the nature of the "self-expressive man," how this man is made present "through his style" and whether that style implicates the culture to any extent.

Among Stephen Whicher's several reconsiderations, briefly detailed in his "Introduction" to his Emerson anthology of 1957, is the observation that as Emerson's "art matured and he found his proper method he became more overtly dramatic. Even *Nature,* where he is least himself, rises to the words of the 'Orphic poet' at the end. In the 1840's he commonly assigned his ideas to appropriate type-characters: the Conservative, the Transcendentalist, the Poet, the Skeptic, and so on. The later essays, too, are sprinkled with imaginary *alter egos* who speak his thoughts for him. Again and again, even when no speaker is named, we find that he has assumed a dramatic personality."[30] Adhering to Whicher's biographical profile of Emerson, Jonathan Bishop nevertheless sees in the later writings a diminution of vitality in what he terms the "experimental self."[31] Lawrence Buell, who values highest among Emerson's personae the universal and exemplary voice, suggests that, in the "early essays, the speaker is primarily an experiencer of the holy, ready to take on the protean manifestations of the soul in nature—to make himself equal to every relation—and to deny them all, too, if the spirit demands.

The later speaker, by contrast, is eminently an observer, experimental in the sense of testing out all possibilities but embracing none." In the later work the resonant universal persona "largely dwindles away." Instead, the "voice of private opinion is used more and more; the essays become more anecdotal; the speaker seems increasingly ready to speak off the top of his head."[32]

In the light of the divergent views a recently published statement is doubly instructive, as a partial explanation of the range of opinion and as a notable alternative to all of these opinions: "Given Emerson's enormous tonal complexity, it is remarkable that so few of the books and articles written about him even pause to consider the subject. . . . Ever since Lowell's characterization of Emerson as a 'Plotinus-Montaigne,' half gold mist, half shrewd wit, critics have tended to assume that Emerson had only two workable tones—the oracular and the Yankee—and that everything not obviously witty must be taken as transcendental."[33]

Emerson himself is the *source* of the problem of reading and hearing him. There are several Emersons and many different personae when one begins to add up the later works. The *problem,* however, lies with us as scholars, whose tendency has been to make strict selections. In "Art" one cannot help but attend carefully to the following passage:

The artist who is to produce a work which is to be admired, not by his friends or his towns-people or his contemporaries, but by all men, and which is to be more beautiful to the eye in proportion to its culture, must disindividualize himself, and be a man of no party and no manner and no age, but one through whom the soul of all men circulates as the common air through his lungs. (*W,* VII, 48)

This passage exemplifies the presiding voice of the essay, a piece Emerson first published in *The Dial* in 1841. Most generalizations about Emerson's development to the contrary, his earlier essay on "Art," published in *Essays: First Series,* exhibits less of the universal, exemplary voice and vision in which individual wealth and commonwealth are synonymous. This is not to say that the second essay on "Art" typifies Emerson's work of the early '40s. The private as well as discreetly confessional voice of "Experience" is already evident in essays such as "Heroism" (lecture version 1837–38), "Self-Reliance" (1839), and "Friendship" (1841). Yet, in these essays, as in "Experience," the frankly honest but intermittent autobiographical touches are part of a game of checks and balances, objection and counterobjection, denial, affirmation, and qualification, in short, a literary ploy as well as a discreetly measured disclosure of the interdependence of Emerson's skeptical, cynical, and affirmative tendencies. One engages a similar persona in "Works and Days" and "Fate," in each of which the persona has one overriding purpose—to establish an aesthetics of control. The essays use this purpose as means to their end—to safeguard and discipline the act of building house and world, acts that require the builder to be at the top of his condition.

The economy of Emerson's major works in the 1840s and '50s is his maturest answer to utopian experiments and their failures, to the politics of the abolitionists and the proslavery constituencies, to Thoreau's lectures on why he went to Walden Pond, to the paucity of political and cultural leaders in the 1840s and 50s, to the growing enthrallment of young America by inventions and popular science, to an American literature under the aegis of the past, to a naïve transcendentalism attributed to him by impatient, intolerant, or intellectually careless contemporaries, and to the necessitarianism that many of our own contemporaries (especially those who still keenly feel the passing of youthful romanticism) associate with the later Emerson.

"An expense of ends to means is fate," the essay "Fate" declares in one of its elementary and profound observations. This fate is nothing less than a life, art, and a readership victimized by their materials. Aesthetics of control, in contrast, combine vital mind and proper economy, a working equilibrium between concentration and permutation, a constantly shifting balance of power and form, and, above all, the courage of the artist to build not only his house but also a world.

Notes

Preface

1. Ralph B. Perry, *The Thought and Character of William James*, 2 vols. (Boston: Little, Brown, 1935), I, 100–1.
2. "The American Metamorphosis," *Emerson: Prophecy, Metamorphosis, and Influence,* ed. David Levin (New York: Columbia University Press, 1975), p. 31.

1. Man Thinking: Emerson's Epistemology

1. *Emerson on the Soul* (Cambridge: Harvard University Press, 1964), p. 221.
2. See part 1 of ibid.
3. Ibid., p. 28. Bishop's terminology for Emerson's instinct— "organic faculty"—is not the best, since Emerson emphasizes a special kind of life, not faculty. Bishop's discussion of the organic dimension of consciousness, however, impressively introduces us to a crucial aspect of Emerson. If the word "faculty" creates problems, so does the psychological language of the unconscious and pre-conscious when applied to Emerson's organicism. The layman popularly conceives of these dark states as a repository within the self, not an instinctive action.
4. In this respect, Emerson's "The Poet" is particularly illuminating. See the discussion of "The Poet" and Emerson's poetry in chapter 6.
5. Occasionally, however, Emerson complained about a lack or excess of animal instincts. Concern over excessive sensuousness appears to underlie his declaration in the journals that "Order & self control are the 'melodies' which I should use to mitigate & tranquillize the ferocity of my Animal and foreign elements" (*JMN*, VII, 425).

6. Bishop, p. 57.
7. The "Language" chapter of *Nature* is perhaps the best statement on this subject.
8. Bishop, pp. 57–58.
9. Ibid.
10. "Introduction," *Selections from Ralph Waldo Emerson* (Boston: Houghton Mifflin, 1957), pp. xviii–xix.
11. Vivian Hopkins, *Spires of Form: A Study of Emerson's Aesthetic Theory* (Cambridge: Harvard University Press, 1951), p. 130.

2. The Artist: Metamorphosis and Metaphor

1. (Philadelphia: University of Pennsylvania Press, 1953), p. 52.
2. "Introduction," *Selections from Ralph Waldo Emerson*, pp. xviii–xix.
3. "Thoughts on Art," *The Dial* 1 (January 1841): 368.
4. (London: W. Strahan, T. Cadell, and W. Creech, 1783), I, 300. See pp. 295–317 for the lecture on "Metaphor." The first American edition of Blair's *Lectures* appeared in 1813.
5. "Three Academic Pieces" in *The Necessary Angel* (New York: Alfred A. Knopf, 1951).
6. Bishop, *Emerson on the Soul*, p. 188.
7. *Emerson's Angle of Vision* (Cambridge: Harvard University Press, 1952), p. 30.
8. "Ralph Waldo Emerson," *Masters of American Literature*, ed. Leon Edel, Thomas H. Johnson, Sherman Paul, and Claude Simpson (Boston: Houghton Mifflin, 1959), I, 269.
9. Precise dates cannot be ascertained for many of these essays. "Literature" and "Fate" belong to the early 1850s; "Works and Days" was first delivered in 1857; "Thoreau" was drafted in 1862 in the two months following Thoreau's death and funeral; "Fortune of the Republic" was composed in 1863 and revised and published as an independent essay in booklet form after the war; "Poetry and Imagination" grew out of several stages of work in the 1840s, '50s, and '60s, but was first delivered as a lecture (in two parts) in 1872.
10. Originally Cabot, Edward Emerson, and Ellen Emerson collaborated in sorting out, editing, and publishing Emerson's publishable literary remains. Eventually Ellen was separated from this work; the production of volumes VIII, X, XI, and XII for the 1884 edition of the *Complete Works* was Cabot's and Edward Emerson's doing. Both had a hand in compiling *Nat-*

ural History of Intellect, but Cabot was the principal editor of the essays that gave the volume its title. What is not known is how complete these texts were at Emerson's death and, if relatively complete, whether Cabot was at least partially responsible for their content. We know, for instance, that he pulled together Emerson's one-hundredth Concord Lyceum lecture, a task much too difficult for the senile Emerson. The essays on the intellect, however, had been delivered as lectures by Emerson on more than one occasion and in more than one version.

11. (Knoxville: The University of Tennessee Press, 1978), pp. ix–xii.
12. Ralph L. Rusk, *The Life of Ralph Waldo Emerson* (New York: Columbia University Press, 1949), pp. 278–79.
13. *Emerson on the Soul,* especially part 2.
14. "Introduction," *Essays and Essays: Second Series* (Columbus: Charles E. Merrill, 1969), pp. vii, ix, xi, x–xi.
15. *The Slender Human Word,* pp. x–xi.

3. Technology and Science: The Science of Power

1. *Technics and Civilization* (New York: Harcourt, Brace, 1934), pp. 182–85; *The Myth of the Machine* (New York: Harcourt, Brace and World, 1967), chapters 1 and 2.
2. For an excellent survey see Leo Marx, *The Machine in the Garden* (New York: Oxford University Press, 1964), chapters 4 and 5.
3. Particularly in "Signs of the Times" (1829) and somewhat more tangentially in "Characteristics" (1831). Materialistic and mechanistic considerations must be integrated into a larger, more authoritative consideration, the moral-aesthetic economy of individual man. This assessment extended to science also. As Carlyle noted in a letter to Emerson, science is "falsely so called" unless it is personal and moral (*CEC,* 573).
4. The subject has rarely been treated in American scholarship, and recently hardly at all. Earlier studies that bear directly or indirectly on the subject are: H. H. Clark, "Emerson and Science," *Philological Quarterly* 10 (1931); Frederick Conner, *Cosmic Optimism* (Gainesville: University of Florida Press, 1949); Sherman Paul, *Emerson's Angle of Vision;* Philip Nicoloff, *Emerson on Race and History* (New York: Columbia University Press, 1961); Leo Marx, *The Machine in the Garden;* Jonathan

Bishop, *Emerson on the Soul*; Michael Cowan, *City of the West: Emerson, America, and Urban Metaphor* (New Haven: Yale University Press, 1967). Clark and Nicoloff deal with the issue of science, Marx analyzes Emerson's views on the machine, Conner is concerned with Emerson's shift to an evolutionary and dynamic conception of nature, Paul and Bishop with Emerson's understanding of mental action (and how, according to him, investigation, discovery, invention, and philosophizing are an intellectual necessity), Cowan with Emerson's attitude toward nineteenth-century American civilization in general. The pioneering essay by Clark is subsumed by subsequent investigations, Nicoloff's treatment is most useful in identifying influences on Emerson and weakest in laying out Emerson's own view, and Marx's brilliant discussion tends to sacrifice Emerson's distinctive view to the larger scheme of *The Machine in the Garden*.

5. Marx should have included Oliver Wendell Holmes and Whitman with Emerson as exceptions to the prevailing attitude of American writers toward the machine.

6. "The Present Age," *The Works of William Ellery Channing, D. D.* (Boston: G. G. Channing, 1849), VI, 152.

7. Although Bentham used the term "technology," he did so in referring to a handbook of technical terms or a treatise on "technics." Technics was the nineteenth-century term for our "technology."

8. *The Myth of the Machine*, p. 9.

9. The first formal engineering degree programs created in U.S. institutions of higher learning were: Harvard (1847), Yale (1850), several state universities in the 1850s.

10. *The Machine in the Garden*, pp. 234–42; *City of the West*, pp. 57–72; *Emerson's Angle of Vision*, pp. 224–28. For Nicoloff the most revelatory material on Emerson's attitude toward science are the journals for the years when *English Traits* and *The Conduct of Life* were in preparation (*Emerson on Race and History*, p. 102). Since "Works and Days" mines much of this material from the journals and shapes it into a sustained and reasoned argument, it is unfortunate that Nicoloff's concentration on *English Traits* did not permit him to incorporate "Works and Days" into his discussion.

11. Friedrich Klemm, *A History of Western Technology* (Cambridge: M. I. T. Press, 1964), p. 326.

12. John B. Rae, "The Invention of Invention," *Technology in Western Civilization*, ed. Melvin Kranzberg and Carroll Pursell

(New York: Oxford University Press, 1967), I, 331. The best-known popular studies of technology and invention in the context of American cultural history are those of Roger Burlingame: *March of the Iron Men* (New York: Scribner's, 1940); *Inventors Behind the Inventor* (New York: Harcourt, Brace, 1947); *Backgrounds of Power* (New York: Scribner's, 1949); *Machines that Built America* (New York: Harcourt, Brace, 1953).

13. Emerson's view here is virtually identical with T. H. Huxley's position some years later against the sovereignty of blind process and in favor of the human reorganization of the environment for the sake of harmonious existence; cf. esp. Huxley's "Prolegomena" to *Evolution and Ethics.*

14. *The Machine in the Garden,* p. 236.

15. *Technology in Western Civilization,* I, 728.

16. *The Myth of the Machine,* p. 293.

17. *The Machine in the Garden,* pp. 232, 23. To be sure, there were transcendentalist friends of Emerson who somewhat fit Marx's characterization of American pastoralism; for examples, Thoreau, Bronson Alcott, Marston Watson, and perhaps Jones Very. But not Emerson. In his notes of Emerson's thoughts and sayings, Ellery Channing the younger reports Emerson to have said of the rural world: "It was well to come out of the city to admire the beauties of the world, but to be continually here, to be present at the baking of the Johnny-cake was not so interesting." "Channing-Emerson Notebook," Pierpont Morgan Library, NNPM MA 609; quoted with permission of the Pierpont Morgan Library.

18. Of these, Newton is cited most frequently. For a discussion of what Newton meant to Emerson see Bishop's *Emerson on the Soul,* pp. 41, 42, 52.

19. I have found several studies and collections helpful in creating the context in which Emerson formulated his views on science: *Correspondence between Spencer Fullerton Baird and Louis Agassiz,* ed. Elmer C. Herber (Washington, D.C.: Smithsonian Institution, 1963); Charles Gillespie, *The Edge of Objectivity* (Princeton: Princeton University Press, 1960); Edward Lurie, *Nature and the American Mind: Louis Agassiz and the Culture of Science* (New York: Science History Publications, 1974); Harold Sharlin, *The Convergent Century: The Unification of Science in the Nineteenth Century* (New York: Abelard-Schuman, 1966); Charles Singer, *A Short History of Scientific Ideas to 1900* (New York: Oxford University Press, 1959).

20. *J,* IX, 498; X, 33, 70–71, 91, 173, 189–90.

21. See my "Emerson and the Civil War," *JEGP* 71 (November 1972): 502–513.
22. *Letters of Henry Adams,* ed. Worthington Chauncey Ford, II (Boston and New York: Houghton Mifflin, 1938), p. 369.
23. *Ralph Waldo Emerson: New Appraisals,* ed. Leonard Neufeldt (Hartford: Transcendental Books, 1973), pp. 6–20.

4. Daniel Webster as Representative Man

1. *Life of Henry Wadsworth Longfellow,* ed. Samuel Longfellow (Boston: Houghton, Mifflin, 1891), II, 193.
2. Mrs. Peabody, mother of the famous sisters and mother-in-law of one of Webster's political adversaries, Horace Mann, reacted to Webster's death without the slightest sympathy: "God took care of Mr. Webster." Louise Hall Tharp, *The Peabody Sisters of Salem* (Boston: Little, Brown, 1950), p. 221. Her harsh judgment of Webster's conduct, although predictable, is also surprising in that her daughter Sophia (Hawthorne's wife) was named after an ancestor only a few generations removed who had been born and reared an illegitimate daughter, the result of a passionate affair between Elizabeth Palmer and the tall, handsome American dramatist of the late eighteenth century, whom Dimmesdale physically resembles. Apparently Sophia was familiar with this family secret, and she must have found it important enough to share with her husband in all its detail. I am grateful to Professor Margaret Neussendorfer for apprising me of this major source for Hawthorne's *Scarlet Letter.* This information is documented in the Peabody Papers Professor Neussendorfer has investigated in preparing her biography of Elizabeth Peabody.
3. An illuminating article on Emerson's intellectual and emotional responses to the fugitive slave debates of the early 1850s and his ambivalence toward Webster at this time is John C. Broderick, "Emerson and Moorfield Storey: A Lost Journal Found," *American Literature* 38 (May 1966): 177–86.
4. *JMN,* IV, 235. Other names surrounding Webster on Emerson's recurrent lists of worthies include Homer, Pericles, Michelangelo, More, Sidney, Handel, Swedenborg, Goethe, Wordsworth, Coleridge, Byron, Carlyle, Tennyson, Canning, Lafayette, Franklin, Channing, Greenough, Alcott, Thoreau, Lowell, Holmes, Samson Reed, Bancroft, Hudson, Bering, and Parry.

5. *JMN,* VII, 198. For typical examples of more general praise see *JMN,* IV, 21, 262, 317; XII, 39–40; V, 483; *RL,* II, 428–29.

6. In the interest of domestic egalitarianism, rational discipline, charitable patronage, and intellectual sharing, Emerson hoped to bring into the family the penniless Alcotts and for a brief time sought unsuccessfully to make the maid a member of the family at the diningroom table.

7. Whicher, *Freedom and Fate;* Bishop, *Emerson on the Soul;* Quentin Anderson, *The Imperial Self* (New York: Alfred Knopf, 1971); Harold Bloom in a number of recent articles and books, most notably *The Anxiety of Influence* (New York: Oxford University Press, 1973), *A Map of Misreading* (New York: Oxford University Press, 1975), and *Figures of Capable Imagination* (New York: Seabury Press, 1976); R. A. Yoder, *Emerson and the Orphic Poet in America* (Berkeley: University of California Press, 1978).

8. To be sure, the journals of 1844–52 do not turn silent on Webster's defects (see *JMN,* IX, 90–91, 357, 380; X, 149; the tirades in XI against Webster and the Fugitive Slave Law; XIII, 63, 72, 82, 88, 109, 110). But his narrowing sympathies continued to allow for Webster's greatness (*JMN,* IX, 237, 248, 360, 373, 374, 389; X, 40, 393–94; XI, 121, 217, 250, 331; XII, 415; XIII, 60–61, 111–12; *RL,* III, 424). In *JMN,* XIV (years 1854–61), the majority of references recall Webster's moral failure on slavery. Still, he appears in a list of luminaries (p. 285).

9. *Journal,* vols. VII–XX of *The Writings of Henry David Thoreau* and also numbered independently from I–XIV, which is the numbering I adopt (Boston: Houghton Mifflin, 1906), I, 338; hereafter cited as Thoreau *Journal.* The *Correspondence of Henry David Thoreau,* ed. Walter Harding and Carl Bode (New York: New York University Press, 1958), p. 135; "Herald of Freedom," *Dial* 4 (April 1844): 511. The journal passage suggests the possibility that Thoreau knew and believed the story (probably apocryphal) of Webster's Indian blood, a story which, George Hendrick surmises, was circulated by Webster's political enemies. If Thoreau accepted the story, he regarded the ancestry as desirable. See *Remembrances of Concord and the Thoreaus,* ed. George Hendrick (Urbana: University of Illinois Press, 1977), pp. 33–34.

10. The first draft includes the following: "We have heard a few, a very few, good political speakers—Webster & Everett—who afforded us the pleasure of larger intellectual (conception—)

strength and acuteness—of soldier like steadiness and resolution." NNPM MA 1303; quoted with the permission of the Pierpont Morgan Library. Within a day or so after drafting this initial text, Thoreau heavily revised it, canceling, among other items, any statements or allusions that deflected from Phillips or diminished him, including the comment on Webster and Everett.

11. See *Reform papers*, ed. Wendell Glick, *The Writings of Henry D. Thoreau* (Princeton: Princeton University Press, 1973), pp. 86–88.

12. Pp. 87–88.

13. Walden, ed. J. Lyndon Shanley, *The Writings of Henry D. Thoreau* (Princeton: Princeton University Press, 1971), p. 232. Compare Thoreau, *Journal*, III, 209–12. For the history and content of versions of the *Walden* ms., see the *Walden* papers at the Huntington Library, CSmH HM 924, and Shanley, *The Making of "Walden"* (Chicago: University of Chicago Press, 1957).

14. *Reform Papers*, p. 97.

15. NNPM 1302, Thoreau notebook #6, Pierpont Morgan #XII; quoted with the permission of the Pierpont Morgan Library. Compare Thoreau *Journal*, II, 351. The missing material was deliberately omitted. Very likely Houghton, Mifflin and Company, the successor to Ticknor and Fields, and not Torrey and Allen, the *Journal* editors, or Sanborn's advice to them, were responsible for the suppression of Charles Emerson's story, in part, perhaps, out of Ticknor's regard for Webster, which survived several generations, but also in part, perhaps, because George Ticknor's nephew George Ticknor Curtis had written the authorized biography of Webster, the two-volume *Life of Daniel Webster.* Propriety and moral concern for the public and Thoreau's legacy, too, may have influenced the decision of publishers and editors.

16. NNPM MA 1302, Thoreau notebook #6, Pierpont Morgan Library; quoted with permission.

17. The possibility of indirect self-revelation seems to escape Thoreau entirely. More than one account by friends and acquaintances, however, attributes similar behavior to Thoreau. Horace Hosmer, for example, recalls how his brother Benjamin walked seven miles to visit Thoreau at Walden only to hear from Thoreau that he had no time for friendship. See *Remembrances*, ed. Hendrick, p. 14.

18. See *Walden* papers "D" and "E," CSmH HM 924, Huntington Library.
19. *Walden* (Princeton), p. 165.
20. P. 166.
21. P. 164.
22. P. 82.
23. NNPM MA 1302, Thoreau notebook #23, Pierpont Morgan #XXIX; quoted with permission. For the entry omitted by the journal editors, compare *The Maine Woods,* ed. Joseph Moldenhauer, *The Writings of Henry D. Thoreau* (Princeton: Princeton University Press, 1972), pp. 252–53. For other entries on Webster see Thoreau *Journal,* VII, 465, and IX, 261–62.
24. See Sherman Paul, *The Shores of America* (Urbana: University of Illinois Press, 1958), ch. 1 for a fuller discussion on this point.
25. The fullest examination of this subject is still Nicoloff, *Emerson on Race and History,* especially chapters 5, 7, and 9.
26. Franklin Sanborn, *Henry D. Thoreau* (Boston: Houghton, Mifflin, 1899), pp. 18–19. In the preceding pages (13–17), Sanborn speculates on the love affair between Louisa Dunbar and Webster, a relationship to which she owed her Christian conversion.

5. Thoreau and the Failure of the Ideal

1. See the *Walden* papers, Huntington Library, CSmH HM 924 ("A"), and Shanley, *The Making of "Walden,"* p. 143.
2. *Walden* (Princeton), p. 91.
3. The Houghton Library of Harvard University, MH bMS Am 1280.212; quoted with permission.
4. "The Succession of Forest Trees," "Walking," "Autumnal Tints," "Wild Apples," "Night and Moonlight," and more than a thousand manuscript pages for the unfinished "Wild Fruits," "The Dispersion of Seeds," and "The Fall of the Leaf." I wish to thank Thomas Blanding, editor of *Excursions* in *The Writings of Henry D. Thoreau* for his willingness to discuss with me the nature writings of Thoreau's late years.
5. *Walden* (Princeton), p. 17.
6. The concluding paragraphs of "Winter Visitors" were added as late as 1853. As these paragraphs and the entries in Thoreau's journal for this period reveal, the relationship had not improved. Otherwise Thoreau would not have slighted

Emerson in *Walden* while treating both Alcott and Channing generously and without ambivalence.

7. Regarding Thoreau's attitude toward "colleges," Emerson undoubtedly recalled how he had once boasted that Harvard College offered most of the branches of learning only to produce the retort from Thoreau, "Yes, indeed, all the branches and none of the roots." John Albee, *Remembrances of Emerson* (New York: Robert Grier Cooke, 1903), p. 33. Emerson is not always accurate in his biographical notations on Thoreau. For example, we would want to correct his observations concerning Thoreau's teaching experience, the date of Thoreau's imprisonment, his description of Thoreau's attitude toward surveying, the unqualified assertion that Thoreau did not write if shut up in the house, and his claim that Thoreau's early death had been unexpected (one suspects, with some surprise, an unawareness of Thoreau's long history of acute bronchial attacks and pulmonary infections). However well Emerson knew Thoreau, biography is clearly secondary here to the profiling and assessment of a colleague who has died young without acquitting his debt to the commonwealth.

8. Whether Emerson actually uttered to the funeral audience this statement about not liking Thoreau cannot be determined. The funeral oration was briefer and undoubtedly somewhat less critical in tone than the essay version he published three months later in the *Atlantic Monthly*. When Emerson began to prepare the text for the *Atlantic Monthly*, he revised and expanded it more than he had expected to, drawing heavily on his journals from as early as 1843, the time when he had begun to record unfavorable observations about Thoreau. Several of the most favorable anecdotes and ideas in the published text came not from Emerson's journals but out of Channing's notebook of transcriptions from Thoreau's journal. A thoroughly reliable edition of Emerson's "Thoreau" based on the printer's copy of Emerson's working manuscript has recently been prepared and published. See Joel Myerson, "Emerson's 'Thoreau': A New Edition from Manuscript," *Studies in the American Renaissance* (Boston: Twayne), 1979 annual, pp. 17–92. Emerson's manuscript, housed at the Huntington Library (CSmH HM 187), is correctly identified by Myerson as a working copy for Emerson and the printer. Ten years ago I conjectured incorrectly that it was to be identified more closely with the funeral oration than with the published text.

9. In this respect the first version of paragraph 36 in Emerson's manuscript takes on added interest. Initially Emerson wrote, "But these foibles real or apparent vanish very fast in every recollection." Why he deleted this statement is not clear, but there is evidence in the published text and in the cancellations and revisions in the working manuscript that many of these foibles lingered in Emerson's memory. The text of the manuscript notebook at the Huntington shows revisions made in several stages. Most of these revisions indicate an effort to prepare a text appropriate for a reading audience and in keeping with a view of Thoreau that emerges from Emerson's journals. The manuscript is quoted here with the permission of the Huntington Library.

10. *Consciousness in Concord,* ed. Perry Miller (Boston: Houghton Mifflin, 1958), p. 162.

11. CSmH HM 187.

12. Thoreau began to admit much the same in the 1850s. See, for instance, his *Journal,* II, 98, 143; III, 146, 262, 400; VI, 165.

6. Metamorphosis of the Image: Emerson and Poetry

1. *Emerson and Literary Change* (Cambridge: Harvard University Press, 1978), p. 2.

2. This view is at odds with the continuing popularity of F. O. Matthiessen's position that one "can hardly assess Emerson's work in the light of his theory of language and art, since there is such disproportion between this theory and any practice of it." *American Renaissance* (New York: Oxford University Press, 1941), p. 5.

3. *Emerson as Poet* (Princeton: Princeton University Press, 1974), chapter 1.

4. As revealing as the essentially Coleridgean context for the Swedenborgian allusions in *Nature* are journal entries such as *JMN,* IV, 92, 288, 317–18, 347, 348, 354–55, and V, 7, 48, 79, 115–19, 180. See also Kenneth W. Cameron, *Emerson The Essayist* (Raleigh: Thistle Press, 1945), I, 247–52.

5. Porter, p. 3. Other important studies of Emerson's poetry and poetics are: Frank T. Thompson, "Emerson's Theory and Practice of Poetry," *PMLA* 42 (December 1928): 1170–84; Carl F. Strauch, "The Mind's Voice: Emerson's Poetic Styles," *Emerson Society Quarterly* 60 o.s. (Summer 1970): 43–59; Michael Cowan, "The Loving Proteus: Metamorphosis in Emerson's Poetry," *American Transcendental Quarterly* 25

(Winter 1975): 11–22; Albert Gelpi, "Emerson: The Paradox of Organic Form," in *Emerson: Prophecy, Metamorphosis, and Influence*, ed. David Levin (New York: Columbia University Press, 1975), pp. 149–70; Hyatt Waggoner, *Emerson as Poet*; and Richard Yoder, *Emerson and the Orphic Poet in America*.

6. To paraphrase Porter, in the poet's ability to see with unmistakable reference to both world and self, these two are reconciled and the world yields its meaning (p. 3). Surprisingly, however, he writes of "The Snow-Storm" that "Emerson's deliverance schema presides over the poem, threatening to exclude a whole contingent world." In his view, the "structural formula" pretty much overwhelms an empirical taking-hold of experience (p. 37). Porter has brought back in a new and interesting guise the old argument that some of Emerson's best-known pieces are known by their generous power and deficient form. Less surprising is Stephen Whicher's romantically charged observation that "The Snow-Storm" is not "the natural or organic poem he described in 'The Poet.' . . . The bardic poem should be a kind of electrical circuit whereby disconnected men could be reunited for a pulse or two with the living truth." *Selections from Ralph Waldo Emerson*, pp. 408–9. Deborah Brassard's research paper on Emerson in one of my graduate courses has been useful in clarifying several image transformations in "The Snow-Storm."

7. *Wordsworth's Poetry: 1787–1814* (New Haven: Yale University Press, 1964).

8. Yoder, *Emerson*, p. 53.

9. For more than a century now "The Sphinx" has produced scholarly uneasiness and apologies, the strongest support found in the view that the poem has something to do with the process of creating art. We continue to be tantalized by the poem's fate in the nineteenth century: "Emerson's contemporaries found the poem impenetrable," and Emerson's son removed it from its lead-off position in the volume of poetry (Porter, p. 80).

10. Harold Bloom, "Bacchus and Merlin: The Dialectic of Romantic Poetry in America," *Southern Review* 7 n.s. (January 1971): 152.

11. Yoder, p. 108.

12. Although *The Bridge* impresses us with its dynamic flow of images, Crane's critical comments on poetry and on his own work indicate that he never fully appreciated the logic of permutation in his work, that he hoped, rather, for some

grand synthesis. Herein, perhaps, lies the explanation for his tendency to veer away from the flow of his images into moments of strained surrealism and arbitrary transformations that act like points without filiation and with no return.

13. Lawrence Buell, *Literary Transcendentalism* (Ithaca: Cornell University Press, 1973), pp. 182–83. An earlier but equally instructive reading is Thomas Whitaker's "The Riddle of Emerson's 'Sphinx,'" *American Literature* 27 (May 1955): 179–95, for which Buell offers both support and corrective.
14. Whicher, *Selections from Ralph Waldo Emerson,* pp. 407–8.
15. Buell, p. 175.
16. Charles Feidelson, Jr., *Symbolism and American Literature* (Chicago: University of Chicago Press, 1953), p. 123.
17. Porter, p. 80.
18. Emerson's understanding of the wide-ranging implications of such a doctrine exceeded Whitman's, which is probably why he considered Whitman's use of the catalogue rather elementary. See Edward Emerson, *Emerson in Concord* (Boston: Houghton, Mifflin, 1889), p. 228n.
19. Feidelson, p. 123.
20. In "The Poet" Emerson argues that every "word was at first a stroke of genius. The etymologist finds the deadest word to have been once a brilliant picture" (*W*, III, 22). A favorite Emerson ploy is to drive words back to their original sense, which he does with "hypocrite," the Greek word for actor, the principal behind the mask and who signifies meaning behind and by means of the mask. The speaker in "Days" should have known that the "hypocritic Days" are and yet are not the "Day."
21. Porter, pp. 128, 98. Matthiessen's view is similar. For him the poem is mixed darkly with the Tantalus myth (pp. 60–61). A contrasting interpretation, Waggoner's, sees "Days" "to mean that our days are often uninspired but might well be filled with meaning if we dared to follow our morning wishes" (p. 173), a view in keeping with most of Emerson's observations on the poet.
22. Buell, p. 183.

7. Tendencies, Forms, and Personae in *Nature*

1. Régis Michaud, *Emerson the Enraptured Yankee,* trans. George Boas (New York: Harper and Brothers, 1930), p. 133.
2. *Spirit of American Literature* (New York: Boni and Liveright, 1913), p. 71.

3. "Emerson the Oriental," *University of California Chronicle* 30 (July 1928): 271.
4. Barbara Packer, "The Instructed Eye: Emerson's Cosmogony in 'Prospects,' " in *Emerson's 'Nature': Origin, Growth, Meaning,* ed. Merton Sealts and Alfred Ferguson (Carbondale: Southern Illinois University Press, 1979), pp. 209–21.
5. William T. Harris, "Emerson's Philosophy of Nature," in *The Genius and Character of Emerson,* ed. Franklin Sanborn (Boston and New York: Houghton, Mifflin, 1898), pp. 339–64; Kenneth Burke, "I, Eye, Ay—Emerson's Early Essay 'Nature,' " in *Transcendentalism and its Legacy,* ed. Myron Simon and Thornton Parsons (Ann Arbor: The University of Michigan Press, 1966), pp. 3–24; Richard Lee Francis, "The Architectonics of Emerson's *Nature,*" *American Quarterly* 19 (Spring 1967): 39–52; Lawrence Buell, "First Person Superlative: The Speaker in Emerson's Essays," in *Emerson's Relevance Today,* ed. Eric Carlson and J. Lasley Dameron (Hartford: Transcendental Books, 1971), pp. 28–35; Barry Wood, "The Growth of the Soul: Coleridge's Dialectical Method and the Strategy of Emerson's *Nature,*" *PMLA* 91 (May 1976): 385–97.
6. Buell, "First Person Superlative," p. 30.
7. Henry James, *Notes of A Son and Brother* (New York: Charles Scribner's Sons, 1914), p. 185.
8. Ralph B. Perry, *The Thought and Character of William James,* 2 vols. (Boston: Little, Brown, 1935), I, 97, 96.
9. Lawrence Buell, "Reading Emerson for the Structures: The Coherence of the Essays," *Quarterly Journal of Speech* 57 (February 1972): 61.
10. For a fuller discussion of the start of Emerson's literary career in Concord see Leonard Neufeldt, " 'The Fields of My Fathers' and Emerson's Literary Vocation," *American Transcendental Quarterly* 31 (Summer 1976): 3–9.
11. The metaphor of expanding the warm day may well have an autobiographical resonance. One recalls Emerson's antipathy to cold weather, which lends additional poignancy to the bare common passage.
12. Ralph La Rosa, *Necessary Truths: The Poetics of Emerson's Proverbs,* in *Literary Monographs,* vol. 8 (Madison: The University of Wisconsin Press, 1976), p. 159.
13. Richard Lee Francis, "The Evolution of Emerson's Second 'Nature,' " *Ralph Waldo Emerson: New Appraisals,* p. 33.
14. Richard Lee Francis, "The Architectonics of *Nature,*" p. 42.

15. See Neufeldt, "Fields of My Fathers," for a discussion of Emerson's uses of the past in the "Historical Discourse."
16. Sealts and Ferguson, *Emerson's 'Nature,'* pp. 46–65.
17. Bishop, *Emerson on the Soul,* chapter 1; Buell, "First Person Superlative," p. 31.
18. *The Friend I,* ed. Barbara Rooke, in *The Collected Works of Samuel Taylor Coleridge* (London: Routledge & Kegan Paul, 1969), VI, 40.
19. See Blair's *Lectures on Rhetoric and Belles Lettres,* the first American edition published in 1813. The popularity and wide use of this book in American colleges accounts for the numerous American editions and several different publishers of the text. From 1820 to 1826, for instance, a new American edition appeared each year. The most useful discussion of Blair's influence on Emerson's writing is Sheldon Liebman, "The Development of Emerson's Theory of Rhetoric," *American Literature* 41 (May 1969): 178–206.
20. Buell, "Reading Emerson for the Structures," p. 59.
21. *A World Elsewhere: The Place of Style in American Literature* (New York: Oxford University Press, 1966), pp. 65–66.
22. I am indebted to Professor Jon Lawry, whose discussions with me on transformation in seventeenth-century English poetry helped to identify similarities and differences with respect to transformation in Emerson's *Nature* and several of his poems.
23. Vivian Hopkins, *Spires of Form,* p. 115.
24. *Ralph Waldo Emerson: His Life, Writings, and Philosophy* (Boston: James R. Osgood, 1882), p. 259.
25. Interest in psycho-economic interpretation of Emerson's life has in recent years fostered the argument that Emerson's early-rooted fear of deprivation was a persistent force throughout his life and a principal factor behind his lecturing. The most recent and extensive discussion of Emerson's economic situation is in Esther D. Lister, "Emerson's process of Composition" (doctoral dissertation, University of California, Irvine, 1978), chapter 2. Lister suggests that economic need continued to be a factor in the 1840s, '50s, and beyond, forcing Emerson to supplement a marginal income with lecture fees. Economics were, indeed, a factor; Emerson hoped to become independently wealthy so as to be able to live entirely on his savings and investments. The 1850 census lists him as a wealthy inhabitant of Concord. One does not want to ignore the obvious, however: on the whole Emerson enjoyed lecturing,

and he often enjoyed the travel associated with it.

26. Bishop's chapter on "Tone" in *Emerson on the Soul,* 1964; Poirier's chapter on Emerson in *A World Elsewhere,* 1966; Buell, "First Person Superlative," 1971, and parts of chapter 10 in *Literary Transcendentalism,* 1973; Donald McQuade, "Convergences of Style: A Study of the Affinities between Robert Frost and Ralph Waldo Emerson" (doctoral dissertation, Rutgers, 1972), part 2; Barbara Packer, "Uriel's Cloud: Emerson's Rhetoric," *Georgia Review* 31 (Summer 1977); 322–42.

27. Alfred Reid, "Emerson's Prose Style: An Edge to Goodness," *Emerson Society Quarterly* 60, o.s., part 1 (Summer 1970): 37.

28. *A World Elsewhere,* p. 66.

29. "First Person Superlative," p. 30. Unfortunately, Poirier's vigorous and promising approach to Emerson's texts suffers the liabilities of his conclusion that "Emerson was primarily an essayist and lecturer, seldom choosing to argue alternative positions within a given piece, and he writes the same way, uses the same style for all aspects of experience. . . . His unalterable consistency of tone . . . is perhaps one reason why he *sounds* rather simple to modern readers" (*A World Elsewhere,* pp. 64–65). Although more useful to an understanding of *Nature* than of Emerson's later work, the observation strikes me as misleading on three counts: an overcommitment to the traditional view of a uniform and strictly presiding visionary voice in every sentence and essay, a lack of distinction between the mode in *Nature* and in the essays of the 1840s and '50s, and a misreading of Emerson's low opinion of the novel, a form that supposedly depends on a variety of voices.

30. *Essays in Radical Empiricism* (London: Longman's Green, 1922), p. 238.

31. This, I suggest, is the cardinal problem in one of the most sensitive and illuminating discussions of Emerson to date, Bishop's *Emerson on the Soul.* According to Bishop, the presence of active soul is confirmed only here and there within Emerson's essays, and "one makes a drastic selection to arrive at these" moments (p. 131).

32. Buell, "First Person Superlative," p. 29.

8. Personae and Vision in Later Essays

1. This passage from "The Divinity School Address" disclaims

precisely what the lecture achieved: it took the student audience by storm.

2. "Emerson," *Atlantic Monthly* 94 (December 1904): 741.

3. *Emerson at Home and Abroad* (Boston: James Osgood, 1882), p. 376.

4. In his essay "Character" Emerson defines "reverberation" as latent power or continuing reserve of force. See *W*, III, 89.

5. Some years earlier the widowed Emerson had become infatuated with Lydia Jackson in part because of her familiarity with and zest for Swedenborg. At that time Emerson shared her enthusiasm for Swedenborg. By the early 1840s, however, she had turned from both Swedenborgianism and Emerson's increasingly radical and skeptical transcendentalism to orthodox Christianity.

6. A. W. Plumstead, *JMN*, VII, xv.

7. Oliver Wendell Holmes, one of the few early biographers to admit Emerson's intolerance for pedestrian and narrow people, wrote that "his equanimity . . . was not incapable of being disturbed, and that on rare occasions he could give way to the feeling which showed itself of old in the doom pronounced on the barren fig-tree." *Ralph Waldo Emerson* (Boston: Houghton, Mifflin, 1886), p. 367.

8. Bishop's view of the later Emerson. See *Emerson on the Soul*, pp. 187–215.

9. *Ralph Waldo Emerson*, pp. 414, 133.

10. This is an altered version of Lawrence Buell's suggestive analysis in "Reading Emerson for the Structures," p. 62.

11. William Scheick, *The Slender Human Word*, p. 53.

12. The two most noteworthy examples are Sherman Paul, *Emerson's Angle of Vision*, pp. 98–109, and Albert Tricomi, "The Rhetoric of Aspiring Circularity in Emerson's 'Circles,' " *ESQ: A Journal of the American Renaissance* 18 (Fourth Quarter 1972): 271–83.

13. Packer, "Uriel's Cloud," p. 335.

14. "Emerson's Tragic Sense," in *Emerson: A Collection of Critical Essays*, ed. Milton Konvitz and Stephen Whicher (Englewood Cliffs: Prentice-Hall, 1962), p. 43.

15. *Emerson on the Soul*, p. 195.

16. *Sartor Resartus*, rejected by British publishers, was first published in book form in the United States in 1836, the year Emerson published *Nature*, through Emerson's dogged efforts and under his supervision. He probably had become familiar with the manuscript in 1833 when he visited Carlyle.

17. On this point see Michael Cowan's helpful commentary in his *City of the West: Emerson, America, and Urban Metaphor,* p. 114.
18. Equating the death of young Waldo with the loss of "a beautiful estate" may, as Bishop has suggested, be a sign of diminishing Waldo's death (*Emerson on the Soul,* p. 197). If so, then by Emerson's norms the analogy is evidence of a poised and active soul, not a deadened one. On the other hand, "estate" meant much to Emerson. Throughout the 1840s he worked hard at becoming financially well-to-do. The 1850 U.S. census identified him as one of the few wealthy citizens of Concord. In other words, Emerson may not be stating his loss of a son "as lightly as he might."
19. Cowan, p. 112. Cowan notes, moreover, that Emerson "intermixes the major section on each lord with subsidiary references to other lords."
20. Cowan, p. 113.
21. The similarities in outer structure between *Nature* and "Experience" also include seven major sections leading to the announcement of prospects. In terms of the nature and function of personae, however, the essays are dissimilar.
22. For additional commentary on this point see Leonard Neufeldt, "Emerson and the Civil War," pp. 502–13.
23. "What Is Writing," *Writing Degree Zero and Elements of Semiology,* trans. Annette Lavers and Colin Smith (Boston: Beacon Press, 1970), pp. 16–17.
24. Phyllis Cole, "Emerson, England, and Fate," *Emerson: Prophecy, Metamorphosis, and Influence,* ed. David Levin, p. 92.
25. Catalogues of disasters leave one wondering, as they do in reading Barbara Tuchman's portrait of the Fourteenth Century, how anyone has survived. Putative laws and explanations of history are human diagrams, however, as much as Emerson's profile of fate is his design.
26. Nine paragraphs in "Fate" open with "But," a practice strongly discouraged by rhetoricians and grammarians of Emerson's era. In addition, "but" appears sixteen times as a contrastive in the closing sentence of paragraphs and at least forty times as a contrastive, disjunctive conjunction or as a qualifier within the paragraph. This is not to mention Emerson's use of "yet," "however," "while," colons and semicolons to poise contrasting clauses, and a balancing of sentences against each other in a procession of variance and continual redefinition.
27. In the words of a recently completed dissertation, "To put it most briefly, Emerson's beginnings are climactic and his end-

ings initiative." Also noteworthy is the related observation that "Emerson's essays end by empowering rather than instructing." Gertrude R. Hughes, "The Cost of Confirmation: Emerson After 1842" (doctoral dissertation, Yale University, 1976), pp. 19, 27. Daniel Shea notes that "As these essays finally right themselves, certain phrases make one wish the metamorphosis could run backwards. . . . The total form of these essays, however, redeems individual expressions and embodies the principle by which their dramas of contradiction have been resolved." "The American Metamorphosis," *Emerson: Prophecy, Metamorphosis, and Influence,* pp. 43–44. Despite the resistance of editors, this structural principle has become the mark of some of America's most impressive modern literary artists.

28. Shea, p. 37.
29. *A World Elsewhere,* pp. 63–64.
30. "Introduction," *Selections from Ralph Waldo Emerson,* pp. xx–xxi.
31. *Emerson on the Soul,* p. 130.
32. "First Person Superlative," pp. 34, 33, 32.
33. Barbara Packer, "Uriel's Cloud," p. 325.

Index

Published works by Emerson, except for his journals and letters, cited or discussed in the text are listed at the outset together with edition and volume and with the page references to *The House of Emerson*.

Title Index

Emerson's prose works:
"American Civilization" (*W*, XI), 90; "The American Scholar" (*CW*, I), 43, 55, 81, 89, 105, 133, 156, 173, 204, 222, 231; "Art" (*CW*, II), 95, 241; "Art" (*W*, VII), 43, 241; "Character" (*W*, X), 73, 75, 101, 259n; "Circles" (*CW*, II), 43, 50–51, 131, 156, 205, 207, 210, 213–18, 221, 222, 224; "Civilization" (*W*, VII), 91; *The Conduct of Life* (*W*, VI), 138, 231, 246 n; "Demonology" (*W*, X), 63, 92; "The Divinity School Address" (*CW*, I), 85, 106, 156, 189–90, 201, 204, 208, 219, 231, 238; "Editors' Address" (*W*, XI), 93; "Eloquence" (*W*, VII), 202–3, 219; *English Traits* (*W*, V), 66, 246n; *Essays: First Series* (*CW*, II), 12; *Es-*

says: Second Series (*W*, III), 12, 152; "Experience" (*W*, III), 13, 34, 42, 55, 92, 107, 108, 118, 126, 137, 156, 157, 162, 165, 195, 198, 207, 213–30, 231, 234, 235, 238, 242, 260n; "Fate" (*W*, VI), 66, 73, 75, 132, 162, 163, 165, 231–40, 242, 244 n, 260n; "The Fortune of the Republic" (*W*, XI), 25, 66, 86, 91, 135, 165; "Friendship" (*CW*, II), 106, 208, 242; "Goethe; or, the Writer" (*W*, IV), 95; "Heroism" (*CW*, II), 106, 208, 242; "Historical Discourse at Concord" (*W*, XI), 107, 180, 185, 187; "History" (*CW*, II), 204–5; "Illusions" (*W*, VI), 231; "Inspiration" (*W*, VIII), 57; "Instinct and Inspiration" (*W*, XII), 69; "Intellect" (*CW*,

263

II), 25–44 passim, 49, 91;
"Lectures on the Times"
("Introductory Lecture":
CW, I), 31; "Literature"
(*EL*, II), 23; "Literature"
[Second Lecture] (*EL*, I),
58; "Literature" (*W*, V), 66,
244n; "Martin Luther" (*EL*,
I), 178–80; "The Method of
Nature" (*CW*, I), 45, 47, 63,
184, 206, 207–11, 214;
"Montaigne; or, the Skep-
tic" (*W*, IV), 49, 123–24,
137, 165; *Natural History of
Intellect* (*W*, XII), 66–67;
Nature (*CW*, I), 2, 16, 25, 27,
28, 30, 33, 35, 36, 37, 38, 39,
40–41, 43, 47–65, 80, 85, 86,
87, 91, 96, 97, 102, 105, 107,
135, 143, 147, 153, 155,
156, 164, 169–99, 204, 209,
211, 222, 227, 260n; "Na-
ture" (*Nature*, Chapter I),
63–64, 180–81, 186,
187–88, 193; "Commodity,"
64–65, 193–94; "Beauty,"
65, 173–74, 176, 193; "Language," 65, 147, 174, 176,
193–95, 244n; "Discipline,"
60, 174, 177, 195;
"Idealism," 170–71, 174,
177, 181, 195–96, 234;
"Spirit," 60, 170–71,
174–75, 177, 181, 195–96;
"Prospects," 58–59, 65, 181,
196–97; "Nature" (*W*, III),
86, 91, 93; *Nature, Addresses,
and Lectures* (*CW*, I), 184;
"Nominalist and Realist"
(*W*, III), 225; "The Over-
Soul" (*CW*, II), 214; "Plato;
or, the Philosopher" (*W*,
IV), 56; "The Poet" (*W*, III),

32, 36–37, 41, 42, 43, 44, 66,
102, 144–45, 146, 148, 149,
150, 152, 154, 156, 157,
160, 164, 165–66, 168,
255n; "Poetry and Imagi-
nation" (*W*, VIII), 66, 244n;
"Power" (*W*, VI), 93; "Powers and Laws of Thought"
(*W*, XII), 66–69; "The Present Age" ("Introduction":
EL, III), 47; "Progress of
Culture" (*W*, VIII), 76, 79,
83, 91; "Religion" (*EL*, III),
47; *Representative Men* (*W*,
IV), 49, 51, 104, 109, 110,
153; "Resources" (*W*, VIII),
230; "Samuel Hoar" (*W*, X),
120; "The Scholar" (*W*, X),
91; "Self-Reliance" (*CW*, I),
51, 208, 209, 231, 242; *Society and Solitude* (*W*, VII), 12;
"Spiritual Laws" (*CW*, II),
89, 194, 198, 211–13, 214,
225, 238; "Success" (*W*,
VII), 82, 92, 94; "Swedenborg; or, the Mystic" (*W*,
IV), 206; "Thoreau" (*W*, X),
66, 127–40, 244n, 252n–
253n; "Thoughts on Art"
("Art": *EL* II and *W*, VII),
51; "The Tragic" (*W*, XII),
36; "Uses of Great Men" (*W*,
IV), 16, 36, 46, 49–50, 51,
82, 96, 120–21; "Works and
Days" (*W*, VII), 66, 81,
83–99, 128, 143, 242, 244n,
246n; "Worship" (*W*, VI),
16; "The Young American"
(*CW*, I), 83–84.
Emerson's poems (*W*, IX):
"The Apology," 167;
"Blight," 167; "Brahma,"
159, 167; "Concord

Hymn," 167; "Days," 145, 146, 161–67, 204, 230, 255n; "Each and All," 167; "Eros," 167; "Hamatreya," 167; "Illusions," 167; "Merlin," 167; "Music," 167; "Ode (Inscribed to W. H. Channing)," 299; "Ode to Beauty," 167; "Seashore," 167; "The Snow-Storm," 145, 146, 147–51, 152, 155, 160, 163, 164, 165, 166, 167, 204; "The Sphinx," 14, 34, 56, 145, 146, 152–64, 165, 166, 167, 168, 203, 204, 205, 207, 209, 210, 215, 216, 226, 227, 238; "Terminus," 167; "Threnody," 159, 167; "The Titmouse," 167–68; "Two Rivers," 167; "Uriel," 51, 97, 134–35, 156, 167, 209, 214; "Waldeinsamkeit," 167; "Woodnotes I," 167; "Woodnotes II," 167; "The World-Soul," 167

Name and Subject Index

Abolitionism: Emerson on, 133, 229, 242
Adams, Henry, 90, 98
Aeneas, 165, 180
Agassiz, Louis, 82–83
Alcott, Bronson, 247n; on Emerson, 190; Emerson's view of, 34, 104, 107, 110, 249n; on Webster, 102
Alexander I, of Russia, 92
American Association for the

Advancement of Science, 83
Archimedes, 95
Aristotle, 54, 137, 175
Arkwright, Sir Richard, 86
Art: Emerson's view of, 25, 27, 47–71 passim, 143–68 passim; the artist, 31, 36, 37, 38, 42, 203, 230
Augustine, Saint, 50, 145
Autobiography: Emerson's use of, 186–88, 193–96, 220–22, 224–25, 228–29

Bacon, Francis, 66
Bacchus, 86
Baird, Spencer Fullerton, 82, 83
Bancroft, George, 108
Banta, Martha, 99
Barthes, Roland, 231
Beckett, Samuel, 62, 70
Bentham, Jeremy, 246n
Berkeley, George, 56
Biography: Emerson's view of, 45–46, 47
Biot, Jean Baptiste, 104
Bishop, Jonathan, 12, 25, 69; approach to Emerson's art, 198, 258n; on Emerson and metaphor, 40; Emerson and science, 246n, 247n; Emerson's loss of faith, 218–19, 220–21, 260n; Emerson's route of knowing, 29, 35, 243n; persona in Emerson, 240
Blair, Hugh: on metaphor, 53; popularity in America, 257n; rhetorical classification and *Nature*, 54, 189
Blake, William, 77
Bloom, Harold 153

Bohr, Niels, 17
Bonaparte, Napoleon: Emerson's view of, 92, 104, 109, 111
Broderick, John C., 248n
Brook Farm, 107, 229
Browning, Robert, 61
Bryant, James Cullen, 103, 108
Buell, Lawrence, 12, 189; on Emerson's "Spiritual Laws," 259n; Emerson's "The Sphinx," 255n; persona in Emerson, 192, 240–41
Burke, Edmund, 104, 105
Burlingame, Roger, 247n

Cabot, James Elliot, 67, 244n–245n
Calhoun, John C., 108
Cambridge Platonists, 54
Carlyle, Thomas, 104, 106, 107, 111, 112, 183; on technology and science, 78, 245n; Emerson's early admiration for, 83; *Sartor Resartus* 193; Emerson's "Experience" compared to *Sartor*, 221; Emerson's efforts to publish *Sartor*, 259n
Catalogue technique in art, 153–54, 159–64, 167–68, 204–6, 216
Ceres, 86
Cervantes, Miguel de, 104
Channing, Ellery (poet): Emerson on, 104, 108; on Emerson's view of the rustic, 247n
Channing, William Ellery: Emerson's view of, 106, 107; on science, 80
Choate, Rufus, 110

Clark, Harry Hayden, 245n–246n
Clay, Henry, 108
Coleridge, Samuel Taylor: Emersonian great man, 104; as Emerson's context for Swedenborg, 253n; influence on Emerson's poetics and poetry, 145, 146–47, 151–53, 163, 174; philosophy as trope, 173; as source of Emerson's "Reason," 55; use of past, 188
Commonwealth: Emerson's view of, 51, 75–76, 125, 138–39, 143, 170, 218, 229, 236; role of scholar in, 51, 75–76, 94–96, 101, 126. *See also* Man thinking; Representative man; Self-reliance
Concord, Mass., 13, 102, 103, 107, 110, 116–17, 120, 126, 128, 165, 178, 179, 180, 199
Conner, Frederick, 245n–246n
Conservative: Emerson on, 29–31, 95, 228–30, 234
Conway, Moncure, 202
Cooke, George Willis, 191
Cooper, James Fenimore, 192
Copernicus, Nicolaus, 94, 104
Cowan, Michael: Emerson on technology, 84; on Emerson's "Experience," 226, 227, 260n
Crane, Hart, 154, 254n–255n
Cudworth, Ralph: correspondence, 172; Emerson's source for Plotinus, 175
Curtis, George Ticknor, 250n

Dalton, John, 83, 94
Dana, Richard, Jr., 102, 108

Dante, Alighieri, 104, 151
Davy, John, 82
Dial, The, (1840–44), 107, 160,
241
Dickens, Charles, 66, 192
Dionysius, 26
Dunbar, Louisa, 120, 251n

Eliot, Thomas Stearns, 173;
The Waste Land compared to
Emerson, 62, 77, 204
Emerson, Charles Chauncy
(brother), 114, 250 n
Emerson, Edward Waldo
(son), 67, 158, 244n
Emerson, Ellen Tucker
(daughter), 244n
Emerson, Lydia Jackson (second wife), 107, 259n
Emerson, Ralph Waldo: on
conservatives, 29–31, 95,
228–30, 234; doubts about
American culture, 47–48,
59, 79, 95–96, 101, 107–10,
132–33, 138–39, 199,
228–30, 231–32, 242; on
the novel, 133, 162, 192–93,
258n; on politics, 101,
103–12, 117–21, 127,
132–33, 138–40; scholars
on the Emerson text, 11–18;
on self-reliance, 45, 51,
75–76, 80; on Thoreau,
102, 110, 118, 123–40, 143,
242, 252n–253n; Thoreau
on, 117–19, 121; visit to
Jardin des Plantes, 52, 83,
175, 177. *See also*
Abolitionism; Alcott, Bronson; Art; Carlyle, Thomas;
Coleridge, Samuel Taylor;
Commonwealth; Concord,
Mass.; Goethe, Johann

Wolfgang von; Holmes,
Oliver Wendell, Sr.; James,
Henry, Sr.; Knowledge;
Man thinking; Metamor-
phosis; Metaphor; Persona
in Emerson; Plato; Plotinus;
Poetry and the poet; Repre-
sentative man; Science;
Slavery; Swedenborg,
Emanuel; Technology;
Thoreau, Henry David;
Webster, Daniel; Will
Emerson, Waldo (son), 107,
222–23, 260n
Emerson, William (brother),
125
Everett, Edward, 249n–250n
Exfoliation of thought, 25–27,
31–34, 38–39, 46, 181

Faulkner, William, 63
Feidelson, Charles, 160
Ferguson, Alfred, 84
Fielding, Henry, 192
Fields, James T., 102
Francis, Richard L., 184, 185
Franklin, Benjamin, 95
Frost, Robert, 68, 149
Fruitlands, 107, 229
Fuller, Margaret, 107

Galileo, 225–26
Gay-Lussac, Joseph Louis, 82
Goethe, Johann Wolfgang
von: influence on Emerson,
104, 151–53 1.62; *Faust,* 30,
153, 157–58; *Wilhelm Meister's Lehrjahre,* 153
Gorham, John, 82
Gray, Asa, 82, 83

Hallam, Arthur, 66
Harris, William T., 61

Hartman, Geoffrey, 151
Hawthorne, Nathaniel, 99, 107, 192, 248n
Hawthorne, Sophia Peabody, 248n
Hedge, Frederic Henry, 146
Hegel, Georg Wilhelm, 153, 162
Hendrick, George, 249n
Henry, Joseph, 82, 83
Heraclitus, 48, 61, 65, 152, 175
Hercules, 109
Hesiod, 88
Hill, Isaac, 110
History: Emerson's view of, 45–46, 47, 144
Hoar, Elizabeth, 129
Hoar, Samuel, 120
Holmes, Oliver Wendell, Jr., 102
Holmes, Oliver Wendell, Sr., 102, 212, 246n, 259n
Homer, 104, 106, 151, 213
Hopkins, Vivian, 44, 169
Howe, Peter, 106
Howells, William Dean, 90
Hughes, Gertrude R., 261n
Huxley, Thomas H., 247n

Instinct: incipience of knowing, 25–33, 39, 41
Irving, Washington, 108
Isaiah, 179

Jackson, Charles T., 82
Jamblichus, 146
James, Henry, Jr., 176
James, Henry, Sr., 12, 48, 111, 175–76, 201
Jardin des Plantes: Emerson's visit to, 52, 83, 175, 177
Jesus, 104, 106, 151, 179

Kant, Immanuel, 55, 145, 146, 152, 174
Kepler, Johannes, 83, 94, 104
Knowledge: route of thinking, 25–44; intellect receptive and constructive, 34–38; knowing as fluxional, 42–44. *See also* Exfoliation; Instinct; Language; Metamorphosis; Metaphor; Nature; Reason; Understanding; Undulation

Landor, Walter S., 143–44
Language: relation to knowing, 38–42, 58–60. *See also* "Language" (*Nature*, Emerson's prose works); Metaphor; Nature; Poetry and the poet
Lincoln, Abraham, 120
Linnaeus, Carolus, 95
Lister, Esther D., 257n
Locke, John, 66
Logos: Emerson's view of, 41, 50, 145, 150
Longfellow, Henry Wadsworth, 102
Lowell, Francis Cabot, 82
Lowell, James Russell, 102, 241
Luther, Martin, 178–80

Mackintosh, James, 104
Macy, John, 171
Mann, Horace, 229, 248n
Man thinking, 17, 31, 32; and culture, 45–46, 77, 143–44, 218, 228; and metaphor, 40–41, 75; and metamorphosis, 51–52. *See also* Representative Man; Self-reliance.

Marsh, James, 146
Martineau, Harriet, 78
Marx, Leo: on American
romanticism and technol-
ogy, 79, 246n, 247n; Emerson and pastoralism 93;
Emerson and technology,
84, 246n; technology, 89
Massachusetts Quarterly, 93
Matthiessen, F.O., 253n
Maya, 163
Melville, Herman, 63
Metamorphosis, 17, 26; law of
permutation in nature and
thought, 29, 31, 47–71,
144–69 passim, 170, 174;
and man thinking, 45–46;
in *Nature*, 182–83, 186–96,
199; and poetry, 144–69,
172; and Pyrrhonism,
213–14. *See also* Knowledge;
Language; Man thinking;
Metaphor; Permutation;
Poetry
Metaphor, 17, 144; as concentration and permutation
of nature and thought,
47–71, 170, 174, 194–95; as
incarnation of thinking, 35,
38–41; and poetry, 147,
150, 152, 153–54; relation
to man thinking, 75;
Thoreau's use of, 135–36.
See also Exfoliation; Knowledge; Language; Man
thinking; Metamorphosis;
Poetry and the poet
Michelangelo, 104
Milton, John, 91, 104, 145,
151, 153, 214
Mohammed, 104
Montaigne, Michel Eyquem
de, 104, 152, 153, 162

Mumford, Lewis, 77, 81, 92

National Academy of Sci-
ences, 83
Nature: Emerson's view of,
47–71 passim, 143–68 pas-
sim, 226, 234, 236; en-
dorsement of in *Nature*,
177–82; importance to
knowledge, 25–38; im-
portance to language,
39–41; relation to art, 47–71
passim, 143–68 passim;
Thoreau's relation to,
136–37; Webster's reliance
on, 105. *See also* Instinct;
Jardin des Plantes;
Metamorphosis; Metaphor
New England Patriot, 110
Newton, John, 45, 83, 94, 95,
104, 247n
Nicoloff, Philip, 245n–246n,
251n
Nietzsche, Friedrich Wilhelm,
214
Novel: Emerson on, 133, 162,
192–93, 258n

Otis, Harrison Gray, 110

Packer, Barbara, 215, 241
Palmer, Elizabeth, 248n
Paul, Saint, 215
Paul, Sherman: Emerson on
mental life, 246n; on Emer-
son and technology, 84;
Nature, 62, 169
Peabody, Elizabeth Palmer,
248n
Peabody, Elizabeth Palmer
(mother), 102, 248n
Peckham, Morse, 69–70

Permutation: principle of,
42–44, 47–71 passim, 143–
168 passim. *See also*
Metamorphosis
Persona in Emerson, 56–57,
62, 70–71, 172, 258n; in
Nature, 190–99; in later essays, 201–42
Phillips, Wendell, 250n
Pitt, William, 104
Plato, 54, 56, 61, 65, 104, 209,
239; art and metamor-
phosis, 145, 153; Luther's
Platonism, 178–79; Neo-
platonists, 54; Platonist
tendency in *Nature*, 170–71,
172–77, 181, 185–86,
194–95
Plotinus, 56, 209; Plotinian
tendency in *Nature*, 170–71,
174–77, 181, 185–86, 195
Plumstead, A. W., 207
Plutarch, 104, 151, 213
Poe, Edgar Allan, 70, 99
Poetry and the poet: analysis
of Emerson's poetry,
143–68; Emerson's lexicon,
61, 145–47, 152–55; Emer-
son's view of, 17, 34, 36–37,
41, 49–50, 58, 59–60, 65,
68–69, 143–68 passim, 184,
227. *See also* "The Poet"
(Emerson's prose works)
Poirier, Richard: on persona
in Emerson, 189, 191, 240,
258n
Polis, Joe, 117
Politics: Emerson's view of,
101, 103–12, 117–21, 127,
132–33, 138–40
Porter, David, 144, 165, 254n
Prescott, William Hickling,
108

Reason: Emerson's view of,
36–37, 55–56, 163, 183
Representative man, 17, 75,
101, 143, 218. *See also* Man
thinking; Self-reliance;
Webster, Daniel
Ripley, Ezra, 107
Ripley, George, 107
Robinson Crusoe, 133
Rowse, Samuel, 120
Rusk, Ralph L., 69

Sanborn, Franklin, 251n
Sanford, Charles, 90
Scheick, William, 69, 70
Schelling, Friedrich Wilhelm,
172
Schiller, Friedrich von, 104
Science: Emerson on, 143,
242; nature of, 27, 52, 58,
81–83, 94–99; relation to
technology, 76–77, 80–81.
See also Newton, John;
Technology
Scott, Sir Walter, 104, 106,
192
Scottish Common Sense phi-
losophers, 54
Sealts, Merton, 186
Self-reliance, 45, 51, 75–76,
80
Shakespeare, William, 45,
104, 105, 106, 145
Shea, Daniel, 15, 261n
Shelley, Mary Wollstonecraft,
78
Sidney, Sir Philip, 145
Sisyphus, 237
Slavery: Emerson's view of,
90, 101, 104, 228, 242;
Thoreau on, 113–14;
Webster's compromise,
108, 110–11. *See also*

Abolitionism
Smithsonian Institution, 83
Socrates, 104, 105, 239
Spiller, Robert E., 207
Stevens, Wallace: and Emerson's "Fate," 237–38; permutation of metaphor, 60–61, 68, 154, 239; "Anecdote of the Prince of Peacocks," 238; "Domination of Black," 238; "A High-Toned Old Christian Woman," 238, 239; "The Idea of Order at Key West, 37, 68, 238; "The Man on the Dump," 238; "The Man With the Blue Guitar," 238; *The Necessary Angel*, 238; "Notes Toward a Supreme Fiction," 13; "A Primitive Like an Orb," 69; "Sea Surface Full of Clouds," 238; "Someone Puts a Pineapple Together," 16, 238; "Sunday Morning," 68, 238; "The Well-Dressed Man With a Beard," 238
Sumner, Charles, 103, 110
Swedenborg, Emanuel, 104, 162, 172, 206, 253n, 259n

Taylor, Edward Thompson, 106
Technology: Emerson on, 76–80, 83–94, 97–99, 242; inventor as man thinking, 58, 97–99, 143; relation to science, 76–77, 80–81. *See also* Science
Tennyson, Alfred, Lord, 104
Thackeray, William Makepeace, 66
Therien, Alek, 30, 138

Thoreau, Henry David, 78, 99, 104, 107, 193, 199, 247n; on Emerson, 117–19, 121; Emerson on, 102, 110, 118, 123–40, 143, 242, 252n–253n; on Webster, 102–3, 112–17, 118–19, 120–21, 249n–250n; "The Allegash and East Branch," 117, 137; "Chesuncook," 137; "The Dispersion of Seeds," 125, 251n; "The Fall of the Leaf," 125, 251n; "Herald of Freedom," 112; *Journal*, 102, 112, 114–15, 116–17, 118, 119, 250n; "Resistance to Civil Government," 112, 113, 119, 138; "Slavery in Massachusetts," 112, 113–14; *Walden*, 112, 113, 115–16, 124, 125, 126, 130, 135, 136, 251n–252n; "Wendell Phillips Before the Concord Lyceum," 112, 119, 249n–250n; "Wild Apples," 132; "Wild Fruits," 125, 251n
Thoreau, Sophia (sister), 130
Ticknor, George, 102, 250n
Timoleon, 213
Transformation: Emerson's practice of, 143–68 passim, 176, 181–83, 186, 188–95 passim, 199. *See also* Metamorphosis
Tyler, Royall, 248n

Understanding: Emerson's view of, 35–36, 55–56
Undulation of thinking, 33–34, 46

Vergil, 165, 180. *See also*

271

Aeneas
Very, Jones, 102, 247n
Vishnu, 162

Waggoner, Hyatt, 144, 255n
Walpole, Horace, 109
Washington, George, 104, 106
Waterville (Colby) College, 184, 207
Watson, Marston, 247n
Webster, Daniel: Emerson on, 101–12, 117–18, 119–21, 127, 138, 143; Thoreau on, 102–3, 112–17, 118–19, 120–21, 249n–250n; Winslow house, 111, 114–17
Whicher, Stephen, 42, 49, 57; on Emerson's poetry 155, 254n; later Emerson, 218, 220; persona in Emerson, 240
Whitehead, Alfred North 76
Whitman, Walt, 61, 209; Emerson's influence on, 169, 190; persona, 195; poetry and poetics, 93, 151, 154, 211, 216; on technology, 93, 99, 246n
Whitney, Eli, 86
Will: Emerson on, 13, 41–42, 43–44, 199, 238
Williams, William Carlos, 68, 154
Williamson, George, 171
Wordsworth, William, 28, 34, 104, 107; influence on Emerson, 146, 147, 151, 152

Yoder, Richard A., 153